# The Photographer's Assistant

# The Photographer's Assistant

**JOHN KIEFFER**

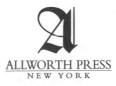

ALLWORTH PRESS
NEW YORK

05   04   03   02   01   00          5   4   3   2   1

Published by Allworth Press
An imprint of Allworth Communications
10 East 23rd Street, New York, NY 10010

Cover design by Douglas Design Associates, New York, NY

Page composition/typography by SR Desktop Services, Ridge, NY

ISBN: 1-58115-080-6

Library of Congress Cataloging-in-Publication Data
Kieffer, John.
     The photographer's assistant / by John Kieffer.—Rev. ed.
          p.     cm.
     Includes bibliographical references and index.
     ISBN 1-58115-080-6
     1. Photographic assistants—Vocational guidance.   2. Freelance photography.
     3. Photography—Marketing.   I. Title.
     TR690.K54   2000
     770'.23'2—dc21                                        00-048478

Printed in Canada

Cover Photo: With the help of his assistant, Brian Mark photographs a high-tech product in his Denver studio. Equipment includes a 4" × 5" view camera with digital back, power supplies, a large ban light, and a back light covered with a blue gel. © 2000 John Kieffer.

# Contents

# Acknowledgments

I'D LIKE TO THANK THE FOLLOWING PEOPLE FOR THEIR CONTRIBUTION TO THIS book. First my wife, Beth, for her help and commitment to both my photographic career and our stock agency, Kieffer Nature Stock. The following photographers were especially helpful: Brian Mark and Christina Dooley for their involvement with the cover photograph; Jim Cambon and his digital expertise and the photographs supplied by Tony Dube (Ulsaker Studio), Bob Kieffer (Pro 1st), Chip Simons, Rick Souders (Sidelight Studios), Mike Tangretti (Sinar Bron), and Jeff Hirsch's Foto Care.

The interviews are a valuable part of the book and I'd like to thank the following photographers for their time and effort: Nancy Brown, Todd Droy, Carl Fischer, Jim Grout, Michal Heron, Pete Saloutos, Shel Secunda, Chip Simons, and Steve Umland. Finally, to the people at Allworth Press, especially Tad Crawford, Nicole Potter, and David Milne.

# 1

# The Assistant and the Photographic Community

MANY OF US EXPERIENCED A SPECIAL FASCINATION WITH PHOTOGRAPHY FROM our earliest encounter, and we continue to nurture the dream of being a professional photographer. Unfortunately, one of the first and greatest stumbling blocks is just getting your foot in the door. The best approach to getting started as a professional photographer is to become a professional photographic assistant.

## THE PHOTOGRAPHIC ASSISTANT

Just what is a professional photographic assistant? In general, it's an individual with both photographic and related skills who assists a professional photographer. Being a photographic assistant can be both a transitional period and a learning experience. It can allow the advanced amateur or recent photography school graduate to turn professional more smoothly. A good assistant has marketable photographic skills but also performs as an apprentice.

Before you can appreciate the importance and responsibilities of the assistant, it's necessary to dispel some *common myths* regarding professional photographers, especially those photographers most likely to hire assistants. Photographers who regularly utilize assistants receive photographic assignments that have budgets for an assistant. They get the better jobs because of their ability to consistently produce a technically excellent photographic product, regardless of the subject or shooting conditions.

Many aspects of high-level photography must be approached very precisely. What is almost perfect is unacceptable. Being a little out of focus, seeing only the edge of a piece of double-stick tape, or overlooking a speck of errant dust on the set is intolerable. Imagine several professionals viewing a 4″ × 5″ color transparency with a magnifying loupe. There's no place to hide mistakes.

Photography is a process where the production of the final image, whether it's a piece of film or digital file, is the result of many small steps. Failure to perform any one of the steps satisfactorily can render the outcome useless. To consistently sustain this high level of output requires both technical and creative skills. It also necessitates a certain fastidious nature, attentiveness to detail, and overall organization by photographer and assistant.

Photography is often mistakenly perceived as a fairly laid-back, almost casual occupation. This is largely untrue for professional photography as a whole, and even more so when assistants are utilized. An acceptable product must be delivered on schedule, often by the end of the day.

Besides the assistant, others might be involved with the day's work—perhaps an art director, the client, a stylist, or a model. Either their schedules or the budget may not allow for extending the shoot. A photographic assistant is an integral part of this creative effort and can be a tremendous asset. Conversely, mistakes can cost thousands of dollars and damage the photographer's credibility.

The bottom line is, the most successful photographers are those who won't let something go out the door until they're satisfied that the work is the best it can be. These are the photographers assistants want to work for the most. Keep in mind, as the day grows longer and the take-out pizza gets colder, only two people are likely to be left in the studio—the photographer and the assistant. As an assistant, you should expect long days and demanding work. The rewards are financial, educational, and an active involvement with a high quality photographic experience.

## THE ASSISTANT'S RESPONSIBILITIES

A clearer view of the photographer's working environment makes it easier to appreciate why the successful photographer needs a competent assistant. Well, what are an assistant's responsibilities? In general terms, the assistant is hired to free the photographer from many lesser tasks. This allows the photographer to concentrate on what's in the camera frame, and ultimately on film.

The best assistants integrate a variety of skills into many different kinds of photographic situations. Besides receiving instructions from the photographer, a good assistant anticipates the progression of the shoot and takes the initiative regarding assisting duties. Finally, the assistant must be in tune with the photographer—a sort of mind reader.

More specifically, assistants work with *photographic equipment*. However, this equipment is rarely the kind mentioned in the popular photography magazines. The 35mm, single lens reflex camera (SLR), so familiar to amateur photographers, is often the format encountered least by the assistant. The 35 mm SLR is likely to be replaced by medium-format cameras (6×6cm and 6×7cm), and large-format view cameras (4″ × 5″). These often have digital backs, completely bypassing film.

The need to produce on schedule requires the photographer to control as many variables as possible—hence the use of constructed shooting environments. *Artificial lighting* is a big part of this controlled environment. The small flash units that attach to 35mm, SLR cameras are replaced by more powerful, electronic flash systems. These lighting systems consist of large power supplies and individual flash heads.

In addition, stands and numerous *light-modifying devices* are used to control this raw light. Some of the assistant's responsibilities are to set up the lighting system, subtly change its position and character, and to tear it down. Reliance on artificial lighting greatly increases the need for an assistant.

Artificial lighting also necessitates the use of *Polaroid*™ instant film, and Polaroid film means more work for the assistant. Generally, a photographer won't go to film until everything is set. Polaroid helps confirm important aspects, ranging from composition and lighting to focus and exposure. Everything must be just right to avoid unwanted surprises. Today's assistant is just as likely to encounter some form of *digital capture,* thereby forgoing film entirely. Here, the set might be reviewed on the computer monitor.

Like an artist, the photographer often starts with only a general idea and a blank camera frame. This means a background or location must be chosen or even specifically constructed.

Both the subject and all props must be selected and everything must then be precisely positioned, by whatever means necessary. The solution may dictate the simple use of a clamp, but frequently demands real ingenuity. It's imperative that everything stays together, at least until the last exposure is made.

A key to being a *good assistant* is the ability to prioritize your responsibilities and be efficient in accomplishing them. At the same time, you keep one ear dedicated to the photographer. There's more to professional photography than what's visible in the final image. To be a successful assistant, you need many skills. Not all are thought of as photographic, but they're still essential in creating successful photography.

## BENEFITS FROM ASSISTING

The benefits you receive by being a professional photographic assistant are almost too numerous to list. In simple terms, it's an incomparable *learning experience*—and you get paid for it. You work with the better photographers, and in the process you're exposed to a vast array of photographic challenges and creative solutions.

By assisting different photographers on countless photographic assignments, the day-to-day tasks of photography gradually become routine. As a result, you'll be far less likely to have difficulties when making the transition from assistant to professional photographer.

Perhaps of greatest value is the knowledge you gain regarding every aspect of light. As your photographic eye evolves, you learn to appreciate its subtleties. If you're perceptive, techniques used to control light can become invaluable tools for use later on.

No one works with the photographer as closely as the assistant. Assisting also gives you a familiarity with a range of photographic equipment that's impossible to obtain any other way. This hands-on experience makes the inevitable purchase of costly photographic equipment less of a gamble.

The assistant is part of a creative team, commonly working with models, stylists, set builders, and other assistants. Working with these people imparts valuable knowledge. Later in your career, many of these same individuals may even be of service to you.

When assisting, your daily routine is likely to include running errands. These will consist of stops at film-processing labs, repair shops, and other photo-related resources. Support services are essential to virtually all areas of professional photography, and many times aren't readily located in the phone directory.

Finally, assisting provides a unique avenue for becoming part of the local photographic community and building a *network* of relationships. As a successful assistant, the transition to professional photographer will be more fluid. Gradually, your employers become your peers.

## THE PROFESSIONAL PHOTOGRAPHIC COMMUNITY

The field of professional photography is extremely diverse, so it's critical to know which areas of photography require assistants and why. The following list discusses areas with the greatest potential to utilize photographic assistants. It's fair to say that several categories might apply to a photographer over the course of a busy year.

### Commercial Photography

Commercial photographers use assistants more than any other group of photographers. These photographers commonly obtain work from advertising agencies, graphic design firms, and larger companies. The images produced are used in some form of commercial endeavor, such as a magazine advertisement, brochure, Web site, or annual report.

　　　　The field of commercial photography isn't precisely defined and holds the potential to expose the assistant to every kind of shooting experience. Commercial work differs from wedding and portrait photography, where the general public is buying the product. Editorial photography and photojournalism aren't considered commercial work because the photography is not directly involved with selling something.

### Product Photography

Product photography is a branch of commercial photography, essential to many businesses and photographers alike. When the objects are small, it's often referred to as table-top or still-life photography. Whatever you call it, you take pictures of things, usually things that are sold. Ideally, this work is performed in the studio, where photographic control can be maximized. Proper lighting is critical, not only to show the product most favorably, but also to elicit a response or convey an idea. Utilizing view cameras, professional lighting systems, and every type of related equipment is the routine.

### Architectural Photography

Architectural photographers also depend on assistants. Whether shooting interiors or exteriors, they are often called on to illuminate large areas. This translates into lots of lighting equipment. Photographers often need to be in two places at once, and when large spaces are involved, what's better than a good assistant? As you'd expect, it's always a location job, and everything must be transported to and from the site; strong backs are required.

　　　　With much of product and architectural photography, capturing the final image is often anti-climatic and almost a formality. Lighting and composition problems will have been solved and verified with Polaroid instant film or by viewing a monitor. Unless an important variable cannot be precisely controlled, like the pouring of a beverage or rapidly changing natural light, a limited number of exposures are made.

### People and Fashion Photography

For some subjects, going to film signals a higher level of activity. This is true when photographing people, especially in fashion. Here the fast handling 35mm and medium-format cameras are most useful, with electronic flash helping to freeze the action.

Due to a model's movements, the photographer cannot control the final outcome and a certain level of tension exists on the set.

This uncertainty means many more exposures are made to assure the photographer gets the shot. As the assistant, it becomes more important than ever to be attentive to the photographer's needs and to what's happening around the set. If there's a delay in the action, it better not be because of you.

## Editorial Photography and Photojournalism

Editorial photography and photojournalism is the noncommercial photography found in magazines and newspapers. The photographers producing this work tend to use assistants less frequently than commercial photographers. Unfortunately, many editorial budgets just don't have any extra money for an assistant.

Besides budget, there is a fundamental difference in the subject matter. In most instances, the editorial subject possesses an inherent quality that makes it interesting to the viewer. A commercial product or idea doesn't have this advantage. It's a box, a thing, and the public often has little interest in it. The commercial photographer has to work hard to evoke any kind of response—that's part of the challenge. But the very nature of editorial photography and photojournalism requires a less contrived approach, which means less need for an assistant.

## Wedding and Portrait Photography

When the lay person envisions professional photography, both weddings and portrait studios quickly come to mind. From an assistant's viewpoint, both share some common traits. First, they draw their livelihood from the general public. This usually translates into a restricted budget. In addition, shooting situations and lighting solutions are less complex. The result is less need for an assistant. It's important to realize, though, that in photography a tremendous opportunity still exists to photograph people, although it's usually related to a commercial job.

## FREELANCING AND FULL-TIME ASSISTING

Another aspect of assisting must be addressed: whether to be a freelance or full-time assistant. As a full-time assistant, you are like an employee of any small business, except that the job is with a photographer who owns an independent studio. As a freelance assistant, you provide services to many photographers on an as-needed basis.

Before deciding if one position is better, it's important to examine the city where you intend to work. There may not be a choice to make. Larger, economically healthy, metropolitan areas have larger photographic communities. These markets hold the greatest potential in finding a full-time position. Metropolitan areas with less than 500,000 people may have only a handful of full-time positions. Wherever the market, there are always more freelancers than full-time assistants.

If given the opportunity to pursue either, understanding how the two positions differ will help you make an informed decision. The word that best describes freelance assisting is diversity. One day you're on location, involved with a fashion shoot. You're working with a medium-format camera, strobe, models, and a stylist. On another day, you're in the studio, fine-tuning a single product shot. Here, the photographer utilizes a view camera, different lighting equipment, and, more importantly, a different viewpoint.

No matter how skilled, no single photographer practices every type of photography or utilizes every valid approach. Freelancing allows you to explore the widest range of photographic experiences. You may become more familiar with those areas you think you want to pursue professionally. But it is just as likely that you will become sidetracked by areas you never even knew existed. Try it, you might like it. If it doesn't hold your interest, don't worry; your next assisting job will probably be quite different.

Working with different photographers means different equipment. Freelance assistants get hands-on experience with a vast array of equipment. This helps you decide which style of photography or particular camera format feels right for you.

Don't conclude that freelance assisting is all pluses. As a freelance assistant, you are essentially running your own business. Freelancers don't find one job and then stop looking. They build a clientele and work at keeping it. So you won't receive a steady paycheck. You'll bill your clients and wait for payment.

When pursuing a full-time position, it's important to evaluate both the photographer and the kind of work he or she performs. The assistant works very closely with the photographer, and a certain degree of compatibility is essential. Does the kind of work the photographer shoots day in and day out fit into your learning and career goals?

## AN INTERVIEW WITH
## SHEL SECUNDA

Shel Secunda is an advertising and editorial photographer in New York City.
He specializes in photographing people,
and his subjects range from children to
celebrities. Currently, he's placing more
emphasis on art photography.

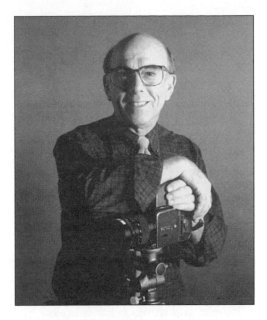

**John Kieffer:** What do you look for
most in an assistant regarding his personal attributes?

**Shel Secunda:** I guess the most important thing to me is how I perceive
their attitude. I am less interested in the
quality of their own photography. If
there's an eagerness and a curiosity, that's
much more important to me than who they've worked for or where they've gone to
school. For instance, if I like them and they're not familiar with the Hasselblad, I'll let
them visit the studio and practice loading my Hasselblad back. That's an important
skill, and it can be learned quickly.

      Also, overall personal appearance is important and I'm not talking about any-
thing as specific as length of hair. A major turn off is someone who looks dirty or
grubby. Beyond that, I require a cheerful attitude, not someone who's a downer on
the set.

**J.K.:**    Do you interview potential assistants?
**S.S.:**    I screen and interview my assistants very carefully, and I tend to interview
those people who have contacted me. That shows they're interested in me. It's often
in the form of a letter saying they've seen my work. Nothing turns me off more than
an assistant calling me and saying, "By the way, what kind of work do you do?" That
indicates a lack of interest, immediately. But most assistants who contact me do so
because they've seen my work in various creative directories and are smart enough to
butter me up a little bit.

      When I interview assistants, I take Polaroid pictures of them, which I keep
with their resumes. Also, I ask them for references, and I check the references. What's
always amazing to me is the number of kids who assume you're not going to check
the references, and apparently a lot of photographers don't. I've had assistants give a
photographer's name as a reference, and I'll call the photographer, and the photographer will say, "He gave you me as a reference? That kid cleaned out my cash box!"

**J.K.:**    Do you like to see an assistant's portfolio and what's important in it?
**S.S.:**    I look for photographs that indicate craftsmanship and attention to detail. It's
nice that they're very artistic and creative, but if somebody shows me a whole portfolio of blurred, abstract pictures, that really doesn't show me very much.

When I look at their work, I like to see their black and white. This gives me an indication of their darkroom skills. I do a lot of black and white, and I need skills in that area.

**J.K.:**    Are most of the people who contact you about assisting graduates from a photographic school, or have many learned on their own?

**S.S.:**    Nowadays, the vast majority are graduates. They come from photography schools such as RIT (Rochester Institute of Technology) and Brooks, or they've gone to a school such as New York University, which has a very fine photography major. In my early days, it wasn't this way.

**J.K.:**    Do you have a full-time assistant or do you use freelancers?

**S.S.:**    Throughout much of my career, I've had a full-time assistant and would hire two to three freelancers, depending on the scope of the job. But now, I have several freelancers who work for me on a fairly regular basis. It works out much better financially and every other way because it also gives me great freedom. When you have a full-timer and things get a little slow, you get anxious.

**J.K.:**    I'm curious, do you have any preference for male or female assistants?

**S.S.:**    Over the years, I've had three women as full-timers and I use women as freelancers. The only thing I'm careful about is that they are reasonably strong. I ask them directly because I don't want to be picking up a heavy case just because I'm concerned about a female assistant not being able to. In many areas, I prefer a woman assistant. There are a lot of things I feel a female assistant can do that a male assistant can't. I do a lot of work with children, and they can be very helpful under those circumstances.

**J.K.:**    Do your female assistants ever get involved with styling, or do you have a stylist on the set?

**S.S.:**    I almost always have a stylist on the set. I never hire a female assistant with the idea of having her function as a stylist.

**J.K.:**    Do you set any ground rules regarding the assistant's etiquette on the set? Do you like assistants to interact with the client, or do you prefer them to stay in the background?

**S.S.:**    I have very firm ground rules on that score, best summed up in two words: "dummy up." I let them know right away, and it's not because of anxiety that they'll steal my clients. Over the years, I've found that a loquacious assistant can be very detrimental to a shoot, whether he's engaging the models in conversation, or the client. He's not only not paying attention to me, so that if I need something I have to first get his attention, but he's also distracting either the model or the client, and I might want their attention. So I tell all my assistants to be friendly, but do not initiate conversation with either the clients or models. I also tell them to make sure to pay attention to me at all times. Anyone who doesn't seem to get the message doesn't work for me very long.

**J.K.:**    Earlier you mentioned the Hasselblad and the importance of loading film. Have you had any disasters caused by assistants?

**S.S.:**    I had one that could have been, but it turned out to be rather funny. Once during a shoot, the studio manager went to the darkroom to start processing film. This left the assistant to load the film magazines and hand them to me. My studio manager had worked with me for a long time, and we had a shorthand jargon worked out. When I would hand him a magazine, I would say, "Dump it." This meant take the roll of film out, and put another roll in.

This kid had never assisted me directly, and I handed him a magazine and said, "Dump it." He handed me another loaded film magazine, and I continued to shoot. After about an hour, I turned and looked at the work cart and asked, "Where's the film?" He replied, "You said, 'Dump it.'" He was methodically watching me shoot the film, and when I'd say, "Dump it," he'd take the film out of the back and throw it in the garbage. Luckily, even though he had not sealed the ends of the rolls, the film had not unraveled too much, and we only had fog on the last shot of each roll. I just marveled that some people can follow orders so literally.

**J.K.:**    Have you had any occasions when the assistant performed above the call of duty and saved the shot?

**S.S.:**    I'm a great believer in praise whenever an assistant does something great. The first thing I tell them before a shoot is that their primary job is to save my ass and to keep me from totally screwing up. Once I get really involved in a shoot, I might overlook some basics, like setting the f-stop correctly or checking depth of field or whether I pulled the dark slide.

Earlier, when I said I didn't want them talking to anybody, it's because I really need their total attention to make sure I don't screw up. And I give them that responsibility right at the beginning of the shoot. I want them to say to me, "Slide? F-stop?" just before I start each roll or each new setup. I need them to pay close attention to me. Whenever somebody catches me about to screw up I'll say, "That's one for you."

**J.K.:**    What do you think of assisting as a way to learn photography?

**S.S.:**    I think it's really an excellent way. I never assisted myself, and I never went to photography school; I'm totally self-taught. I did several other things before I became a photographer, and I came to it accidentally. At the time, I was a theatrical press agent, and my employer knew that I was a fairly capable photographer. He'd seen my work and asked me to photograph one of the Broadway plays he was handling. I soon realized that I really loved photography, but not that kind of photography. I asked around to find out where the money was, and I was told it's in advertising; so here I am all these years later.

Assisting certainly would have been helpful—I had to learn a lot of things the hard way. I read a lot and joined photography organizations. That's how I learned, but I'm sure it's much faster to go to school or assist. I'd say that assisting is absolutely essential nowadays because there's just so much to know. When I started twenty-five years ago, it was so much simpler. For one thing, there were far fewer photographers.

**J.K.:**    Do you have any advice for aspiring assistants or comments about photography in general?

**S.S.:**    I would pass on to aspiring photographers what was advised to me by a consultant. It might sound very simplistic, but if I'd had that advice years before, my career might have been even more rewarding and richer than it has been, and I'm not complaining.

I showed all these commercial things I had done, along with a sprinkling of personal pictures. It was what I felt the market wanted. I guess it was obvious to the consultant that I really wasn't shooting that much from the heart. So I started adding more and more of my personal pictures to my portfolio. The reaction was wonderful. My work picked up. I still include the commercial work, to let them know that I can follow a layout and satisfy their requirements. However, I also want to give them a hint of my vision.

I would also emphasize to any beginning photographer the importance of satisfying the needs of the client. In advertising, if you get a layout from an art director, you can bet that it has passed through many hands—all of them stamping their approval. When the final photograph goes back to the client and it doesn't somewhat resemble the layout, there are going to be a lot of questions.

# 2

# Making the Most of Your Skills

BEFORE RUNNING OUT THE DOOR TO LOOK FOR WORK AS AN ASSISTANT, IT'S BEST to have a strategy. One aspect of any approach should be to determine what skills are most marketable. Then, ascertain which skills you have to offer and work to develop the others. With this base information, you can begin to capitalize on your unique attributes.

## ASSISTING SKILLS

To make this task easier, now is the time to begin your *Skill List*. The list found in this chapter is merely a starting point, a way to highlight some of the basic skills needed by assistants. More importantly, it shows there's more to assisting than just photography. So try to become aware of how your unique background relates to assisting. Blank spaces are provided to record your insights.

A well-kept skill list serves several functions. It's a way to develop a list of talents specific to you—a pool of raw information that can be drawn from to construct promotional material. Later, it will make follow-up phone calls more productive, by quickly reminding you of what you have to offer. Start your skill list now; as it grows, so does your confidence.

## EXPANDING YOUR REPERTOIRE

Most of this book is directed toward what the assistant needs to know to perform effectively. However, a wealth of photographic information is readily available to help you perfect your skills. The key is to tap into the varied resources now. Many are free or relatively inexpensive.

## RESOURCES

Many excellent sources for information are consolidated in the appendixes at the back of this book. In addition, you should visit your public or college library, perhaps a well-stocked magazine or bookstore, and of course the Internet. You will probably come across a book or two on the view camera or basic lighting. But most importantly, the periodical room at your library or the magazine racks of a good news store will provide a valuable introduction to the abundance of professional magazines and journals. If you're not familiar with the following publications, you're missing out:

*Photo District News (PDN), Photo Electronic Imaging (PEI), Studio Photography and Design, Digital Imaging,* and *ASMP Bulletin.* Most of these publications have a Web presence as well, where useful articles and information can be found. Appendix D provides contact information for these publications.

These periodicals are directed to a professional audience and address a broad range of technical and business matters. Some trade journals routinely attach free subscription cards and easy-to-use literature-response cards.

Professional photographic *equipment literature* can also be of value by providing information on the kind of equipment rarely mentioned in the amateur photography magazines. Literature can take the form of a large, general-purpose catalog, containing all the basic and not-so-basic items. It might offer more esoteric items, such as background materials or artificial ice. All of it can be informative and lend insight into the nature of professional equipment.

Another important source of information is the *creative directories.* Basically, directories are large print books in which commercial photographers buy advertising space. The photographers and the kinds of photographs selected are very representative of much of the work associated with assisting. These vital resources and their associated *Web sites* serve several functions and will be discussed more thoroughly later.

## The Internet

All companies and professional organizations have Web sites, and these can be a great resource for information. There are also group Web sites for professional photographers to advertise their services. The appendices at the end of this book list many company names, addresses, and Web addresses (URLs).

## Professional Organizations

Learn which professional organizations are most active in your area. Their meetings are one of the few places where both photographers and assistants get together. The *American Society of Media Photographers* (ASMP), at *www.asmp.org,* is the largest national organization, and I think it is the most valuable. Local chapters have regular gatherings that are open to nonmembers for a nominal charge. Topics covered range from business practices to presentations by world class photographers. Most local chapters also publish a newsletter, which is often available at the local pro labs. See if there are any services or listings for photographic assistants.

The *Advertising Photographers of America* (APA) is likely to be useful in larger cities, like Los Angeles and Chicago *(www.apanational.org).* The Advertising Photographers of New York has a Web site *(www.apany.com)* for its members, and it also has an online *Assistant's Directory.*

One of the best ways to meet potential clients is to volunteer at ASMP and APA meetings. Believe me, they can always use a helping hand. Also, don't be afraid to ask other assistants a question or two. Like relationships between fellow photographers, other assistants can be competitors or friends; some may help now and then.

In most circumstances, it will be necessary to contact an organization's national office in order to find a local representative. See appendixes for additional contact information.

**Professional Resources**

Become familiar with the film-processing labs, retail stores, and rental shops utilized by the local professionals. These often have bulletin boards for posting a variety of professionally oriented material. All will provide valuable information and names of the photographers most likely to use assistants.

## GETTING HANDS-ON EXPERIENCE

Not even the best photographer knows everything about every piece of equipment. So how do you go about filling in some of the inevitable gaps? Acquiring printed material is fairly easy. Obtaining hands-on experience with unfamiliar equipment can be a bit more difficult.

Try visiting a professional retail store or rental shop during off-hours. Bring in a roll of 120 size, medium-format film and practice on a Hasselblad. Examine a couple of different power supplies and related lighting hardware. The rental shop probably carries what's most popular with local shooters. Doing this while referring to the information presented in this book can be very useful. When you are working and have time after a day's shoot, ask for the photographer's indulgence. This can be a good time to examine unfamiliar equipment or to ask the photographer a question.

## MAKING THE MOST OF YOUR NONPHOTOGRAPHIC SKILLS

In addition to taking the pictures that provide the revenue, most photographers run all aspects of their own one-person operations. If you take on the job of assisting such a photographer, everything from answering the phone to running errands may fall on your shoulders.

## CREATING SOMETHING FROM NOTHING

At the start of many jobs, the photographer is often faced with little more than an empty studio and an idea. The studio must be filled with the subject, background, and props. Consequently, one area of particular importance includes carpentry, painting, and a familiarity with tools in general. An active participation in the maintenance of the average home or an interest in arts and crafts provides a good foundation. When combined with a little ingenuity, handyman skills become even more useful.

This is especially true for commercial studio photography, where a shooting environment or set is routinely constructed for one shot. Building even a simple wall utilizes a range of talents. With time, you'll apply paint using a variety of techniques on an even greater variety of surfaces. You can't appreciate a perfectly painted surface until it has to withstand the scrutiny of a photographer behind a view camera.

If you've ever been labeled a *perfectionist,* then take advantage of this attribute. Whatever's in frame must be exactly as desired and every component of the shot must come together at a singularly critical moment—the exposure. If you are going to make it all work consistently, you don't have the luxury of glossing over minor details.

## LOCATION AND TRAVEL SKILLS

Due to the rigors of location work, an assistant can become a necessity. The location shoot might be just down the street or involve an extended stay out of town. Here again, what nonphotographic skills do you have that make you an asset and not a liability? You'll find that being *articulate* and *resourceful* is more important to a corporate-annual-report photographer than being an accomplished black-and-white printer. These attributes allow the assistant to function most effectively in this type of environment.

If you wish to travel, and you have related skills, capitalize on the skills. Extended location assignments always have an element of uncertainty, and it's reassuring to be able to call upon a self-sufficient assistant—one who can also get to the airport on short notice. Assets might include excellent physical conditioning, coupled with a health-insurance policy. Add to these a passport, immunization shots, and a fluency in a foreign language, and you could be the perfect candidate. A second language can be of value even in the United States. An assistant in Miami, who's fluent in Spanish and has a good knowledge of the city, could be indispensable.

When thinking of location, *think environmentally.* The environment might be corporate America or America's heartland. Are there places you feel particularly attuned to? If you live in a smaller market or in an environment to which photographers travel, explore related possibilities. My outdoor-oriented experience, coupled with a passion to shoot large-format landscapes, led to assisting on location and location scouting assignments.

## BEING OBJECTIVE

An honest self-critique is important when evaluating your assisting skills because mistakes cost time and money. A thorough familiarity with the Hasselblad doesn't translate to an equal finesse with a Mamiya medium-format camera. Nowhere is this concern more valid than in working with film. Here, you can do something 99 percent correct and still end up with 100 percent disastrous results—useless film. So you shouldn't state that you're familiar with something when you're not. If questions arise after you've carefully examined the equipment, be honest and ask. Lack of a particular assisting skill won't make or break anyone. Assisting is a learning experience, but one in which limited mistakes can be made.

## ASSISTANT'S SKILL LIST

### Small Format Cameras (35mm SLR)

Familiar with these models: _____

Familiar with lenses and filters: _____

Film handling: _____

Polaroid film back: _____

Digital capture: _____

## Medium-Format Cameras

Familiar with these models: —————————————————————

Familiar with lenses and filters: ————————————————————

Film handling: ———————————————————————————

Polaroid film back:   ——————————————————————————

Digital capture: ————————————————————————————

## Large-Format View Cameras

Familiar with these models: —————————————————————

Familiar with lenses and filters: ————————————————————

Film handling: ———————————————————————————

Polaroid film back:   ——————————————————————————

Digital capture: ————————————————————————————

## Lighting

Electronic-flash systems:   ——————————————————————

Familiar with these models: —————————————————————

Small on-camera flash: ———————————————————————

Tungsten: ————————————————————————————

Soft boxes: ————————————————————————————

Umbrellas: ————————————————————————————

Stands, booms, clamps: ———————————————————————

## Computers

Mac (Apple): ———————————————————————————

PC (Windows): ————————————————————————————

Photoshop (photo manipulation): ———————————————————

Burn CD-Rs (toast software):   ————————————————————

Film scanning: ———————————————————————————

Software programs: ——————————————————————————

Storage devices (Zip and Jazz drives):   ——————————————————

Digital printers: ————————————————————————————

Web/Internet knowledge: ——————————————————————

## Photo Related

Utility knife and straight edge: ————————————————————

Surface preparation: ————————————————————————

Mounting prints: ————————————————————————————

Sewing: —————————————————————————————

Hair styling and makeup: ——————————————————————

## Background Materials

Seamless paper: _____

Formica and Plexiglas: _____

Black velvet: _____

Support systems: _____

## Set Building

Painting: _____

Carpentry: _____

Power and hand tools: _____

Model building: _____

Locating props: _____

## Darkroom

Black-and-white film processing: _____

Film formats: _____

Black-and-white printing: _____

Color printing: _____

E-6 processing: _____

Slide duplicating: _____

## Location and Travel

Excellent physical conditioning: _____

Health insurance and disability insurance: _____

Foreign language: _____

Intimate knowledge of area: _____

Skills specific to an area: _____

Climbing, rafting, etc.: _____

Location scouting: _____

Travel experience: _____

Credit cards: _____

Current passport and immunization: _____

## General Employee

Resourceful: _____

Problem solver: _____

A fast learner: _____

Articulate: _____

Reliable: _____

Attentive to details: _____

Good with people: _____

Tactful: _____

Driver's license: _____

Knowledge of city: _____

## PROMOTIONAL MATERIAL

It's time to begin integrating your skills with what you know about assisting. This process will help you design effective promotional material that fits into an overall marketing strategy. The following is a combination of traditional approaches, general observations, and new ideas. The availability of the personal computer has made it easier than ever to make unique promotional material. And the Internet, with e-mail and Web sites, gives you the opportunity to take completely new approaches.

### The Résumé

The résumé is still fundamental to almost any job search, even in today's electronic world. It may be quite conventional, such as a chronological listing of education, work experience, and related skills. But if you have less formalized photographic training, a less structured approach might be better. Try listing skills and attributes in appropriate categories, such as studio, location, camera formats, lighting, or whatever best illustrates what you have to offer.

Regardless of your résumé's structure, it should be designed to be *easy to read*. Don't make it an effort for the photographer to get to know you. Also, don't assume the photographer knows anything about you. Convey what you feel is important, clearly and concisely. Keep your résumé to one well-designed page. Additional thoughts can be expressed in a cover letter.

Mailing or faxing your résumé may be the first contact you have with the photographer. If it's ineffective, it may be the last. Avoid misspellings and grammatical errors. Remember that overall appearance can tell much about you and how you relate to assisting. A hastily prepared résumé doesn't bode well when the work you seek often demands meticulous care.

A résumé can provide some *direction* to your career. That is, it should represent you in such a way that it leads to the work experience needed to reach your specific goals. For example, you do not need to mention the goal of becoming an accomplished food photographer. However, you must convey information that makes you invaluable to food photographers. At the other end of the spectrum, résumés can be directed to a wider audience, allowing for a broader range of photographic experiences.

Your résumé can also illustrate *desirable traits* that can be difficult to state credibly. It's easy to say that you're reliable. Unfortunately, by itself it doesn't have any substance. It doesn't prove that you're reliable, nor does it convey that you appreciate how important being reliable is in assisting. Find ways to present intangible, but important traits by giving substantive examples.

My own assistant résumé contained the phrase, "Years of rock climbing assures precise foot placement and a sure grip while on the set." This served several functions. First, it informed the photographer that I was aware of how critical it was to be careful while working on a crowded set. Second, my past experience lent credibility to the statement. Finally, it was a way to solicit more demanding outdoor assignments.

A successful photographic session can be characterized by many qualities, such as cooperation and teamwork, creativity, resourcefulness, attention to detail, and commitment to excellence. It's difficult to gain validity by simply stating that you're resourceful and ingenious. Try to draw on past accomplishments and experiences to illustrate these qualities in a photographic context. A successful photographic assistant should possess the basic attributes that make anyone a good employee.

## The Cover Letter

A short cover letter should accompany any résumé. In fact, it's often more important than the résumé. A conventional résumé lists your experiences. It's also written for a general audience and printed in large quantities. A cover letter allows for a more personalized introduction of you and your services.

### Quality versus Quantity

There are two basic approaches to cover letters: those produced in large numbers, much like a résumé, and those composed for a specific photographer. A *personalized cover letter* is obviously more difficult and time-consuming to write. Although not essential, it should be seriously considered.

It's really a matter of quality versus quantity. You cannot write nearly as many personalized letters as the "Dear Photographer" variety, but an individually written letter is of much greater value in that more photographers read it and respond favorably. This approach makes your subsequent contact with the photographer more effective. People in general are overwhelmed by impersonal mail, and "Dear Photographer" doesn't give the best first impression. You can at least sign a preprinted cover letter, but a personalized cover letter holds far more promise.

When a personalized cover letter is written to an individual photographer, it provides the opportunity to comment on some aspect of the photographer's work. Visiting her Web site is an easy way to view the work and determine if working with that person is of particular value. With this insight, you're in a good position to mention particular skills that may be most beneficial to a specific photographer.

Whether personalized or not, both kinds of cover letters share some similarities. They serve as an introduction to you and your services as an assistant. Cover letters allow you to expand upon statements made in the résumé and to elaborate on less defined attributes. You can mention how you enjoy the meticulous and precise nature of product photography. Or, you can state that you're at your best when things are most hectic during a fashion shoot.

At this stage of contact, avoid bringing up any potential conflicts, such as schooling or a second job. You must be accessible and available for work. If appropriate, state that you have a portfolio and that you intend to contact the photographer by phone. Let the photographer know you would like to meet with him or her at a convenient time. Don't plan any spontaneous visits.

Incorporating both preprinted and personalized cover letters may be productive. Consider mailing or faxing a relatively large number of preprinted cover letters and résumés to less established photographers. Send personally written letters to more established photographers, those who tend to receive a greater number of inquiries regarding assisting. To convey a sense of professionalism, résumés and cover letters are best printed and not photocopied. A good quality, twenty-pound white paper is commonly used.

## Business Cards

Business cards serve many functions, especially for the freelance assistant. They are used to advertise your services or ensure that someone has your contact information. You'll probably use more business cards than any other piece of promotional material, so take care in its design.

### *What to Convey*

A business card should contain enough information to be useful, but shouldn't become cluttered. Basic information to consider is your name, PO Box, phone number, pager number, cell-phone number, Web address, and e-mail address. Next, tell something about your services. Possible terms include "Freelance Photographic Assistant", "Professional Photographic Assistant", or "Studio Assistant." The title will occupy a prominent position on the card and might be italicized in a bold typeface or in a larger print size. Remember, you're promoting yourself as an assistant and not as a professional photographer.

Subheadings are used to provide additional information. A generalist might print "Studio and Location." An experienced assistant can print "All Formats, All Strobes," to signify a familiarity with most equipment. The phrase "Love to Travel" suggests location work. If you intend to specialize, be sure the market is suitable or design two different cards.

### *Technical Details*

After deciding what's to be printed and where it's to be positioned, determine the style of print or type face. Clean, simple styles are easier to read than more ornate ones. Then, establish the relative size of what's to be printed. The personal computer has made design much easier. Try to get the basic design on paper and then take it to a print shop specializing in business cards. Software is available to design and print your own cards, which might be a cost-effective approach if you're printing limited numbers or if you want color. The only drawback is that the ink isn't waterproof.

## ELECTRONIC MEDIA

Using a traditional marketing approach consisting of a portfolio, résumé, and business card is no guarantee and isn't cheap. If you have embraced the digital world, I would certainly give it a try. The approach might also lead you to photographers who are more cutting edge. They'll feel more comfortable looking at your work online or perhaps on CD-ROM.

### The Internet

The Internet has changed much of the way we do business, and it can provide a real opportunity to help your promotional efforts. Two ways to use the Web are with a *Web site* and *e-mail*. One approach would be to have a portfolio and description of your services at your Web site. A variety of software portfolios are available both through private vendors and on the Web. Most are set up to show your photography in a slide-show format. Many service providers include a couple megabytes of space, which is ample for a small site.

The PC computer I use came with a program called Publisher. It's easy to use and lets you make simple brochures, but there's more. Just about anything you can do in Publisher can be readily placed on your Web site. It is a simple and economical way to get a basic Web site up and running. Macintosh has a similar program called AppleWorks. High-end software programs include Dreamweaver from Macromedia and Adobe GoLive. Less sophisticated programs are Adobe PageMill, Microsoft FrontPage, and FileMaker Home Page.

Keep your Web site simple and concentrate on showing your photography and assisting skills. Also, simple Web sites are more likely to run smoothly on all browsers.

Another approach might be to incorporate some form of regular e-mailing to a list of potential clients, although this sounds like spam to me. Again, try to keep e-mails short and maybe add a personal note. You can send a photo via e-mail by using an attached file. I don't recommend sending attached files if you're unknown to the recipient, since opening attached files from unknown sources is a way to get viruses. Some photographers and assistants send e-mail, with a link to their Web site, to prospective employers. If the receiver is interested, it is very easy for her to click on the link and look at what the potential employee has to offer. Again, you want to be selective when using this technique; you don't want to be considered part of the barrage of spam.

One problem with a Web site is that you'll have to get the photographers to visit it. It's unlikely that they'll find your site unless you direct them to it. Therefore, it may not yield you much work by itself. As mentioned, many local chapters of ASMP and APA have Web sites available. Check the ASMP, APA, and APNY to see what's available through their Web sites and newsletters. See appendixes for detailed contact information.

## CD-ROMs and Floppies

You may also consider placing your photography on a CD-ROM or a floppy disk and mailing it to selected photographers. Once you have a CD-ROM burner, you can duplicate a CD for about a dollar. Print a cover for the jewel case, and it's a promo piece the photographer is likely to look at and hold on to. *Kodak Photo CD* offers an economical way of getting 35mm slides scanned to CD-ROM. You can then use these moderately high-resolution scans for a variety of purposes, such as a letterhead, résumé, or promo piece.

## ALTERNATE APPROACHES

The aforementioned approaches might be considered safe because they're unlikely to offend or be misunderstood. Safe doesn't always mean best. You may want to strike a balance between the business and creative appearance of your promotional material. There's also a delicate balance between presenting yourself as a professional photographic assistant and not as a professional photographer.

As an assistant, you'll come into contact with many different people, including the photographer's clients. You are hired to assist unobtrusively, not to compete. Is it possible to look too professional or to invest more than necessary or even desirable on promotional material?

Few circumstances dictate slick promotional material or large expenditures of money. However, this doesn't mean you shouldn't break with tradition. If you think you're in a highly competitive market and that the conventional goes unnoticed—or if you're just unconventional—then certainly try other approaches. Often something is done differently to get attention or to stand out from the crowd. But to be really effective, it needs to be remembered. You will most likely be remembered if whatever you put your name on is kept by the photographer.

Before going much further, it's important to decide when the promo piece is to be used. If it's intended to serve as your initial contact with the photographer, it should be relatively inexpensive to produce, since it's likely to be used in large numbers. When it's to be given to the photographer after your interview, far fewer will be needed.

*The following ideas are presented to stimulate your creative process:*

❏ It's not uncommon to produce a photograph or digital file, print it, and mail it. Photographers do it all the time as a means of self-promotion. Use a black-and-white piece to keep costs down or make copies on a digital color printer. If the photo conveys what you want it to, there won't be need for elaborate copy. You might consider being in the photograph, perhaps carrying or surrounded by the equipment you can operate. The use of a personal computer and color printer can be an effective means of producing marketing material in limited numbers. With Kodak Photo CD scans and Photoshop, all that's required is your imagination.

❏ The fax machine and e-mail can be used to send material or a note directly to the photographer. They can also be a way to intrude on the photographer, so a little additional ingenuity might be in order. If you intend to take advantage of the devices, consider sending a discount coupon for your services. Don't send attached files with an e-mail message without the photographer's knowledge; aware of the possibility of computer viruses, photographers will not open such files.

❏ You'll find that scheduling one worthwhile interview will require you to contact several photographers. To simplify the process, enclose a self-addressed, stamped envelope (SASE) and questionnaire along with your résumé. Ask if they utilize assistants, how often, and if they like you to call them.

## THE PORTFOLIO

A portfolio is a critical selection of your photography. Both the material and how it's presented provide information about you. The relative value of the portfolio can depend on individual circumstances. Graduating from an established photography school imparts a certain level of credibility. Here, portfolio pieces might be less personal and more likely graduation requirements. As such, they may say less about you. If you are self-taught, a portfolio can lend credence to what you've said or stated in your résumé. Therefore, it might take on greater significance.

## What's Important

Professional photographers often show a certain style of photography in order to obtain similar work. However, it's often how the assistant's portfolio is put together that determines the response. While the assistant's portfolio is unlikely to contain high-level commercial work, it should be technically correct and presented in a well-thought-out manner.

The assistant is required to handle a variety of precious materials with the utmost care, and presenting scratched transparencies and tattered prints sends all the wrong signals. Scrutinize your work. Make certain that what's supposed to be in focus is in focus and that it's properly exposed. Any piece requiring excuses has no place in your portfolio.

The most obvious benefit from a portfolio is employment. But there are other advantages. Critically reviewing your photography while putting together a portfolio can be very enlightening. It tends to raise your standards. Knowing that it will be shown to many established photographers is even more incentive to do your best.

### *Maximizing Your Potential*

One usually begins the selection process by sorting through everything that's been shot during the last couple of years. It's easy for your portfolio to become a reflection of what you like to shoot, but a well-executed portfolio conveys much more. It represents specific *skills* and provides insight into your *personality*. When evaluating your selections, remember that more than photographic skills are required to be a competent, well-rounded assistant.

By carefully integrating selected pieces, you maximize what you have to offer. Presenting 4″ × 5″ color transparencies can be used to represent multiple skills. First, it shows that you are familiar with a view camera and its many related tasks. The specific subject matter can illustrate other talents. For instance, studio product shots reflect an understanding of that kind of work. If you are comfortable with a computer and Photoshop, have your portfolio reflect this. Digital images can often be printed out for relatively little cost.

A photographer may not care about your lighting technique, but will care about the different kinds of electronic flash systems you've handled. For some photographers, a shot that shows you built and then positioned everything on the set in an apparently impossible way might be most important. Look for components of a shot to address other skills.

Careful selection also holds true for a well-executed black-and-white print. A finished print demonstrates you can properly expose, process, print, and mount black-and-white material, a long sequence that requires care and different techniques at each stage. Besides showing that you care about your work, it demonstrates you're adept with a utility knife and straight edge. You might spend more time using these two items than working in the darkroom.

### Editing Your Work

By defining your skills, the material you have available, and what's expected of an assistant, you are in a position to begin editing your work. A good starting point is to organize material into *categories*. First, compile all color transparencies into their respective formats, such as 35mm and 4″ × 5″. It's easier for the photographer to examine all color transparencies at one time, since a light box is needed.

Next, sort each format into *subjects* or *themes*. It's difficult to display any depth in your work when jumping from subject to subject. If you want to integrate different camera formats, consider having duplicates or *dupes* made. You might have several very-high-quality 35mm slides that are best included with your 4″ × 5″ material. These slides can be duplicated onto 4″ × 5″ film. Because a good dupe is not easy to make, use a quality lab.

Placing your photography on the Web requires a little additional thought. I've found that many photos do not translate well to the Web, particularly when small. Generally, photos that are very graphic or have a simple, strong subject look best on the Web. It is also an advantage to have a fast-loading, thumbnail-sized photo come up first. Then give the viewer the option of seeing a larger version of the photo, as it will take longer to load. I'd also keep the overall design simple. Remember, the photographer is there to view your photography and credentials.

## Preparing Your Material

Color transparencies are generally mounted on black *presentation boards*. Professionally manufactured boards usually hold sixteen to twenty 35mm slides. Here, mixing vertical and horizontal 35mm slides isn't a problem because the photographer doesn't have to rotate the presentation board when a horizontal image follows a vertical one.

However, this isn't the case with the premade presentation boards designed to hold four, 4″ × 5″ transparencies. Therefore, it's best to mount each transparency on a separate presentation board. This has a couple advantages. First, it maximizes the impact of each transparency, because it can be cropped to its best dimensions. Second, individually mounted transparencies let you restructure your portfolio quickly and easily. Chapter 10, "Scanning Film and Using Digital Files," has more information on using film scans for multimedia presentations.

### Photographic and Digital Prints

Printed material, whether photographic or digital, should be neatly trimmed and dry mounted. Standardize on a good quality, acid-free mat board. Try a white or black color, with a not-too-textured surface. Also, stick to one size of mat board, regardless of print size. These two procedures can lend continuity to prints produced over a period of time. To facilitate viewing, put together effective sequences of horizontal and vertical prints.

If you want to produce black-and-white material but don't have a darkroom, check out rental darkrooms. Some introductory photography courses provide access to darkrooms at more reasonable rates. Another resource is the self-service framing shop. These shops supply everything needed to mount prints and color transparencies.

Everyone likes large prints, but large prints require an even larger portfolio case. A standard, 11″ × 14″ print is usually mounted on a 16″ × 20″ board. Unfortunately, it can be difficult finding cases that accommodate 16″ × 20″ material. Don't discount using larger pieces, but it's a good idea to examine some portfolio cases to know your options. I'm not suggesting you design your portfolio around your case, but make sure you're material can fit into it.

## Presenting Your Material

A common concern is how many pieces to put into your portfolio. Several sources on portfolios for the professional photographer suggest a total of about fifteen to thirty pieces. However, an assistant's portfolio has greater variability. First of all, you may not have enough material that even qualifies. Ten excellent pieces will be more effective than those same items padded with five mediocre ones.

If you wish to convey greater photographic range, more pieces may be necessary. For example, showing both black-and-white prints along with color transparencies tends to increase the total number. So will a desire to show more than one kind of photography. Although an exact figure is hard to pin down, efforts to convey all that you know through a large portfolio can end up being counterproductive.

It can be helpful to *practice* showing your portfolio, like saying a speech in front of a mirror. Practice can point to areas with too much material or awkward transitions. Later, while showing the portfolio to potential clients, be attuned to their subtle responses—the good, the bad, and the indifferent. When most photographers consistently thumb through the last four or five pieces, their hurry signifies that it is too long. Thin out redundant pieces or try a little reorganization. It's worth the interview just to have your work critiqued by a professional photographer; take advantage of it.

Generally, it's best to let the portfolio speak for itself. Your work shouldn't need much explaining or excuses. During the process, however, be alert for occasional opportunities to mention other skills. This is when knowledge about the photographer is especially helpful. At the very least, examine what's hanging on the studio wall.

## AN INTERVIEW WITH MICHAL HERON

Michal Heron is a freelance location photographer based in New York City. She's involved mostly with editorial and corporate photography.

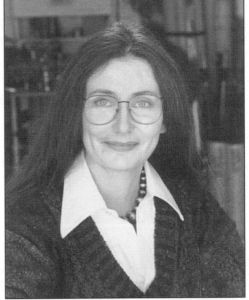

**John Kieffer:** What do you feel are the most important personal attributes for an assistant?

**Michal Heron:** The thing that pops into my mind first is an attitude that nothing is too much trouble, an open willingness. This is worth its weight in gold to me. The number one attribute and also the number one problem is attitude.

**J.K.:** What do you look for regarding photographic skills?

**M.H.:** I expect familiarity with the standard equipment that's used in the business. Assistants should have a good understanding of the commonly used camera bodies and lenses, Polaroid systems and strobes—the basic equipment. That I expect without question because if I don't have an assistant with those basic skills, then I have a trainee.

Besides a familiarity with equipment, I want an assistant to have an understanding of lighting. When I explain the lighting I want, they must understand what I'm talking about. They need to have a feeling for the quality of light and how to achieve it, especially when I'm working on location. Then I'm free to discuss other things with the client, rather than instructing the assistant step by step. There's a very fine line here, the photographer wants to design the lighting, but wants an assistant who can carry it out.

Good assistants are knowledgeable apprentices. They already have a considerable background, but are assisting to learn the business and to fine-tune their skills. I don't have the time to train anybody, but I'm more than happy to share my experience with someone who's ready to learn. That's interesting and enjoyable. When using a good assistant, an assistant who contributes to me, I find that I enjoy the process of giving them information—the little hints and shortcuts. It's a way of sharing what I've learned in the business.

**J.K.:** Considering the amount you travel, what kind of photographic equipment do you use most often?

**M.H.:** I work primarily with 35mm and to a lesser extent medium-format cameras. I use the Mamiyä RB-67, which I like for its rectangular format. I would say it's 20 percent medium format and 80 percent 35mm. In my corporate work, I do a lot of interiors that require strobe lighting. I also photograph people—one of my specialties is ethnic and cultural groups around the world, especially Native Americans.

**J.K.:**    Do you use a small, on-camera flash unit or a larger electronic flash system?
**M.H.:**    It's rare for me to use on-camera strobes for a professional job because I do very few of the PR (Public Relations) events that require on-camera strobe. I generally use a monolight system, so there isn't a battery pack on the floor. I carry between 1200 to 2400 watts per second for most jobs and more for anything really big.

**J.K.:**    Do you have a full-time assistant or do you utilize freelancers?
**M.H.:**    I use freelance assistants on a regular basis.

**J.K.:**    Do you look at an assistant's portfolio?
**M.H.:**    I like to see a portfolio because it tells me who the assistant is technically and creatively. It isn't essential, but is certainly desirable.

**J.K.:**    What do you look for in a portfolio?
**M.H.:**    I would say overall professionalism. If people are presenting themselves as professional assistants, then they should have arrived at a stage in their career where they can present their portfolio in a professional way—this means clean, attractively presented, technically proficient, reasonably creative work and no fast-shuffling excuses for dog-eared prints. If I don't see professionalism in the preparation of the portfolio, then I may be uneasy.

**J.K.:**    What don't you like in an assistant?
**M.H.:**    The death knell for me is the assistant who gossips about other photographers. I don't want to hear about all that, and it isn't the assistant's business to repeat it. Also, I know that I have to be on my guard because I have a viper in my midst. This is a person I can't trust to be professional. Assistants are exposed to privileged information, so discretion is a critical personal attribute.
        You want assistants to feel they're contributing something important to the shoot. I'm delighted when an assistant picks up on something. That's what I feel they're there for, to help me by being another pair of eyes. I welcome that, but that contribution has to be done in a way that's helpful to the photographer and not disruptive.

**J.K.:**    Do you feel female assistants are as capable as male assistants?
**M.H.:**    Yes, absolutely. But if you're a woman looking for an assisting job, it's important to confront the issue of physical strength. A female assistant should diffuse any possible bias by making it clear that she not only knows the technical aspects of the job, but also that she is strong and willing to lift heavy equipment.

**J.K.:**    Have assistants been responsible for any disastrous mistakes?
**M.H.:**    There have been a lot of common technical mistakes, such as not making sure the power supply is properly adjusted after taking a meter reading or the film not advancing in the camera. Mistakes can be the result of a certain casual arrogance that some assistants get about doing the simple tasks. You can't develop a blasé or cavalier attitude just because you've loaded a thousand rolls of film. If an assistant makes a mistake, the first thing to do is to try to rectify it, but it's also important for an assistant to take responsibility for mistakes.

# 3

# Finding the Right
# Photographers

IN MANY WAYS, THE PROFESSIONAL PHOTOGRAPHIC COMMUNITY IS A REFLECTION
of the local environment, and your marketing strategy should take this into
account. Therefore, when utilizing the following resources to develop a list of
potential clients or employers, it's important to view your market in a broad sense.

## DEFINING YOUR MARKET

One of the most important factors influencing the marketing of your assisting services is population. In larger cities you have the opportunity to become involved with
almost every type of photography or pursue a more specialized direction.
Intermediate-sized cities offer plenty of diversity, but perhaps fewer chances to specialize. In small cities you have to be endlessly creative just to keep busy.

Market size can influence your marketing approach in another way. For
example, a complete listing of every qualified photographer in a large metropolitan
area will be overwhelming. You'll either need to be more selective or find ways to
take advantage of many names. As the market size becomes smaller, every photographer and potential avenue for employment becomes increasingly important.

In addition to its population, is your market known for anything specific?
Whether you live in a community based on hi-tech manufacturing firms or tourism,
you can expect it to influence what the local photographers shoot. Unique environments, man-made or natural, are also likely to attract out-of-town shooters.

### Creative Directories

One of the oldest and most useful resources used by photographers to market themselves is the creative directory, also referred to as a photography annual and sourcebook. Commercial photographers use creative directories to advertise their services
to graphic design firms, advertising agencies, and larger companies that regularly use
commercial photographers.

#### Full of Information

Creative directories provide several kinds of information for the aspiring assistant.
Directories show excellent quality work, much of it similar to the photography you'll

be associated with as an assistant. Individual ads often contain a client list, which provides further insight into the assistant's working environment.

If a photographer's ad consists of carefully crafted still lifes, coupled with a second-floor address, then you can expect to assist in small-product photography. An advertisement that shows work produced on location, accompanied by a list of national accounts, would indicate a photographer with a very different specialty.

This information gives you a good idea of the photographer's needs in an assistant. If you have an interview with a location specialist who relies on a 35mm SLR camera, don't waste everyone's time by discussing your expertise with the view camera. You'll mention many skills, none of which are of benefit to that particular photographer.

A better perspective regarding the field of commercial photography can be obtained by viewing almost any creative directory. However, as you begin to produce and distribute your own marketing material, more specific directories are needed. At this later stage, the directory must address your marketplace and should ideally be the most recent edition. Creative directories are fairly expensive, so use discretion if you intend to make a purchase.

Older directories can often be obtained from used-book stores, especially those specializing in graphic arts and photography. Also, ask anyone you know who's involved with any aspect of commercial photography or advertising. You might also inquire at those libraries associated with photographic institutions.

## Kinds of Creative Directories

It's important to realize that directories are produced for a particular market or region. *National* directories represent photographers from across the country and are distributed nationally or even worldwide. As you would expect, such coverage can be prohibitively expensive.

Besides the cost consideration, this kind of advertising also doesn't meet every photographer's need. Consequently, only a relatively small proportion of the photographers in your local community will purchase advertising space. Even so, a national directory can be an excellent starting point because of its index. The index provides a listing of many photographers throughout the United States.

To meet the needs of more photographers, there are both *regional* and *local creative directories*. A directory might cover the New England region, California, or Chicago. A local directory gives an indication as to the quality and nature of photography in the area. It also includes the most complete index of local photographers.

## The Index

An important part of every directory is its index. However, to utilize it best, you must understand that the index only provides a name, address, and phone number—nothing personal. Also, a photographer can usually get his name on the list simply by doing some paperwork. Therefore, while an index contains many excellent names, it takes time and effort to isolate them.

Depending on the market, a directory's index might yield too many names. For those of you faced with this dilemma, cross-reference the indexes from several

directories and construct a list of those photographers found in more than one directory. The assumption is that these are more established photographers, taking advantage of every directory.

An alternative is to compile a complete list and narrow it down by zip code.
This allows you to direct your efforts within a smaller, yet concentrated, area. A final
note: many local creative directories provide a free listing for assistants.

## Online Searches and Web Sites

The concept of the traditional creative directory has been taken to the Web; many
creative directories have Web sites. The hurdle faced by most photographers, and consequently by assistants trying to find photographers, is finding the Web site to begin
with. Because the Web is global, it's important to narrow your search to your location. This is one reason Web sites host groups of photographers or offer links to the
photographers' individual Web sites.

Perhaps the most reliable place to start is with the *American Society of Media
Photographers* (ASMP) Web sites. You can first go to the national site *(www.asmp.org)*
and search for photographers by name, a region, or a specialty. If the search engine
finds photographers that match your search criteria, it will provide you with the photographers' locations and phone numbers, as well as with the URLs for their Web
sites, which will allow you to learn more about the photographers' specialties. The
national site also has contact information for the forty regional ASMP chapters
around the country, including local Web site addresses for many of them.

The *Advertising Photographers of America* (APA) is also an excellent resource. The
APA chapter in New York has a Web site *(www.apany.com)* for their photographers, and
it also has an *Assistant's Directory*. The APA also has chapters in Los Angeles and Chicago.

See the appendixes for more Web addresses for photographers. Many of them
are specifically targeted to help professionals hook up with potential clients. For
instance, Adobe, makers of PhotoShop software, has a Web site to try to link photographers to clients *(www.adobe.com/job-connection)*.

## Alternate Approaches

Besides actively contacting selected photographers, you may use more passive
approaches. One is to post information in strategic locations and wait for the phone
to ring. Every photographer requires support services, such as equipment stores, processing labs, repair facilities, and rental studios. These businesses rely on a regular flow
of professional photographers, and they often have bulletin boards. Use a pushpin to
post a stack of four to five cards, so photographers can readily take one.

### *Corporate America*

Larger companies can be located anywhere and may offer opportunities. Look for
national companies that manufacture a product or advertise heavily. Those of you living in a smaller community will hardly have to look for them; if they are there, they
probably occupy a prominent place in the local news and economy.

Once you have located a company, simply call and ask whether there's a photographic *studio* or *in-house photographer* at the facility. If so, contact the appropriate

individual about any assisting needs. But if the receptionist doesn't immediately respond and you feel the receptionist thinks you have a wrong number, don't give up.

If it's unclear whether there's an in-house photographer, find a more knowledgeable source, such as people in the personnel or marketing department. Try to determine if the company uses a local photographer and who it is. In small communities, it's very possible that an out-of-town photographer—perhaps a freelance location photographer or a staff photographer from another facility—is brought in to do the necessary product or annual-report photography.

Once you find the appropriate individual, explain the assistant's value to the success of the shoot and ask if you can send your résumé. A local assistant is of great use to a location photographer in an unfamiliar setting.

### Solicit Out-of-Town Shooters

If you've concluded that your area might attract location photographers, consider a different slant to your advertising. Becoming a member of ASMP or APA will provide national exposure through their membership lists, both in chapter newsletters and online at their Web sites. Another excellent source is *Photo District News,* a monthly publication addressing the varied needs of the commercial photographer. A classified in this widely read periodical is affordable.

Word of mouth or *referrals* also hold potential. Many photographers only require assistants occasionally. Consequently, they'll meet with you, but may only need you periodically. This doesn't mean they aren't familiar with what's going on in the photographic community. If you feel the interview went well, ask if they know anyone who needs a good assistant, including the occasional out-of-town photographer.

In larger metropolitan areas, determine if there is an *assistant's group.* This will be through ASMP, APA, or a local college or private photographic institution. These are becoming more common and can provide informal instruction and a free exchange of ideas.

## CONTACTING PROSPECTIVE CLIENTS

While developing a list of prospective clients or employers, you will come across not only names and addresses but also more useful information. Later when you start contacting these photographers, you'll obtain even more information. However, for it to remain useful, it must be kept organized. Obvious ways might be an address book or a file of index cards, but a more productive tool is the Call Report.

### The Call Report

The call report is a form that helps you keep track of all the information that is going to accumulate. Begin the call report before contacting a prospective client. When filling in the photographer's name and address, include a description of his or her work and where you saw it. Photographers often spend considerable time and money promoting themselves. Consequently, they're usually curious as to how you became familiar with them. The remainder of the call report can be completed during the natural sequence of events.

It's not uncommon to feel apprehensive when contacting someone for the first time. One way to be more relaxed is to prepare a few questions beforehand, especially the kinds that require more than a simple yes or no answer. Also, use the call report to write down any specific points you want to be sure to convey.

In many cities, photographic studios are located in certain areas, often referred to as photo districts. When arranging interviews, it can be helpful to organize your call reports geographically. This can maximize your efforts.

Call reports can also be organized alphabetically. When a last-minute job or interview comes up, you can grab one piece of paper and be out the door. It might have essential directions to a hard-to-find studio, or possibly the photographer's home phone number. If anything is going to delay your arrival, you need to be in touch with the photographer. Reliability is critical.

When you're relatively inexperienced or unfamiliar with a particular photographer, a call report can aid in your mental preparation. A quick review on the way to the studio can be helpful. By knowing the type of equipment you'll be using, you can mentally load a certain film magazine or recall the specifics of a power supply. After the day is over, any pertinent information can be readily added.

## Maintaining a Clientele

An established freelance assistant often comes to rely on the same group of busy photographers for a sizable portion of his or her bookings. Unfortunately, if the workload of several of these key photographers slows down, the freelance assistant is quickly affected. Call reports allow you to reconnect with photographers with whom you may have lost touch. You were probably fortunate to have been booked the last couple of times they called. Well-organized files make this latter marketing effort relatively painless.

## Your First Phone Call

In most cases, a promotional mailing merely helps you make a more effective follow-up phone call. This phone call may only be as productive as being asked to call back at a later date. It could also lead to an interview or a job that very day, so be prepared to make the most of any response.

### Preparation

Before calling, take a moment to review what you know about the photographer. It can be helpful to write down what you intend to say, at least an opening line or two. Because the assistant often answers the studio phone, an articulate phone demeanor is an asset. If the photographer is too busy to talk, state that you're an assistant and inquire as to a more appropriate time to call. This question alone will often establish any assisting needs and can save you the trouble of calling back.

In the early stages, it can be helpful to evaluate your telephone conversations. An objective review can lead to a better response on your next call. Like an interview, you'll find that many of the same questions are likely to be asked, so plan ahead.

### Timing the Phone Call to Your Mailing

It's important to consider how to correlate phone calls and mailing. No matter how distinctive a promo piece, as more time elapses it becomes increasingly difficult to associate the person on the phone with a piece of promotional material. A typical

## CALL REPORT

Photographer: _____

Studio: _____

Street: _____

City/State: _____

Phone: (w) _____ (h) _____

Web Address: _____ E-mail: _____

Other Individuals: _____

Use of Assistants:   Freelance _____; Full Time _____; None _____;

Comments: _____
_____

Contact Date and Comments: _____
_____
_____
_____

How did I find photographer's name?: _____
_____

Type of Photography: Studio _____%   Location _____%

Comments: _____
_____
_____

Type of Equipment

Camera Formats/Manufacturer: _____

Digital Cameras: _____

Lighting/Manufacturer: _____

Computer in Studio: Mac _____ PC _____

Software _____

Comments/Questions: _____
_____

Location and Directions: _____
_____

scenario might be to mail fifty resumes and begin calling the recipients in a week or two. You'll inevitably get interviews and a few jobs. Undoubtedly, these will undermine your time on the phone. After a month, few photographers will recall your name or what you sent. It might be better to distribute your material in batches, thereby allowing you time to follow up.

### Scheduling Interviews

If the photographer utilizes assistants and feels you have potential, the next logical step is an interview. It makes sense to try to schedule several appointments in the same area on the same day. Unfortunately, this is easier said than done.

Photography can be a spontaneous business; an unexpected job might come in at the last minute. At other times, the day's shoot can be put on hold until a product arrives. Because of this kind of uncertainty, photographers tend to refrain from making appointments several days in advance. Consequently, it's impractical to expect to arrange three to four appointments for the same day the following week.

I've found a way to get around the problem. When you leave for an appointment, bring some appropriate call reports with you. These could be for photographers in the same area or for those you especially want to contact. After the scheduled interview, position yourself close to these photographers and phone them. Inform the receptive photographer that you're just a couple of minutes away, and ask if he or she has a spare minute to meet with you. If schedules permit, a photographer who's otherwise hesitant to book an appointment will see you on short notice, especially if you're just down the street.

Being *strategically positioned* allows you to take advantage of a photographer's less busy moments. However, don't assume you can drop by unannounced. Even when a photographer isn't shooting, there's much to be done. Unannounced visits are counterproductive and an indication that you don't understand the nature of professional photography.

### The Inevitable Answering Machine

Phone answering machines are commonplace, as is caller ID. Know exactly what you intend to say before calling; disjointed messages don't leave the best impression. If you only connect with an answering machine, note it on the call report, regardless of whether you leave a message. If you call two or three times over a few months with no response, it's probably best to spend your time elsewhere—unless you know the photographer uses assistants.

### How to Become a Regular

After you contact a number of photographers, you'll find that photographers who utilize freelance assistants tend to have their regulars. However, don't make the mistake of disregarding these photographers and their call reports. Very likely, some of them will need an additional assistant in several months. A well-prepared call report makes a follow-up call very straightforward, and you'll have more experience to offer. Don't plan on building a good clientele overnight.

## The Interview

You've probably already succeeded in one interview—your telephone conversation. As with the phone conversation, your personal interview will be more successful if you anticipate questions and develop positive responses. It's not uncommon to be asked whether you attended a photographic school. If you didn't, don't reinforce the negative by saying, "No, I didn't attend a photo school." State that you're mostly self-taught, and explain how you gained experience.

Don't feel that developing photographic skills through personal study and perseverance is a liability. This is exactly how most top photographers did it and why they continue to get better.

At first, your interview may seem a little informal for a job interview. You won't need a suit and tie, and you probably won't be opposite someone sitting behind an imposing desk; but don't be misled, you're looking for work. Regarding your attire, a neat overall appearance is sufficient, though T-shirts and worn tennis shoes may a bit too casual. Keep in mind that first impressions are important, and it's best to err on the side of caution.

### Questions are for Both of You

A little knowledge about the person you hope to work for can always pay dividends during an interview. Whether obtained from a creative directory or a perceptive scanning of the studio, this insight should yield some worthwhile questions.

Questions are an excellent way to direct an interview and to reinforce what you have to offer. When fortunate enough to receive a studio tour, be alert. If a well-equipped workshop is on the premises and you're adept with tools, say so. This goes for computers, too. Paying attention now will also make your first day on the job a little easier.

Photographers are often interested in knowing if you're familiar with specific kinds of photographic equipment. It's imperative to be honest about your skills. Trying not to dwell on what you can't do is one thing, stating you can do something you can't is entirely different.

You may be asked about your goals beyond assisting. Most individuals are involved with assisting as a way to learn and to transition to professional photography. If you have aspirations similar to those of the photographer, you might be viewed as motivated and having a desire to learn. Or you can be seen as a future competitor. It's possible that both interpretations are valid and exactly how you're perceived often depends on the photographer.

Either view can be further reinforced by what you say, so be guarded and aware of what you want to convey. You may think you're playing it safe by stating you hope to experience all kinds of photography and then decide on a specific direction. This could be viewed as either nonthreatening or uncommitted, and illustrates that analyzing your interview can be interesting to say the least.

## AN INTERVIEW WITH JIM GROUT

Jim Grout is a freelance assistant living within commuting distance of New York City. He assists for a variety of photographers both on location and in the studio, while transitioning to professional photographer.

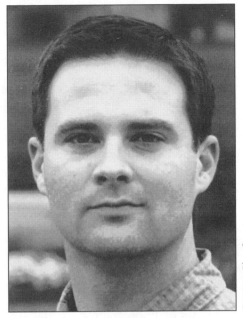

**John Kieffer:** How did you get your photographic training? Did you go to a photo school or were you self-taught?

**Jim Grout:** I went to SUNY (State University of New York), but I first got interested in photography in high school when I discovered I was good at it. In college I was a visual arts major, which required me to take a whole range of art courses besides photography. It was good, but it seemed like a lopsided education. I also wanted to learn things like history. Ultimately I got a more rounded BA degree in Media, Society, and the Arts. However, I think I learned the most about photography from my years working in a camera store as a salesperson. I did this part-time while going to school full-time.

**J.K.:** How did you learn about assisting?

**J.G.:** I learned about assisting while I was at the camera store. I'd try to learn who the professional photographers were and network. First, I met an assistant who worked for a famous car photographer, and he traveled all over the world. It sounded glamorous; he was heading off to Spain for two weeks to scout locations. He introduced me to someone who produced still-photography shoots, and that person helped me out big time and filled me in on the secret world of photography. Through him, I ultimately got a list of names to start calling.

**J.K.:** Did you send these photographers your résumé, or did you just call them on the phone?

**J.G.:** I began by calling them up. In some ways, most photographers don't care that much about your résumé and portfolio, they just want to know if you can do the job and if you're cool to hang out with.

**J.K.:** How long have you been freelance assisting, and how many photographers have you assisted?

**J.G.:** I've been assisting about two years and have worked for probably twenty to thirty photographers.

**J.K.:**   How did you build up such a clientele? Do you advertise?

**J.G.:**   I started out making a lot of phone calls, and I still do. When I work with other assistants, I might ask which photographers are good and good to work for. I also look at creative directories and just keep an eye out for new names. My résumé lists some of the photographers I've assisted, and I fax it to photographers. Then I make follow-up phone calls. I also do mailings, something short that mentions equipment I know.

**J.K.:**   How did you learn what assistants did and that being an assistant was different than being a photographer?

**J.G.:**   I learned from the photographer. I met with one of the photographers I had called and showed him that I was willing to bust my ass and learn. That's all you really need in the beginning. You need a good attitude and a healthy work ethic. Also, I was honest. If I didn't know something, I said so. He appreciated that tenfold and told me that my main job as an assistant was to make the photographer look good.

The first day he paid me fifty bucks because I didn't know anything. The next day he paid me $75, and he kept bumping me up $25 a day, until I was at $175 a day. Keep in mind, I'd been working at a camera store for a long time, and I thought I knew about photography. I could load film, but it's a whole different story when you're on the other side of the camera. Like being able to get the photographer something before he asks for it—I didn't know any of that.

**J.K.:**   What's the current day rate in the New York City metro area for an experienced assistant?

**J.G.:**   If you go into the city for a standard day, let's say you're shooting models and working eight to five, you're going to make about $200 a day. However, if you're with a car photographer, and you're shooting eighteen hours a day, you might make $325. I don't charge a half-day rate because I figure they're keeping me from working a full day.

**J.K.:**   After you invoice the photographer, how long does it usually take to get paid?

**J.G.:**   It depends on the photographer. Sometimes it's right after the job, but usually it's within a week. Some photographers hold off until they get paid. That's bad because you can wait up to three months to get paid.

**J.K.:**   How long do most of your freelance jobs last?

**J.G.:**   Most of them are one-day jobs. For instance, this week I'm only booked three days. Yesterday, I worked on location. Today, I was the photographer because a photographer I work for farmed me out to do one of his jobs.

**J.K.:**   When a photographer's shoot is cancelled, do they ever pay you a cancellation fee because you may have lost a day's work?

**J.G.:**   There seems to be a rule that if they cancel before twenty-four hours, there's no problem because you can scramble around and get another job. In reality, it depends on the photographer. If I like working for the photographer, I'm not going to worry about it. But I've had instances where photographers have paid me half the day rate, particularly when I've turned down work for that day.

**J.K.:**    Do you have a preference for the kind of jobs or photographers you like to assist?

**J.G.:**    Personally, I'd like to shoot car photography, but in the beginning I was told to work with everybody, and I think that's a good thing. I work with whoever hires me. One day it's a corporate job and the next it's journalism. It can be a studio still life or on location, so you get a feel for everything. I like a well-rounded education.

**J.K.:**    Have you ever been brought in as an assistant and found yourself being a model?

**J.G.:**    It depends on the type of photography. If you're working with someone doing editorial photography or working for a magazine, they have such low budgets they aren't going to pay you for anything. No overtime, no cancellation fees and they're not going to pay you as a model.

**J.K.:**    Do you meet many women assistants?

**J.G.:**    I've worked with women assistants, and they've known their stuff, worked hard, and were cool to hang out with. But I think some photographers avoid using women assistants. Not because they can't lift stuff—they can. But they can't lift as much as a guy. One photographer told me that he's found women less likely to want to just run up a ladder to secure something heavy.

**J.K.:**    Do you have a plan as to how you'll transition from assistant to professional photographer?

**J.G.:**    I haven't marketed myself directly as a photographer yet, but I do shoot a variety of jobs. Photographers I assist for may farm something out if they're busy, since they know I know my stuff. I also make contacts when I can. This past Sunday I was at the Mets game shooting my own photography from the press box, right off third base. I try to hustle and do all I can to get more experience behind the camera.

After assisting a few years you've learned the technical things, but I think a lot of it has to do with how you interact with people, both in the studio and on location. I worked with a corporate photographer who got in front of a CEO of a big company and fell apart. He was so nervous. On the other hand, I've worked with photographers who'll have a conversation with them, talk about current events, and it's a good experience all around. That's what's good about working for lots of photographers; you can learn from the bad experiences as well as the good.

**J.K.:**    What are some things beginning assistants should avoid?

**J.G.:**    One sign of an inexperienced assistant is giving directions to the talent or talking to the clients. They just kind of stick their nose in where it doesn't belong. That's a humongous no-no. When the photographer is shooting film, the assistant needs to keep their mouth shut and focus on their job. There are some assistants who worry about everything and loose sight of the fact that their job is to be helpful to the photographer. There are so many little things, like making sure the lights are firing and everything is secure. Just yesterday, I was on an outdoor location shoot. I was working film, and the other assistant was with the lights. An unexpected gust of wind came up, and he had to hustle to keep a light from falling over.

Your attitude is also important. When you're going across the country with a photographer, you're staying in the same hotel, going to restaurants together. He needs someone he enjoys being with.

**J.K.:**      How many days a year do you spend overnight on location?

**J.G.:**      This year I've been doing a lot, anything from car jobs to annual reports. At first it's kind of cool, but now it's getting old. In one recent week, I flew to Ohio, St. Louis, and Chicago, with three different photographers. After that, I'd rather have one full week of work in the studio. It's not like you get to go to Chicago and see all the sights. You get there and haul the equipment into a rental car and drive. You never see Chicago.

**J.K.:**      A couple of years from now, do you think you'll be using assistants instead of being an assistant?

**J.G.:**      I hope so. I do think it's important to have goals and to think about where you want to be at a certain time. You've got to keep taking pictures and building your portfolio. When you're around the set, you can ask the photographer how they got into the game and how it all works. People are friendly, and they'll tell you what they did. Hopefully, they also tell you where they went wrong and what you can avoid.

**J.K.:**      What do you like about assisting?

**J.G.:**      When assisting, every day I'm doing something different. Sunday I was shooting at the Mets game, yesterday I was on location shooting stuff underwater, today I shot my own job, and tomorrow I'll be in a Manhattan studio. I really like being out in the elements, compared to in the studio. I used to work with the computer to retouch photos, but I found I can't stand always being in front of the computer.

# 4

# Business Matters

T HE FREELANCE ASSISTANT CAN'T ESCAPE THE FACT THAT ASSISTING IS A BUSINESS. If you hide from this, you'll surely fail. Plan to track all income and expenses from the start, both to remain solvent and for tax purposes. In addition, you'll need to make proper business decisions in order to maintain a viable clientele.

## ESTABLISHING YOUR RATES

For those of you considering a full-time position with a photographer or studio, the financial arrangement is fairly simple. Assistants are usually paid a set salary, not an hourly rate. The photographer should withhold all state and federal taxes, including workmen's compensation.

As a full-time employee, you might be eligible for personal health insurance at a reduced rate. Be advised, a personal health-insurance policy may not cover an on-the-job injury. Workmen's compensation is probably necessary. It's difficult to give absolutes because workmen's compensation is administered by each state, and health insurance is administered through independent, private companies. You must know where you stand because assisting can be strenuous.

The photographer may opt to give a full-time assistant a set salary but not withhold taxes. Here, you are being viewed as an independent contractor. You would then have to handle all income as a freelance assistant, although the photographer's arrangement is probably not legal.

In general, freelance assistants are viewed by photographers as self-employed, independent contractors. However, because the photographer tells assistants when to arrive on the job and what to do, this classification is probably not correct. A problem arises when an assistant is injured on the job. If the freelance assistant is not really an independent contractor, the hiring photographer should be paying for workmen's compensation. But if the freelance assistant is an independent contractor, the assistant should acquire a private health-insurance policy to cover work-related injuries.

## The Market Rate

When it comes to freelance assisting, financial matters are more complicated than for a full-time assistant. Being self-employed, you establish a set of rates. The *market rate* is the amount an experienced assistant can expect to charge for a particular service in your city. Most freelance assisting jobs are for one to several days, and your fee might be referred to as your *day rate.*

It follows that a necessary starting point is to determine what experienced assistants are charging. With this information you can decide how much to alter your basic rate, depending on experience or as circumstances vary. If you are relatively inexperienced, you might begin by charging 75 percent of the market rate. For example, if experienced assistants charge $175 to $200 for one full day, you might consider charging $130 to $150.

This also serves as a sound base from which to develop half-day or overnight-travel rates. To find out what a professional photographic assistant makes in your city, ask some assistants and photographers who use assistants. If you inquire about experienced assistants, day rates are not likely to vary too widely. The same resources utilized to promote your services will provide access to suitable names.

Mileage and other transportation costs must be worked into the equation. The photographer expects you to get to and from the studio at your expense. Record your mileage and any tolls because these are tax deductible. For 2000, the tax deduction was $.33 per mile. Generally, if you take the per-mile tax deduction, you do not need to keep itemized receipts for gas and repairs.

Once you get to the studio or work site, the photographer ultimately picks up all expenses. If you use your car while on the job, charge at least $.33 per mile. You'll then invoice or bill the photographer, and you'll be reimbursed.

## Full-Day Rates

Before establishing your day rate, you should understand what is meant by a full day. A full day is usually as long as it takes to complete the day's work. A ten-hour day is not uncommon, and even longer days are by no means rare. Also, don't expect to be let off work at a designated time, because most jobs must be completed on schedule and to the photographer's satisfaction. If you have firm commitments, and you know you must leave at a certain time, the photographer must know.

There are several ways to structure a *rate schedule* for a full day. First, you simply charge a fixed amount and work until the day is over, hoping for a generous photographer to pay extra for excessively long days. You can also decide that ten hours constitutes a full day. Afterwards, charge an hourly rate on top of your full-day rate. Finally, it might be easiest to simply charge by the hour. A note regarding meals, usually lunch: Meals are paid for by the photographer, whether in the studio or on location. This is only fair because assistants are not provided an official lunch break.

## Half-Day Rates

A photographer may inquire about a *half-day rate.* A few points should be noted with regards to half-day jobs. First, it's difficult to accomplish much in less than four to five hours, and half days have a tendency to run longer than expected. Consequently, a half-day rate needs to be open-ended. Also, you can't book another job on the premise that a half-day job will finish up on time.

Establish a minimum rate for half days, perhaps four hours. Remember, you must invest time and transportation to get to and from the studio. After four hours start billing on an hourly rate, so at the appropriate time you reach your full-day rate. For example, if your full-day rate is $200, charge $125 for a minimum half-day. After four hours, charge $20 per hour.

A dilemma facing most freelance assistants is the difficulty in booking four to five days a week, week after week. Even if you have five days in requests, several are bound to be for the same day. On top of this, the photographer you turn down will end up calling another assistant. After this scenario is repeated a few times, the photographer will call the second-choice assistant first. Your frequency of calls will then decrease. The full-time assistant is not faced with this predicament. Consequently, the freelance assistant requires a day rate greater than the daily salary of the full-time assistant.

## Overnight Travel

A freelance assisting job typically runs anywhere from a half day to a week, with one- and two-day jobs most common. However, it's possible for overnight travel to become part of your routine. When setting rates, it's important not to expect travel to be all fun wherever you go. It's unlikely you'll have much free time to yourself, and the term "full day" takes on new meaning. Therefore, your day rate should be on the higher end of the scale. The photographer will, or should, pay all travel expenses up front, such as airfare, lodging, and meals. Before leaving, verify that this is true. Accept nothing else. Always travel with your own credit card for emergencies.

When away from home, it's possible you'll have to make some long-distance phone calls. You can't let messages accumulate on your answering machine and expect to return to a happy clientele. To alleviate this burden, change the outgoing message to state your services are booked through a certain date. To be safe, you might need to add a day or two as a buffer. Unfortunately, this may impact short-term bookings. These factors need to be considered when establishing overnight travel rates.

## Alternative Rates

You don't need to be so conventional in what you receive for your services. One of the oldest ways of conducting business is *bartering*. Bartering should be viewed both as a way to actively solicit work and to acquire equipment and services. This may seem like a novel approach, but photographers and models often exchange services. To maximize its potential, you must appreciate that far more than photographic equipment is required to start a small business.

Where do you look for bartering opportunities? An excellent source is the photographers for whom you already work. Many photographers acquire new equipment and unneeded items end up in the corner. A studio may also have a computer and scanner. These might be just what you need to put together an online portfolio, and you could barter your services in exchange for usage of this equipment.

The classified ads in professional newsletters and ads pinned up where commercial photographers congregate may also hold potential for setting up barters.

Responding to a classified ad or posting most likely begins with the phone. Before calling, be prepared with what you feel is a reasonable proposal. For example, if a tripod is listed at $300 and your day rate is $200, suggest two days assisting in exchange. Be flexible; offer what you feel good about while inviting the photographers' input. Don't be discouraged with a neutral response; this proposal may catch some photographers off guard. It may also get them thinking, so always leave a name and phone number.

A better opportunity is when a photographer either relocates to another city or sells the studio. Either undertaking is made more bearable with the help of a good assistant. The newspaper classifieds often have these listed as studio sales. At other times the wording is more discrete. Watch for entire camera systems, professional lighting equipment, and items specific to photographic studios. Associated with any move is plenty of back-breaking work, and some material may never be moved. For most, moving is a good time to trim down one's possessions.

## BOOKKEEPING

Maintaining accurate records is an integral part of business. All expenses and many activities related to running your business must be documented and organized. To accomplish this, it's essential to have an efficient system and to use it. Every assistant has basic start-up costs. There's your portfolio and related marketing materials. Later, there will be transportation costs associated with the job search. As an established freelance assistant, you'll routinely bill clients and record income.

I have no intention of discussing taxes in detail. It's an ever-changing subject. If you keep organized records and total all your expenses, a good tax preparer won't charge too much. However, I will offer a few general guidelines. Have a bank account solely for business and retain all receipts related to assisting and to your own photography. It's useful to organize receipts as they accumulate into labeled envelopes. Categories might be: office supplies, postage, film processing, transportation, and equipment purchases greater than $100.

You must have commuting-expense receipts and a *Mileage Log* to record mileage to and from assisting jobs and for errands related to your business. See the aforementioned section called "The Market Rate" for more details.

### Invoicing the Client

Once an assisting job is complete, you send a bill or invoice to the photographer. Invoice forms can be purchased at any office-supply store, or you can design something on your computer. Just be sure to have the word "INVOICE" in big, bold letters at the top. Before you mail too many invoices, set up a filing system consisting of two envelopes, one for unpaid or *open accounts,* and a second for paid or *closed accounts.*

Preparing a preprinted invoice is fairly simple, although a few points are worth noting. Begin by numbering each invoice in a logical sequence that can be followed throughout the entire calendar year, such as 2001–01. Establish whether an account or job number should be included. If not, briefly describe the shoot and its date.

The most important part involves a billing for all services and expenses. Here it's critical to itemize your figures into two categories, *income* and *reimbursement of expenses*. The largest figure is likely to be taxable income generated from your assisting. Other figures will be for expenses incurred while on the job. When making a purchase for the photographer that's to be reimbursed through your invoice, retain the sales receipt for your records to verify it's an expense.

When using your vehicle to run an errand for the photographer, record all mileage and bill the photographer. If you charge equal to or less than the government allowance, it is not taxable income. As mentioned above, in 2000 this was \$.33 per mile. Come payday you'll only receive one check, so itemizing the invoice ensures that you know what's taxable income. To simplify matters, use the photographer's petty cash for all purchases.

The billing process is a formality when the figures reflect what was made clear before the shoot. If you are not paid within two weeks, send a second invoice. If you're still not paid within thirty days, call the photographer and ask when you can expect to be paid. In this respect, assisting is based on trust, as few contracts exist.

## BUSINESS PURCHASES

A prerequisite for success as a freelance assistant is accessibility and reliability. This usually means a telephone and answering machine, but can include a cell phone, pager, and e-mail. If you anticipate changing your residence, an answering service and post office box will make you more accessible over time. A final note regarding telephones: keep a *log book* to record messages. This provides a quick reference for names, dates, and phone numbers.

The following items are used to maintain records and help keep you organized. A large, *desktop calendar* is especially useful. It provides plenty of space to write down appointments and business tasks. Another is a *mileage log* for recording mileage to interviews, freelance assisting jobs, and business errands.

A self-inking *rubber stamp* with your name and address on it will come in handy from your first promotional mailing to your last invoice. Be sure to acquire a good *city map,* since studios and photo-related resources can be almost anywhere.

## ETHICAL CONSIDERATIONS

A discussion about business issues wouldn't be complete without addressing a few potentially difficult situations. Tentative bookings and cancellations are two unavoidable occurrences, which can quickly add an element of uncertainty or conflict into the schedule of even the most adept freelance assistant.

### Tentative Bookings

In preparing for a shoot, the photographer needs to correlate many things, only one of which is making certain there's an assistant on the set.

Unfortunately, there can be any number of variables over which the photographer hasn't any control. If any of these are subject to change, this uncertainty is passed onto the photographer and then the assistant. The result is being asked to *"pencil in"* or hold a day open.

These troublesome requests are quite understandable. As photographers work with you more often, they begin to appreciate your services and want to secure you for an important job. It's easy to espouse a philosophy of "first come, first served," but a more practical approach is probably a combination of flexibility and diplomacy.

## Cancellations

The second predicament is a cancellation, another hazard of the trade. It's usually a last-minute call from the photographer, saying the job has been postponed or cancelled. You probably won't line up another job for that day, but on top of that, you may have turned down another request for your services. Do you bill the canceling photographer for all or part of your rate? This is not always accepted practice. It's probably best to forget about photographers who consistently call with tentative bookings and cancellations, while giving your better clients some latitude.

## Difficult Questions

Photographers often ask whom you've worked for as a way of judging your experience. They might also inquire as to who's been keeping you busy. This is to be expected, but it shouldn't go much further. For instance, you might be asked specific questions concerning the type of shoot or client. This is privileged information. If pressed, state that you make it a policy not to discuss other photographers and their jobs. Speaking openly and without concern is likely to be appreciated only momentarily. When you leave the studio, the photographer will be left to wonder how much of his or her information you will take to your next job.

It takes considerable time and money for a photographer to find accounts. The result of that work is right in front of you. Assistants are exposed to what might be considered inside information. After ten hours on the set, you'll know the art director, the client, possible future jobs, and more. Will you go home and write it all down, show up at the advertising agency with your portfolio, or hand out a business card when the photographer's back is turned? For your sake, I hope the answer is no to all of the above.

A final consideration relates to equipment. As an assistant you'll work with equipment all day, every day. What if you break something? For the photographer's sake, it had better be insured. What if you're shooting in a busy public building, moving from site to site? You were careful, but there's a camera body missing at the end of the day. You probably won't be assisting at the next shoot, but again, the photographer had better be insured. As you see, an assistant has many equipment-related responsibilities and must be careful, but the financial loss will be born by the photographer.

## AN INTERVIEW WITH TODD DROY

Todd Droy is a commercial photographer based in Denver. Most of his work is performed in the studio and is used for advertising.

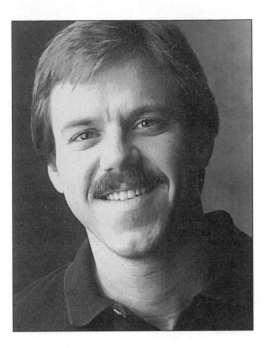

**John Kieffer:**  Could you elaborate a little as to the kind of photography you do?
**Todd Droy:**     The majority of work I do is best described as tabletop; I shoot more things than people. Probably 80 percent of my work is shooting a wide range of objects in the studio. One day it could be a high-tech shot, the next a beverage shot. The majority of the time I use artificial light; this is mostly electronic flash, but I also integrate some tungsten. When conditions warrant on location, I'll use available light and supplement it with artificial light.

**J.K.:**    Since you spend much of your time in the studio shooting smaller objects or products, what camera format do you work with most often?
**T.D.:**    Because so much of my work is tabletop, I prefer a 4″ × 5″ view camera. When shooting people, I use a Hasselblad, and a couple of times a year I dust off my 35mm.

**J.K.:**    For your kind of photography, what do you look for in an assistant's personality?
**T.D.:**    One of the first things I look for is how they present themselves, their overall level of confidence. When I talk to them or look at their book (portfolio), I look for enthusiasm, and I try to sense whether they're excited about photography. I'm not as concerned about the work in their book, but to see if they're excited. This excitement usually translates into working harder in the studio.

I like an assistant who isn't too self-centered, because an assistant is there to help me. Some assistants come into the studio with about forty pictures in their book, and they could weed it down to about three or four. When I ask about that, tell them that their book is too long, some haven't got any idea about which ones they would take out and which ones really belong. I usually show these people the door because they haven't got a clue, and they aren't nearly critical enough of their work. It's rare to see work in an assistant's portfolio that tells you they're good enough to shoot; most of the work is from school, and you can tell.

I also like assistants to be friendly and at ease. You can tell when they are tense—usually it means they're relatively new at assisting—but I like someone who can relax and talk to me. At times it's hard to put a finger on it, but by the end of the interview I've usually decided if I'm going to try someone or not.

**J.K.:**    What do you look for as far as technical skills?

**T.D.:**    Since I work so much with a view camera, I really want to know that they can load sheet film. Fortunately, most assistants that come in can. I also think they should be able to load a Hasselblad. That's what I use, so I don't care about the others. I also like to see 4″ × 5″ in their book, so I can tell if they understand the camera movements. It's not that most of the assistants are going to be operating the view camera, but if I mention pulling focus, I want them to know what I mean and how it can be achieved other than just by closing the lens way down.

I also ask about what other equipment they are familiar with, and how they respond often tells me if they know what's important for an assistant. Assistants have certain responsibilities, and good ones know what they are without me telling them.

A knowledge of strobe lighting is certainly important because so much of artificial lighting centers around it. I met with an assistant yesterday who had a fine arts background and very little knowledge of strobe. He had a fairly high day rate so I asked him why I should hire him, when for a few dollars more I could get a very experienced assistant. When I suggested he should lower his day rate, he took offense. I also suggested he could be a second assistant in the studio as a way to learn some of the basics, and he wasn't interested. He won't work here.  Many years ago when I started assisting in Chicago, a photographer said he'd like to use me, but he'd pay me less until I could be of greater help in the studio. I took it because I was fresh out of school and didn't really know what assisting was all about. It wasn't long before I was up to the standard day rate.

**J.K.:**    You've alluded to interviews. Do you interview all your assistants?

**T.D.:**    I don't think I've ever hired an assistant without meeting him or her first. At the very least, I want to avoid getting stuck with someone who doesn't know his or her place, especially while there's a client around. I also like to see the look on potential assistants' faces when I suggest that they can empty the trash if there's down time on the set. If they get turned off by that, then I don't need them here. An assistant's responsibilities can include an extremely broad array of tasks.

**J.K.:**    When you interview assistants, do you set any ground rules as far as how you want the assistant to interact with the client?

**T.D.:**    No, not at all, because I can usually intuitively tell during the interview whether they can act responsibly. I'm not always right because I did have an art director tell me he was approached by my freelance assistant for some shooting work while I was away from the set. When I do use an assistant for the first time, I try to use him on a smaller, less demanding job. It can be hard to tell beforehand if an assistant is going to be able to sense when to be right over my shoulder and when not. It's always kind of scary trying someone new on a big project; there are just too many things going on.

**J.K.:**    Are you worried the first time you send an assistant in the darkroom to load your sheet film holders?

**T.D.:**    Sure. I think some assistants are put off when I show them what I expect as far as cleaning film holders. I expect clean holders, and fortunately I haven't had anyone make a major mistake either loading or down loading film. I want an assistant to take the necessary time whenever handling film.

**J.K.:**    When looking for assistants, do most find you, or do you ask fellow photographers?

**T.D.:**    Most of the time, assistants call me and I probably get a call a week from a new assistant, and more when school lets out. It's only when I'm at the bottom of my list that I call a photographer for a new name.

**J.K.:**    What is the best way for an assistant to meet with you?

**T.D.:**    I get a lot of résumés, but they don't help me that much. I know a lot of assistants mail résumés and then call, but I think it's probably more effective to just call me and try to meet with me. Basically, if I don't have a face to link to a mailing, it doesn't mean anything to me. When assistants do call me, I may not meet with them for a month or it may be that day. But I tell them not to give up.

After I meet with someone, it's probably best to leave me a business card to file. It has just enough room to write a few notes, ranging from "good potential" to "bad attitude." There is a delicate balance between keeping in touch and calling the studio too much.

**J.K.:**    Considering that photography can be physically strenuous, do you have a preference for male versus female assistants?

**T.D.:**    When I interview women assistants, I ask them if they can lift power supplies and heavy cases. Most of them say they can; now, if they can or not I won't really know until I try them out. But at least they know I expect it of them. If I know I'm going on location, I do prefer a guy. For instance, if I'm working in the studio and I notice that a woman has a problem hanging a heavy canvas background, then I might make a mental note not to take her on location.  I do know a woman assistant who's as strong as any guy, and she made it a point in the interview to mention her capabilities. She also mentioned that when she began assisting, a photographer commented that she seemed to be having problems with some of the equipment, and at that point on she began lifting weights.

**J.K.:**    What do you think about assisting as a way to learn more about photography and as a means of breaking into photography?

**T.D.:**    I don't think there is a way around assisting. Even if you are an exceptional photographer, you can still benefit from assisting. In fact, you can still be learning after two years. You learn more than just how to make an exposure or use a power pack, but all the nuances of how a shoot goes.

Today, so much of running a photography business is nonphotographic—more than most people want to know. Yet most people who go to school still come out and need to learn how to run a studio. Sure you need to know how to make good photos, but there's much more. Even if you feel anxious to open your own studio, you'll ultimately advance much quicker when you do finally open up the doors of your own place, if you've assisted.

**J.K.:**   What percentage of assistants that you've worked with have made a successful transition to professional photography?
**T.D.:**   Well, of course it depends on your definition of success. It's only a guess, but
I'd say about 40 percent end up making photos for a living. However, not more than
5 to 10 percent are making nice pictures, but that's a subjective judgement.

**J.K.:**   Do most of today's assistants come from a photography school?
**T.D.:**   I would say that most have come from the local two-year photography school
and a few from Brooks (The Brooks Institute in California).

**J.K.:**   So is the road to success easier if you go to a photography school and then
assist a couple of years?
**T.D.:**   If I were interviewing an assistant today and I could tell from his book that
this individual works hard and has really been trying to learn a lot, I would respect
that person more if he didn't go to school. Because I could see that he wasn't just
cranking out school assignments and that he had a lot of initiative and drive. School
has just become the common path, but not necessarily the best one and certainly not
the only one. College was good for me because it gave me the time and opportunity to focus on photography. It allowed me to be in an environment with other enthu-
siastic students, where there's an interchange of ideas.

**J.K.:**   Do you have any parting advice for aspiring assistants?
**T.D.:**   You've probably heard it before, that there are too many photographers and
not enough jobs, but I can't change that. I do think that if you have reasonably good
photographic taste and are a hard worker and persistent, you can make it. But these
people would probably make it in whatever they pursue. As competitive as photography has become, I don't think a photography studio will ever amount to anything
as far as a business if you go at it halfway. You have to go at it pretty much flat out,
with the realization that you'll put in a lot of hours.

# 5

# Your First Day
## on the Job

T HE PROFESSIONAL PHOTOGRAPHIC ASSISTANT HAS A LONG LIST OF POTENTIAL tasks and responsibilities. To consolidate and clarify this information, I will present both text and an outline describing a day in the life of an assistant. Although you'll see unfamiliar terms, you can at least begin the next learning phase with a clearer idea of how the information pertains to the assistant. I suggest rereading this chapter after reading the book or before your first job or two.

## PRELIMINARY INFORMATION

The process really starts several days before the shoot, with a phone call from a photographer checking your availability. Besides establishing when and where you'll meet, obtain some background information regarding the day's work. Will you be in the studio or on location? Will it be a series of product shots or a fashion shoot?

By knowing the camera format, you can make certain you're familiar with related film-handling responsibilities, including those for Polaroid instant film. Also, having an idea of the day's activities before you walk into a busy studio can be very helpful in the early stages of freelancing.

## BEGINNING YOUR DAY

Plan to arrive a few minutes early for every assisting job. Before leaving for the studio, take the appropriate call report so you'll have directions and phone numbers. The photographer is very dependent on a good assistant and must be notified in case of a delay. In addition, you'll always need a wristwatch and possibly other items.

Upon arriving at the studio, try to become familiar with the studio's layout when given the opportunity. Key items include the camera, lighting equipment, and the set cart. Important areas will be those used to store background materials and lighting-related hardware, and the workshop. Don't forget the telephone. If it's only you and the photographer, you'll be answering it.

Occasionally, there can be two assistants on the set. The two might be referred to as the *first* and *second assistant*. The first assistant has greater experience and is responsible for the second assistant. There might also be two freelance assistants of equal standing. Whatever the exact relationship, make certain you understand who is responsible for what. This is especially important when it comes to critical tasks, such as film handling. You don't want to find yourself saying, "I thought you were going to do it."

## Prioritize

Throughout the day, the photographer will have much for you to do. But whatever it is, it's important to *prioritize* and work at *integrating* several tasks. Your to-do list might begin with taking down yesterday's set, followed by straightening up the studio and setting up a new background material. Once a background is in position, the subject and props need to be prepared, and the basic lighting should put in place, among other tasks.

Let's say the day's schedule consists of four different shots, and the photographer expects to expose eight sheets of film per shot. The schedule requires a total of thirty-two sheets of film, loaded in sixteen holders. Cleaning and loading all sixteen film holders is time-consuming. It's more expeditious to begin by loading eight holders and finish the remainder as time permits. This provides film for the first two shots and allows you to return to more immediate tasks on the set. Learn to integrate several responsibilities to avoid delaying progress on the set because of your actions.

## Working on the Set

Before much progress can be made, the background needs to be put in place. The background might be a roll of seamless paper, a piece of painted canvas, or a specially constructed backdrop. As an assistant, you're often working with several backgrounds throughout the day, and knowledge of their care and handling is essential.

With the background in position, you can begin to bring some artificial lighting into the shooting area. The exact lighting requirements differ for each shot. Most often, however, as the shot evolves, more lights, light-modifying devices, and related hardware are gradually incorporated. Before proceeding much further, the photographer needs a camera. View cameras usually remain attached to a camera stand. If so, roll it into place. Small- and medium-format cameras are likely to be used with a tripod. Now is an appropriate time to bring the set cart close to the work area. Don't forget the reason for all this effort—the subject. It, and everything else in frame, must be precisely positioned and their surfaces properly prepared.

## Pay Attention and Anticipate

The assistant works closely with the photographer; as you become more familiar with a particular photographer, you begin to understand what is meant with less explanation. One way to arrive at this point more quickly is to pay close attention both to the photographer and to what's occurring on the set. For example, when the photographer grabs the flash meter, it is a cue that it's time to take a meter reading. So act accordingly. Knowing whether the flash meter is set in the cord or non-cord mode influences how you respond.

Being able to anticipate the photographer's intentions allows you to perform most efficiently. If by observing you know the photographer is interested in metering only one of several flash heads, you should make arrangements to fire that specific light by turning off unnecessary flash heads.

## WORKING WITH EQUIPMENT

If it's the first exposure of the day, recheck the camera. It must be synced to the master power supply, and the camera's *shutter* should be set at the appropriate sync speed, usually one-sixtieth of a second. The large-format lens found on a view camera requires several additional steps before being operational. You must be familiar with this procedure.

Next, make certain the power supply is turned on and its ready light illuminated. Additional power supplies must be connected to the master power supply, via flash slaves or radio receivers. When multiple pops or long exposures are required, both the modeling lamps and studio lights are turned off.

## WORKING WITH FILM

You might hear the photographer comment to the stylist or art director that it's time to shoot another Polaroid. More than likely, this remark is also directed to you. Long before now, you should have made sure the Polaroid film holder is loaded and that there's an adequate supply of film at room temperature. Polaroid film is a wonderful problem-solving tool, but to be most useful, each instant print needs to be numbered sequentially and pertinent data noted.

During the shoot, it's critical to monitor film usage. When using sheet film, it can be important to record exposure data for each sheet of film. A film holder containing exposed film can then be correlated to an appropriate Polaroid print.

Due to the time it takes to clean and load film holders, it's very important to track film usage. If the photographer is exceeding earlier estimates, make time to load more holders. You don't want to be holding up a shot's conclusion because there aren't any loaded film holders. If utilizing roll film, plan to notify the photographer when nearing the end of the roll and have unexposed film immediately available.

## KEEPING ORGANIZED

During the evolution of the lighting arrangement, a large soft box may be exchanged for a smaller one or perhaps a silver fill card will be replaced by a white one. As the assistant, you must strike a balance between keeping the studio organized and overdoing it.

The decision to put aside or to put away is influenced by several factors, one being studio size. Smaller studios have little extra space for unneeded stands or soft boxes, and can quickly begin to feel crowded. Larger studios let you set objects aside for possible use later in the day. Another point to consider is how many shots remain. If much still needs to be done, minimize your organizational efforts. Later, as the day winds down, begin to put things away as time permits.

The assistant's day isn't over just because the last shot is complete. If the photographer has seen some film from the day's shoot, it's possible that the set will need to be torn down and everything associated with it returned to its appropriate place.

The exposed film is extremely valuable and requires proper handling. Some or all of it may need to be taken to the processing lab on your way home. If the film has been kept well organized from the beginning, this should be a straightforward task. Remember, you may not be at the studio tomorrow. The photographer may be alone with a lot of unanswered questions if you didn't do things right.

## FINISHING UP

As the end of the day draws near, consider asking the photographer whether there's anything you could do to be more useful. This feedback can help you to be more effective, not only with that particular photographer, but with others as well. When the day is finally over, take some time to reflect on the day's activities while they're still fresh in your mind. Were there mistakes or things you'd do differently? Reflecting can be one of the best ways to learn and improve.

## THE DAY'S SHOOT

On this hypothetical day, the schedule calls for the completion of three different product shots. The work will be performed in the studio, utilizing a 4″ × 5″ view camera, exposing film, and an electronic-flash lighting system.

### Agenda

| | |
|---|---|
| 7:50 AM | Arrive at the studio a few minutes early. |
| 8:00..... | Gain a general understanding of what's on the day's schedule, especially camera format and film requirements. This information will help establish how much time must be allotted for film-handling responsibilities throughout the day. |
| 8:10..... | Clean and load nine 4″ × 5″ sheet film holders with color transparency film. |
| 8:30..... | Confirm the type of Polaroid instant film to be used. Load the Polaroid film holder and place an adequate supply on the set cart. Begin to familiarize yourself with the studio, as time permits. |
| 8:40..... | Prepare the shooting area, so work can begin on the first of three shots. |
| 8:50..... | Set up the background material. Shot number one requires a roll of seamless paper to be suspended from a crossbar and swept onto a sheet of elevated plywood. |
| 9:15..... | Bring the required lighting equipment onto the set, including power supplies, flash heads, stands, and light-modifying devices. |
| 9:30..... | Position the camera and have the set cart nearby. |
| 9:45..... | Prepare the subject and props and then start to position them on the set. |
| 10:00..... | Adjust the lighting and composition until both are far enough along to warrant the first Polaroid print. |
| 10:30..... | Prepare to expose Polaroid film by readying the camera and strobes. Expose a sheet of Polaroid film and annotate it. |
| 10:40..... | Fine-tune the lighting arrangement and composition. The number of Polaroid prints may range from as few as a couple to as many as a dozen per shot. |
| 11:30..... | When everything is as desired, prepare the camera to expose film. Medium-format cameras require the film magazine to be attached and additional film made immediately available. |
| | Large-format camera lenses must be made ready, and the appropriate number of film holders should be brought onto the set. |

11:40..... Reexamine the set. Confirm that everything is still clean and positioned as desired. If you must work on the set at this point, it's imperative not to disrupt anything.

11:45..... Position yourself close to the photographer during the process of exposing film. The photographer must always have film available. Be ready to remind the photographer of any filter changes or variations in the exposure sequence.

Make certain the photographer doesn't outpace the power supply's recycle rate.

Noon..... After the exposure process is complete, organize film and correlate it with a Polaroid print. Then place the exposed film in a safe place. Determine whether any film needs to be processed at this time.

12:10..... Prepare the set for the next shot.

12:30..... Establish which materials are to be reused on the second shot. These might be the background material, lights, and light-modifying devices. Necessary items should be left on or near the set, and unneeded items can be put away.

12:45..... Prepare the subject and related props.

1:00..... Like the previous shot, the lighting equipment and composition will be fine-tuned and confirmed through a series of Polaroid prints.

1:50..... Prepare to go to film. The art director has decided on a slight variation in composition, so the second shot is designated as shot 2A and 2B.

2:00..... With two of the three shots finished, the photographer instructs the assistant to unload one sheet of film from shots 1, 2A, and 2B. This is the middle exposure of a tight bracket. All three sheets will be processed normally.

Clearly label the film with regards to contents and processing instructions.

2:10..... Everyone breaks for lunch.

Turn off power supplies.

While getting the take-out lunch, the assistant takes the film to the lab, noting exactly what time it will be ready later that day.

2:45..... After lunch, the assistant cleans up.

When an opportunity presents itself, call your answering machine to check for messages related to freelance assisting.

3:00..... Load more film holders, due to the unexpected variation on the second shot.

Check supplies of Polaroid film.

If necessary, make time to organize the exposed film.

3:15..... The third and final shot requires the background of seamless roll paper to be exchanged for a sheet of Plexiglas. Carefully clean its surface.

3:30..... As before, follow the progress of the shot through the exposure process. Time permitting, begin to put away items that have accumulated around the set's perimeter.

4:00.....    Be sure to monitor the clock. The photographer wants you to pick up the processed film from the prior two shots.

               Leave for the lab.

4:20.....    Upon your return, the photographer checks film for exposure, sharpness, and color.

5:30.....    Finalize the third shot by exposing film.

5:45.....    Now, make certain you understand exactly what the photographer wants done with all the exposed film. At the very least, it must be well organized and clearly labeled.

               Due to the client's immediate need for the film, the remaining film from shots 1, 2A and 2B, and all from shot 3 is down loaded and will be run normally.

               As soon as the final shot is complete, turn off the flash head's modeling lamp and let the fan cool the head.

6:00.....    Establish whether you should tear down the set.

               Begin to take down the set. Due to their relatively fragile nature, it's a good idea to remove the camera first, then the lights.

               If the flash heads have not had time to cool down, keep the flash tube protected with a reflector until the reflector can be replaced with a flash-tube protector.

6:20.....    Objects on the set are now readily accessible.

               It's important that everything is returned to its proper place. You may not be there tomorrow to help find anything.

6:40.....    If appropriate, ask the photographer how you did.

6:50.....    Before leaving for home, grab the film and take it to the lab. It must be labeled with instructions, and it will be ready early tomorrow morning.

7:00.....    Reflect on how the day went, what you learned, and things you might do differently next time.

## List of Essentials

❑ Call report for the studio's address, phone number, and directions

❑ Wristwatch with a sweep hand to time the development of Polaroid instant film

❑ Indelible pen (Sharpie brand) to annotate Polaroid prints

❑ Local map to aid in running errands

❑ Spare clothes for dirty jobs, like painting and darkroom work

❑ Hip belt/fanny pack to hold useful items, especially for location work

❑ Small flashlight for working in dark studios

❑ Emergency food for those unanticipated late nights.

# 6

# The 35mm Single Lens Reflex Camera

WHATEVER SPARKED YOUR INTEREST IN PHOTOGRAPHY, IT MORE THAN LIKELY led to the use of a 35mm single lens reflex camera. This is true of most professional photographers, regardless of the format they utilize now. As an assistant, you'll continue to use the 35mm SLR, but you will also expand your equipment repertoire to include other formats. Now, some 35mm cameras use digital capture instead of film. These cameras are discussed in the chapter 11, "Capturing Digital Images."

## CHARACTERISTICS OF THE 35MM SLR

The 35mm SLR has qualities that are unmatched. Of the three most commonly used formats, it's undoubtedly the easiest to manipulate and the least expensive to operate. Due to the 35mm camera's light weight and small size, a tripod is often unnecessary. Entire systems consisting of several camera bodies, multiple lenses, and an on-camera flash can often be carried by one strong-shouldered individual. At 36 exposures per roll, overall film handling is minimized.

Unfortunately, these very characteristics tend to limit the necessity for an assistant, but all is not lost. For assignments calling for a large selection of lenses, especially of longer focal lengths, the 35mm system is unequalled. Jobs characterized by a diverse shot list coupled with plenty of activity are more readily accomplished using a lighter, more varied camera system. Finally, some fast-paced events can only be captured with an endless supply of film and a motor drive. You might find that the conditions necessitating the use of the 35mm camera can dictate the need for an assistant after all.

Although most assistants are familiar with their own 35mm SLR camera, as a group SLRs can be confusing. There are many manufacturers, and the different models and features tend to change more quickly than the medium- or large-format systems. Now add to the mix digital cameras and a host of new manufacturers. When confronted with a manufacturer's newest camera body, you might find that you're not as comfortable with it as you first thought.

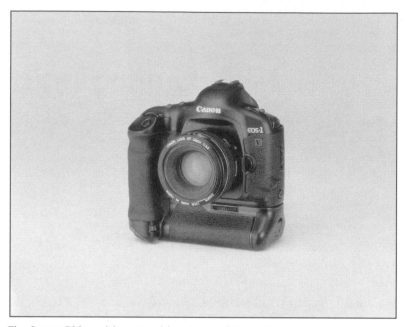

The Canon EOS 1 with motor drive. Be careful. A 35mm camera with a motor drive can easily outpace a strobe's recycle time, leading to underexposed film. © 2000 Canon Cameras.

## THE ASSISTANT'S RESPONSIBILITIES

Many of your responsibilities involving the camera are related to *film*. Due to the speed at which 35mm SLR cameras can be operated, the most important task is often just keeping the photographer supplied with film. To do this, the assistant must be able to do more than properly load and unload film.

Assisting jobs often begin at a fast pace, which generally gets faster as the day progresses. If this is the case and you're confronted with an unfamiliar camera, concentrate on what's important to your job. Some aspects of the camera's operation are absolutely essential, whereas others hardly matter. Prioritize.

### Prerequisites to Loading

Before you can begin loading the camera, you must be certain you understand the day's film requirements. Exactly what type of film will be used? When there is more than one kind, it must be kept well organized so mistakes don't occur. For example, a photographer might have one camera body for black-and-white negative film and a second body dedicated to color transparency film. Clearly differentiate the two camera bodies with regard to film type.

Whether assisting in the studio or on location, try to find a clean, level surface before you begin to handle film. While on location, you have to make due with what you can get, perhaps by using the top of a camera case or your lap. Regardless, plan on keeping the camera and all film away from anyone not directly responsible for it.

### Be Sure the Camera is Empty

You're still not ready to load the camera body with film. First, confirm it's empty. Ask the photographer or check the frame counter. *If the film counter indicates the letter "S," the camera should be empty.* If the counter indicates frame 36, the back hasn't been opened since frame 36 was exposed; therefore, check the rewind crank knob for resistance. When the rewind crank freely moves both clockwise and counter-clockwise, the camera is either empty, or the exposed film has been rewound into the film cartridge.

In either case, attempt to rewind the film just to be sure. Now it's safe to open the camera back. The camera back is most commonly opened by pulling up on the rewind crank. Once open, examine the film chamber for dust. If necessary and when time allows, carefully clean the film chamber with canned-air or an anti-static brush. Do not touch the shutter curtain and avoid blasting it with air.

## Loading the 35mm SLR Camera

I suspect that virtually every reader is familiar with the 35mm film cartridge and how it's loaded into the camera. However, it's useful to reread your camera's instruction manual for a good standard procedure. In addition, here's a general outline with potential hazards to avoid.

1) Begin by installing the film cartridge into the camera's film-cartridge chamber. This is located on the left side when looking into the back of the camera body.
2) Make sure the cartridge is held securely by the forked rewind post.
3) Now insert the film leader into a slot found on the take-up spool.
4) Advance the take-up spool with your finger or by using the film advance lever. Then make *absolutely certain* the film is held tightly by the take-up spool. If the film leader slips out of the take-up spool, the film will fail to advance.
5) Before closing the camera back, check that the perforations found along the film's edge are properly aligned with any sprocket teeth.
6) Close the camera back and use the film advance lever or motor drive to advance the film to frame number one. While doing so, *check to see that the rewind knob rotates* and is under tension. These conditions indicate that film is moving through the camera. It is good practice to occasionally check these two points occasionally throughout the exposure process.

A minor note: When a photographer is utilizing the *motor drive,* you should continue to use it when changing film. Alternating between manual advance and the motor drive can cause problems. Also, before considering the job finished, *check that the camera's ASA, f-stop, and shutter-speed settings remain as desired.*

## The Exposure Process

Before the photographer begins to shoot film, you should establish whether it will be exposed in a particular sequence. The photographer may want to expose color film first and finish each individual shot with black-and-white film. With this basic under-

standing, you're in a position to set up the appropriate camera and film at the beginning of each shot.

You're also better able to anticipate when the photographer might change
from one film type to another. Now you can be sure to have the correct camera ready
and waiting. When changing film types, it's always a good idea to restate it to the photographer to make certain there is no misunderstanding.

Before going to film, prepare for the inevitable accumulation of exposed film.
By being organized from the start, you can avoid confusion. To aid the process have
a couple of plastic bags to segregate exposed and unexposed film, or possibly different film types. A pen with indelible ink, like the Sharpie® brand is necessary so you
can write directly on the metal film cartridge. When unavailable, a grease pencil will
suffice. Notes might include the shot number or processing information.

## Monitor Film Usage

Because the assistant is responsible for keeping the photographer in film, it's important to know when the photographer is nearing the end of the roll. It can be difficult to see the frame counter and almost impossible to keep count, but try.

When the photographer does run out of film, the assistant must have unexposed film immediately available. It's either loaded in a different camera body, or you
need to have a fresh roll ready to be loaded into the camera in use. Note: Some photographers like to be told when there are only a few frames remaining so they can
better decide how to finish a particular shot.

## Unloading the Camera

After you are handed a camera containing exposed film, be sure to rewind it. When
the rewind crank knob loses tension and rotates freely, the film is inside the metal cartridge. Then open the back and remove the film cartridge. It's always worth numbering each roll of film sequentially. Depending on the photographer's preferences, you
might also include a shot number or correlate the film to a Polaroid print. There's
more than one way to process a roll of film. It can be *pushed* or *pulled,* or perhaps the
photographer may want a *clip* or *snip test* done.

When handed a camera with unexposed film, note how much remains.
Under some situations, it's best to change rolls when given the opportunity, especially when only a few frames remain on the roll. Imagine the stylist is finally done,
the model is holding a precarious position, and the photographer begins. Unfortunately, after a couple of exposures the camera is out of film. You just got very
busy and everyone is waiting. The voracious appetite of a motor drive can often
complicate matters.

Note: Both 35mm SLR and medium-format cameras utilize roll film, and
many film-related tasks are common to both formats. Because potential assistants are
likely to be less familiar with medium-format cameras, additional details are presented in the next chapter, "The Medium-Format Camera."

## LENSES AND FILTERS

Not every camera-related task involves film. The assistant will need to change lenses and filters. Lenses are usually attached to the camera with some form of bayonet-style mechanism and removed by depressing a lens-release button and rotating the lens. When not in use, both the front and rear elements should be protected with lens caps. If you encounter a dirty lens or filter, use a blower brush or lens tissue. First blow off any dust particles which could scratch the lens and then wipe gently with the tissue.

Any lens might need to have a filter attached to it. The most common are glass filters, which screw onto the front lens element. However, you will certainly encounter other kinds. Another group of filters is designed to be held in a *filter frame*. The filter frame either clips onto the lens barrel or screws onto its end. The filters are made from a variety of materials, but measure about 3″ × 3″ or 4″ × 4″. Because these filters are most likely to be used with large-format view cameras, their handling characteristics are presented in that section.

### Lens Shades

You'll find that lens shades are standard equipment among professional photographers. Most lens shades screw onto the end of the lens, much like a filter. However, each is designed for a specific focal-length lens. Long lenses have long, narrow lens shades, whereas wide-angle lenses require a short, wide lens shade. Incorrectly placing a lens shade designed for a 105mm lens on a 50mm lens will greatly crop the film image.

# 7

# The Medium-Format Camera

IN MANY WAYS, THE MEDIUM–FORMAT CAMERA IS SIMPLY A LARGER VERSION OF THE 35mm SLR. Ideally, it retains many attributes of its smaller relative, while providing larger film size. Both utilize roll film, Polaroid film holders, built-in light meters, and bayonet style, interchangeable lenses.

However, there are far fewer manufacturers of medium-format cameras, and there is greater stability in their design. This is an advantage for the freelance assistant, as most assistants don't own medium-format cameras. At first, you may need some on-the-job training, but you'll find that regardless of manufacturer, your assisting responsibilities are very similar. Like other cameras, medium-format cameras can be used with a digitizing back in place of film. The same digital back can often be used on a view camera. Hence, they're discussed in chapter 11, "Capturing Digital Images."

## KEY CHARACTERISTICS

Medium-format camera features are directed toward professional photographers. To meet their diverse needs, the cameras tend to be more modular in design. One unique feature is the *interchangeable film magazine*. A film magazine, or film "back," holds the film and is designed to be attached to and removed from the camera body quickly. Having several film magazines allows the photographer to change film type in mid-roll and reduces downtime when out of film. Also, Polaroid instant film is readily integrated into the system, so the photographer can quickly alternate between a film magazine and a Polaroid film holder.

The medium-format camera is likely to be used while mounted on a tripod, partly due to its weight and size but also because of the critical nature of the work for which it is used. However, when necessary it can be hand-held. The medium-format camera is well suited for work both in the studio and on location.

But wherever you're working, its qualities are best highlighted under fast-paced or quickly changing shooting conditions. The ability to view through the lens while exposing film is indispensable when the subject isn't static. The camera's usefulness is further enhanced by the fact that the film can be advanced quickly, either manually or with a motor drive. All of these features increase the likelihood of getting the shot, while supplying a larger film size than the 35mm SLR.

If you are only familiar with the 35mm SLR camera, you've probably taken the features listed here for granted. However, the alternative when larger film size is required is the view camera, a rather cumbersome camera in fast-changing shooting conditions.

## MEDIUM-FORMAT FILM

As with any camera, there are film-handling responsibilities integrated throughout the assistant's day. Here are a few general notes concerning medium-format roll film. There are two standard sizes of roll film, designated 120 and 220. Both sizes are the same width, and the figure denotes the length of each roll—the 120 format being the shorter of the two.

The absolute *number of exposures* per roll will depend on the exact image size or format size of the camera. For example, the three more common image sizes found in medium-format cameras are 6 × 4.5 cm (2¼″ × 1⅝″), 6 × 6 cm (2¼″ × 2¼″), and 6 × 7 cm (2¼″ × 2¾″). The number of exposures per roll of 120-size film is 16, 12, and 10, respectively. The 220-size film provides twice the number of exposures. Please note that 120-size film must be used in film magazines designed for 120-size film; 220 film must be used in magazines designed for 220 size.

Roll film doesn't have the protection of a metal film cartridge. The film and its protective backing paper are wound around a spindle and secured with a paper tab. There are times during the loading or unloading process when roll film can unravel, if dropped or mishandled. Therefore, extra care is required. If you haven't seen a roll of medium-format film, buy one and take it apart. This will help clarify why things are done a certain way.

Because it's usually the assistant's responsibility to keep the photographer in film, here are a few manufacturers you're most likely to come across. The Hasselblad provides a 6 × 6 cm format, and with Mamiya and Bronica, all three formats can be found.

## THE FILM MAGAZINE

In principle, the various models of film magazines are quite similar, but be aware that there are subtle differences. Film magazines differ in how they attach to the camera body and how the film compartment opens and closes. Aspects concerning placing the film in the magazine and advancing it to the first exposure also differ. Such seemingly minor points can cause major problems. Fortunately, a digital back attaches to the camera housing using the same mechanism to attach the film magazine.

The film magazine consists of two main parts. An *exterior housing* protects the film from light and physically attaches to the camera body. The *film holding assembly* or *film carrier* holds the film and is enclosed within the housing. A film magazine is opened and closed using some form of locking mechanism. Once opened, the two parts can be completely separated. Add a roll of film, and you have your hands full.

When unfamiliar with a specific model, examine it and ask for help. Always view film handling as critically important. If you've never handled a camera produced by one of the three aforementioned manufacturers, try to get some hands-on experience, the Hasselblad being the camera of choice.

## Cleaning the Film Magazine

1) While the film-holding assembly is removed from the housing, clean the two pieces with canned air.

2) Be sure to remove the metal *dark slide* from the housing unit and examine the border defining the image area. Look for any small, hair-like particles that may ultimately lie on the film surface.

3) When using canned air, it's easy to nonchalantly blow out the inside and assume it's clean. Make it a point to look. As time permits, it's also a good idea to check for dust when changing film.

4) Before handling film, check that the dark slide is completely reinserted and the film take-up spool is on the correct side.

## Prerequisites to Loading

Make certain you understand the day's film requirements before you load any film. Establish whether more than one type of film will be used; if so, mark each film magazine accordingly. You should also know if there's a particular *exposure sequence* or whether the film should be designated in any way. This basic understanding allows you to be more efficient and minimizes errors.

## LOADING THE FILM MAGAZINE

It's best to standardize a film-handling procedure and refine it with experience. This will help you keep your wits when tensions heighten. Because film magazines come apart into several pieces, try to find a relatively clean, level work surface before you get too involved.

An interchangeable film magazine can be loaded and unloaded, regardless of whether it's attached to the camera body. In the following description, imagine that the entire film magazine has been removed from the camera body.

## Preparing the Film Magazine

1) Check that the magazine is *empty*. You're generally safe when the frame counter indicates anything other than a number. If in doubt, try to wind any film onto the take-up spool by trying to advance the film. You can also check the film magazine in a darkroom or ask the photographer.

2) The empty film spool must first be moved over to the film take-up position. Understand that an empty film magazine has one film take-up spool. The exposed film is wound onto this spool.

It is *important* to know that you do not rewind medium-format roll film. Once the last exposure is made, the remaining film and its protective backing paper are advanced entirely onto the take-up spool. So the empty take-up spool is always supplied by the last roll of film. The empty spool is thus situated where the new, unexposed roll needs to go. Therefore, the empty film spool must first be moved to the film take-up position.

## Magazine Operation

### Loading the Magazine

The magazine may be loaded on, or off the camera. If it is to be loaded off the camera then the magazine slide must be inserted, its flat side towards the rear. This facilitates removal of the film holder for loading. Follow the procedure below.

1) Fold out the film holder key.

2) Turn the key **counter-clockwise** and withdraw the film holder.

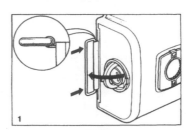

3) An empty take-up spool should be placed under the splined knob of the spool clamp bar. Insert a roll of film under the other end of the bar, ensuring that it is turned the same way as in the illustration. Be careful to remove **all** the paper tape that surrounds a new roll of film.

4) Turn the film holder key **clockwise** to open the film clamp. Pull 8 - 10cm (3 - 4 in.) of paper backing off the film roll and slide the edge under the clamp.

5) Insert the tongue of the backing paper into the slot in the take-up spool.

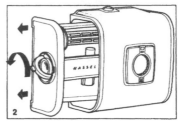

6) Turn the splined knob **clockwise** until the arrow on the paper backing is opposite the triangular index on the spool clamp bar, but no further.

7) Turn the film holder key **counter-clockwise** and insert the film holder into the magazine – jiggling it a little if it does not click into place. Lock the film holder into the magazine by turning the key **clockwise**.

8) Fold out the film crank and rotate it **clockwise** about ten turns until it stops. Turn the crank counter-clockwise and fold it in.

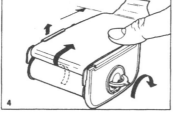

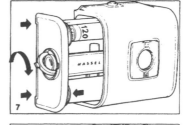

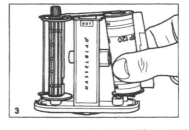

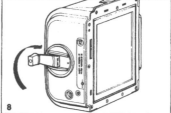

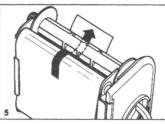

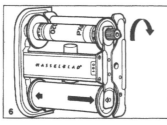

Number 1 will now be displayed in the frame counter window and the magazine is loaded – ready for use.

The magazine's film winder crank is only blocked at frame 1. A partially exposed film may be wound off at any frame thereafter.

The frame counter is automatically reset when the film holder is withdrawn from the magazine.

Loading the Hasselblad medium format film magazine. *Courtesy of Victor Hasselblad, Inc.*

## Loading the Film

1) The film is held securely in the film carrier by inserting the two posts, found at the top and bottom of the film carrier, into each end of the film spool.

2) The unexposed roll must also be positioned so that film and not the paper backing will be exposed. This positioning is critical.

3) Now completely remove the paper tab that keeps the film from unraveling, making certain that no stray paper is left in the film back. *The paper leader must feed out from the underside of the roll, not over the top.* When done correctly, the black, inside surface of the backing paper is facing out as it's pulled across the pressure plate and inserted into the take–up spool.

4) The *backing paper* must wind onto the take-up spool by going under the spool, versus over the top. The backing paper is then wound further onto the take-up spool, until the arrow found on the backing paper lines up in a designated position on the film carrier. This procedure assures that the film is in the precise starting position.

5) Once the film is in place, reinsert the film carrier into the magazine housing and *lock the housing compartment*. The latching mechanism does not automatically lock when snapped shut, like 35mm SLR camera bodies do.

## Advancing the Film

1) With the film carrier secured within the housing, make certain the dark slide is fully inserted.

2) Use the *film advance lever* to advance the film until it stops. The frame counter is now on number one. This procedure advances the backing paper and film, until the film is in position to be exposed. Failure to do this results in the loss of exposures one and two because you'll be exposing the backing paper and not film.

3) Now attach the film magazine to the camera body. Remember, the film magazine can be safely removed from the body in mid–roll so long as the dark slide is fully inserted.

## THE EXPOSURE PROCESS

During the exposure process, track film usage closely; ten or twelve frames can be exposed very rapidly. When only one or two exposures remain on the roll, inform the photographer in an unobtrusive manner. At this time, the assistant needs to have another film magazine loaded. Have it in your hands and stand next to the photographer. If you sense the photographer might shoot a Polaroid, have the Polaroid holder loaded and immediately available. When the shooting stops, don't let it be because of you.

## UNLOADING THE FILM MAGAZINE

After the last exposure is made, the film must be advanced entirely onto the take–up spool. The film isn't rewound like 35mm film. Often, the photographer advances the film, but do it yourself, too, just to be safe.

1) Advance the film using the film-advance lever. The procedure is done just like you would if you were advancing from exposure nine to ten, only it doesn't stop. When the film is completely wound onto the take-up spool, the film advance lever has much less resistance.

2) It's now safe to open the film back and carefully remove the film.

3) When you open the film magazine, the free end of the backing paper is loose. If the roll is dropped, it could unravel. It's sealed by using a paper tab, similar to that torn-off at the beginning of the roll. Moisten it and wrap it around the film.

4) Work close to the table to reduce the likelihood of any mishandling.

5) Have a separate storage container for exposed film. It doesn't take long to accumulate four to five rolls. An empty, 50-sheet box used for 4" × 5" film is especially useful. Whatever you use, try to store exposed roll film in subdued light.

## FILM PROCESSING

For any film, both you and the lab need to know how it's to be processed. Immediately after the film is exposed is the time to include any pertinent information regarding its processing. Generally, properly exposed film is processed normally or "normal." However, both roll and sheet film can also be pushed or pulled by varying amounts. In order to determine if the development process should be altered, a photographer might request a clip test.

### Alternative Film Processing

A *clip* or *snip test* can be performed on both small- and medium-format roll film. Here, the processing lab cuts off a short length of film from either the beginning or end of the roll, as directed by the photographer. This portion of the film is usually processed normally, but could be pushed or pulled. Afterwards, the photographer views the processed piece of film and decides how the remainder of the roll should be run or processed.

For example, let's say a clip test with color transparency film appears a little dark or under exposed, when processed normally. This can be corrected by push processing or *pushing* the remainder of the roll to lighten it up. The lab gives the film a little more time in the developer. Conversely, overexposed film or a light clip test will dictate pulling the remainder of the roll. Less time in the developer yields denser film.

The amount in which the development process deviates from normal processing is measured in *stops,* for f-stops. For example, a roll that is underexposed by one-half f-stops will be pushed one-half stops or, as written on the instruction sheet, "Push, +½ stops." A roll that is overexposed by one-half f-stops will be pulled one-half stops and written as "Pull, -½ stops." I like to add either a plus or minus sign to be certain there's no misunderstanding. These terms regarding altering film processing are common to both roll film and sheet film. However, you don't perform clip tests on sheet film.

## THE ROLL FILM HOLDER AND VIEW CAMERA

It is also possible to shoot medium-format, roll film with a view camera. Roll film holders are available in a variety of formats for view cameras having the International style back and locking system. These holders are very similar to the film magazines for medium-format cameras, with regard to the loading and unloading of film.

Before a roll film holder can be attached to a view camera, the ground glass must be removed. There are two spring-loaded levers on each side of the ground glass. These are depressed, and the ground glass and its frame slide out. The roll film holder is slipped into place and secured with two other sliding latches. A sliding digital back is often attached to view camera using the same mechanism to attach a roll film back or ground glass.

## LENSES, FILTERS, AND THE COMPENDIUM

Medium-format lenses are handled much like those for 35mm camera systems. However, there's less tendency to frequently change lenses during a shoot, partly because there are simply not as many lenses to choose from with respect to focal length. It's also due to the fact that medium format cameras tend to be used in a more methodical manner than 35mm SLRs. Lenses are attached and removed utilizing a bayonet-style mechanism and a lens-release button. Regarding Hasselblad lenses, it is *important* to note that you can only remove the lens when the camera has been cocked. Once cocked, depress the lens-release button and rotate the lens counter-clockwise until it stops.

When required, glass filters can be screwed onto the front of the lens. However, medium-format lenses have a rather large diameter front lens element. This means that owning a wide selection of glass filters can get very expensive. Consequently, a *filter frame* that holds interchangeable filters is far more cost effective and provides access to a much greater selection.

Instead of purchasing an individual lens shade for each lens, medium-format systems often incorporate what's called a *compendium lens shade*. This connects to the lens and resembles an accordion-shaped bellows. A compendium lens shade is extended or compressed depending on the focal length of the lens. A calibrated scale is provided to ensure the bellows is extended the proper distance. In addition, the compendium lens shade has provisions to accept various filters. The fine points about the compendium lens shade and filters will be presented in chapter 8, "The View Camera."

## USING A TRIPOD

The medium-format camera is used with a tripod more often than not. Unless instructed otherwise, begin by setting up the tripod to a height of about four to five feet, making sure it is level. Before attaching the camera, tighten all knobs related to the extension legs and tripod head. Attach the camera body using the mounting bolt found on the tripod head, much like with a 35mm camera. Unlike 35mm cameras, many medium-format cameras require a larger, ⅜-inch diameter mounting bolt. Therefore, when the camera is to be mounted to a tripod head having the smaller, ¼-inch bolt, a ⅜-to-¼ *reducing bushing* is required. It's critical to remember this vital accessory when packing for location shoots.

# 8

# The View Camera

T HE VIEW CAMERA IS THE CAMERA OF CHOICE FOR MANY PHOTOGRAPHERS AND a necessity for certain kinds of photography. No camera is better suited for use in the studio, and it follows that the assistant needs some proficiency in its use, at least in specific areas. As with other cameras, view cameras can be used with various digitizing backs in place of film. Many of these same backs can also be used on medium-format cameras. Hence, they are discussed in chapter 11, "Capturing Digital Images."

## KEY CHARACTERISTICS

The view camera provides several advantages over the two smaller formats, the most obvious is increased film size. A $4'' \times 5''$ sheet of film yields higher quality than a smaller size film, and it's easier to evaluate. Perhaps more important is the ability to control both the plane of sharp focus and perspective. View cameras are also available in $5'' \times 7''$ and $8'' \times 10''$ formats, but these are becoming increasingly rare.

### Plane of Focus and Perspective

The portion of the image that is in focus or acceptably sharp is called the *plane of sharp focus*. With a view camera, you can place the plane of sharp focus in the most useful position and maximize available depth of field. This can be parallel to the shooting surface, perpendicular to it or anywhere in between.

Being able to control the plane of focus is critical to much of photography, especially product work. Here, the camera is often positioned close to the subject, which results in a very limited depth of field. It's not uncommon to have a depth of field measured in inches, even at f32.

*Perspective* is the appearance to the eye of objects, with respect to their relative distance and position. Controlling perspective allows the photographer to create the feeling of three dimensions or depth in a two-dimensional photograph. In architectural work, the photographer must make a structure appear natural or normal to the viewer. By properly manipulating the view camera, a building's vertical lines can be made to look truly vertical. The lines may also be permitted to converge slightly, if more appealing. The divergence and convergence of horizontal lines can also be controlled.

### The Camera Movements

Both perspective and the plane of focus are adjusted by using what are called the camera movements. The view camera allows for independent movement of the film and lens. This affects how the image falls on the film's surface. The film and the lens can *tilt* forwards or backwards; *swing* or pivot to the left or right; laterally *shift* to the left or right; and *rise* or *fall* up or down.

A 35mm SLR or medium-format camera has the lens and film fixed parallel to each other. Being fixed, the camera can produce an uncomfortable amount of convergence among parallel lines. When pointing the camera upward at a tall building, the resulting convergence makes the building look as if it's falling back. Also, the plane of sharp focus is fixed in a position parallel to both the lens and film plane. Hence, there is little control over its placement.

A thorough presentation of view-camera technique can be found in numerous books and does not appear here. I suggest that you have at least a familiarity with the terms describing the camera movements: swing, tilt, rise, fall, and shift. You should also understand the *Scheimpflug Rule,* which defines how to control the plane of sharp focus. Until you've worked with the photographer a considerable length of time, you won't be responsible for adjusting the view camera.

A good way to strengthen your view-camera technique is to note how the photographer has adjusted the camera's front and rear standards, then see if you understand why. Keep in mind, assisting is not one long question–and–answer session. Limited questions can be asked, but at appropriate times.

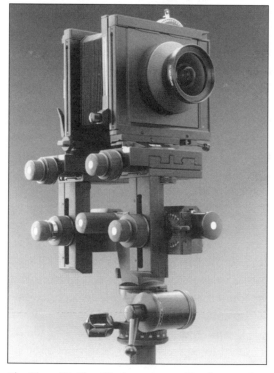

The Sinar P2 4" × 5" view camera. The front and rear standards attach to the monorail, which slips into the rail clamp. The rail clamp screws onto the tripod head, which finally connects to a tripod or camera stand. *Courtesy Sinar Bron, Inc.*

## VIEW CAMERA BASICS

What follows is basic information that's of particular importance to the assistant. Most likely, you'll work with what is referred to as the studio view camera, as compared to the more compact field view camera. Both styles function the same way, but the studio camera's modular design allows it to be used in a greater variety of applications.

In its basic form, the studio view camera consists of the *front standard,* which holds the lens, and the *rear standard,* which holds the *ground glass* and film. The two standards connect together with the accordion-shaped *bellows.* This is attached to a monorail, which is attached to a rail clamp or mounting base. It's the rail clamp or mounting base that screws onto the tripod head.

### Camera Stands and Tripods

View cameras are supported on a camera stand or sturdy tripod. When asked to attach the camera to a stand or tripod, proceed carefully. You'll find that view cameras are more awkward than heavy.

First, make sure the tripod and tripod head are secure, with no loose knobs. Then screw the *rail clamp* to the tripod head. Now, the monorail can be positioned in the rail clamp. The monorail serves as the foundation for the rest of the camera.

## LARGE-FORMAT LENSES

Once the camera is attached to the tripod head, there's still some set-up work to be done. Most of it revolves around the lens. The lens itself is held in a flat, square *lensboard*. The lensboard is then fitted into recessed grooves found on the front standard. Once positioned, the lensboard is secured in place using a locking mechanism.

Though not standardized, this locking mechanism is usually simple in design, and it is fairly apparent how it operates. It will be found at the top, or at both the top and bottom, of the front standard. The same mechanism is used to remove the bellows and rear standard. If perplexed as to its operation, ask for help. Errors can cause light leaks or the lens to fall off.

### Preparing the Lens

Using a large-format lens adds several steps to the set-up and exposure process. To begin with, a lens always needs a *cable release,* one identical to those used with other cameras. However, the cable release attaches to the lens, not to the camera body.

When electronic flash is used, a *sync cord* or radio transmitter must connect the lens to the light source. The sync cord and its connection to the lens are identical to that found in small and medium camera systems.

Now is a good time to check the *shutter speed.* One-sixtieth of a second is a reliable choice when the lens is synced to electronic flash or strobe. If natural light is all or part of the exposure, the shutter speed will be determined by the photographer.

Besides shutter speed, exposure is controlled by adjusting the *lens aperture* or f-stop setting. But with large-format lenses, as the lens is stopped-down, less light reaches the ground glass. When the lens is set at f32, the ground glass is fairly dark. Consequently, the lens must be opened up to its maximum aperture for viewing, commonly f5.6. To make an exposure, it must be closed-down to the working aperture, f32, for example.

At this point, you're not done yet. The lens' *shutter* must be switched open to view the ground glass and switched closed before exposing film. By looking through the front of the lens, you can see the shutter open and close as the switch is moved back and forth. Finally, cock the shutter. Both the switch to open and close the shutter and the lever to cock the shutter are located on the lens.

### *Summary of Lens Preparation*

When you set up a view camera for *viewing,* the lens should be prepared as follows:

1) Attach the cable release and sync cord.
2) Switch the shutter open.
3) Set the appropriate shutter speed and adjust the f-stop for the largest aperture.

To make an exposure:
1) Switch the shutter closed.
2) Stop-down to the working aperture and cock the shutter.
3) Test by plunging the cable release to make certain the shutter works and the strobes are firing.
4) Recock the shutter and pull the dark slide.
5) Plunge the cable release to expose Polaroid or film. Replace the dark slide.

## Compendium Lens Shade

The photographer will probably utilize a *compendium lens shade*. This kind of lens shade utilizes a bellows and attaches to the front standard, not directly to the lens. *Lens flair* caused by extraneous light can be a real problem; it can usually be seen reflected on the front lens element. Position the lens shade or compendium until the reflection is gone. Then look through the camera at the working aperture to make certain the lens shade isn't in view. In addition to a lens shade, black cardboard is often positioned close to the lens to block off or *flag* stray light.

## Filters

An important item associated with the lens is the filter. You've probably handled the glass filters that screw onto the front of the lens. These are used with the view camera, but less often. View-camera lenses have large front elements, necessitating large, expensive filters. Photographers commonly rely on what are referred to as *gelatin filters,* such as Wratten gel filters.

Gelatin filters resemble thin, flexible plastic. They measure either 3″ × 3″ or 4″ × 4″. Although rather fragile, they offer several advantages. First, gelatin-style filters are relatively inexpensive and come in a wide variety. The most common are the *color-compensating (CC) filters.* These are available in red, blue, green, cyan, yellow, and magenta. In addition, each color also comes in precise, varying strengths. The weakest yellow color-compensating filter is designated as *CC025Y,* and the strongest as *CC50Y.* Color-compensating filters are used to achieve the desired color on film. For example, if a film's emulsion is running a little cool (bluish), a magenta (pinkish) color-compensating filter might be used to make it neutral. These can also be used when integrating several light sources—perhaps a building's fluorescent lighting with daylight-balanced film.

### Attaching the Filter

Gelatin filters must be held in a *filter frame.* Most commonly, the frame clips onto the rear lens element of the large-format lens (inside the bellows). Placing the filter on the rear element requires a smaller filter and reduces lens flare. When positioning the filter, care must be taken to assure the filter lays flat and it doesn't develop any kinks or creases.

Gelatin filters are very delicate. They should be touched only along their edges and cleaned with a soft brush. Absolutely no moisture can come in contact with them, or you'll see why they are called *gels*. Some newer gelatin-style filters are sturdier but should still be handled with care.

Gaining access to a gelatin filter placed on the rear lens element can be difficult, especially after the camera is positioned. When practical, remove the lens, and then the filter can be handled. Unfortunately, when there's a compendium, sync cord, and cable release attached to the lens, this can be disruptive. Under these conditions, get to the filter by removing the bellows at the point where it attaches to the front standard.

Another option is to remove the back of the camera holding the ground glass and reach through the bellows. This is most practical when a shorter focal length is used and the bellows is fairly compressed. Ideally, the photographer should not have to refocus after working with a filter. The bellows and ground glass are locked in place with the same mechanism used to secure the lens.

## Focusing Aids

After preparing the lens, make sure there's a *dark cloth* or *focusing cloth* nearby. The dark cloth restricts background light and aids in viewing the ground glass. For focusing, the photographer needs a *magnifying loupe* or *focusing loupe*. Place the loupe directly on the ground glass and then rest your eye on the loupe, in a similar manner to viewing a color transparency. You focus by extending or contracting the camera bellows.

It takes time to feel comfortable viewing the ground glass. The image is upside down and backwards, and at first glance it appears rather dark. However, for both the photographer and the assistant, viewing through the camera is the best way to critically review work performed on the set.

It's common to refer to the viewing area as the ground glass, but you are probably working with the *fresnel lens*. The fresnel lens snaps over the ground glass and provides a more evenly illuminated area. Because it's easily removed, the fresnel lens is also the best surface to place an acetate overlay or make marks with a grease pencil. The overlay and grease pencil might be used to define the exact proportions or layout of a shot.

## SHEET FILM

One of the most time-consuming tasks associated with the view camera is film handling. An assistant can begin and end the day handling film, so a thorough knowledge of the following film-related tasks is essential. This encompasses:

1) Cleaning, loading, and unloading of sheet-film holders
2) Correct identification and organization of exposed film to ensure proper processing
3) Delivery of film to the lab for processing and pickup after processing

If you're not completely familiar with sheet-film holders, I suggest you purchase a 4″ × 5″ sheet-film holder and practice, practice, practice. Go to a professional processing lab and ask for discarded 4″ × 5″ sheet film. If necessary, buy a box of ten sheets.

Fortunately, virtually all sheet-film holders are universal in design. The standard 4" × 5" holder will fit any 4" × 5" view camera and is the most commonly used size. In addition, 4" × 5", 5" × 7", and 8" × 10" film and their respective holders are handled identically; they just differ in size.

## PREPARING THE SHEET-FILM HOLDER

Each time a film holder is used, it must be recleaned and loaded with film. Before you can begin cleaning, a few preliminary chores need to be accomplished. With time, you'll load film holders in many different places. Some photographers have special changing rooms for film handling. At other times, you'll be fighting for a small, clean space in a darkroom. By adhering to a standardized routine, you eliminate errors.

### Preliminary Tasks

It's essential to establish the type of film to be used and the amount needed. This information gives you a good idea of how many holders need to be prepared. Each holder holds two sheets of film. Once you've assembled the required number of holders, remove all unnecessary holders from the immediate area. This reduces the chance of grabbing a wrong holder. Don't assume any film holder is empty. Ask the photographer. If in doubt, recheck the holder in the dark. You can try shaking a holder and hear if a piece of film moves inside, but this is more akin to Russian roulette.

### *Film Requirements*

Now is the time to make sure there's plenty of film at room temperature. Larger quantities of film might be stored in the refrigerator, and it takes one to two hours for film to reach room temperature. It's important to wait, because condensation can form on the film's cold surface when handled in a warm room.

Every film is given an *emulsion number* as an indication of when it was manufactured and as a means of quality control. Verify that each type of film has the same emulsion number. This figure is printed on the side of the box and on the data sheet enclosed with the film. Photographers prefer to use the same emulsion for the entire shoot. This provides consistency with respect to film speed and color. If there isn't enough film of the same emulsion to finish to shoot, the photographer may not use it. Confirm one way or the other before loading any holders.

### Labeling the Holder

Oftentimes, the photographer or assistant needs to make pertinent notes on the film holder. These can be written in pencil on the small white label provided on the holder. Any irrelevant notes must be erased before cleaning begins. A more common procedure is to place masking tape over this area. The tape can be readily removed after each use.

The masking tape or white band is useful for noting what film type is inside the holder. Color-transparency film might be written as "E-6," black-and-white negative as "B+W," and color negative as "C-41." Details depend on the diversity of film to be used and the photographer's preference.

## Identification Cards

Now make some identification cards. The white cards found in sheet-film boxes are ideal. These cards are used to clearly identify the status of various holders and minimize any confusion. Remember, shoots can be hectic, and you must eliminate any errors when working with film.

You may need to run an unexpected errand for the studio, and the photographer will continue without you. The photographer must then be able to quickly determine the status of all holders. For example, a card might read, "Loaded/E-6/Unexposed." When there is a lot of film usage, it's easy to have a combination of loaded holders and clean but as-yet-unloaded holders. The two can look identical. Label the second set of holders as "Clean/Empty."

Annotated *Polaroid prints* are very helpful when organizing film. When more than one type of film is used, blatantly clear labels are even more critical.

## The Dark Slide

The film holder's dark slide does provide some information, but not enough. The top of each dark slide has a white pull-tab on one side and a black pull-tab on the other side. The pull-tab that faces out and is visible reflects the status of the film inside. A dark slide with the white tab facing out indicates unexposed film. A dark slide with the black tab visible indicates exposed film. Remember, white is for unexposed film, and black is for exposed film.

When making an exposure, the holder is placed in the camera, and the dark slide is removed entirely. After the exposure the dark slide is reinserted with the black tab facing out. You can place a rubber band around the film holder to ensure the dark slides don't inadvertently open.

## CLEANING THE FILM HOLDER

Once the necessary holders are segregated and marked with the day's film type, you can begin cleaning. Keep in mind that no dust is permissible. Today, virtually all film is scanned, and removing dust spots is minor when compared to film retouching. However, it still pays to be very careful because Photoshop fixes cost time and money. To prepare for cleaning, follow these steps:

1) Wipe off the work area, ideally with a damp sponge.
2) Organize the following items: a natural bristle brush, canned air, two zipper-locking plastic bags, and a clean pair of hands.
3) When holders are used exclusively in the studio, they tend to remain fairly clean. But don't assume so. All holders must be cleaned before each film loading.

## Removing Dust

It is important to note that the top of the sheet-film holder is where the two dark slides are first inserted into the holder. Also, the top is where the two white bands for notes are located. To clean, follow these steps:

1) Blow or brush off the entire holder before removing the dark slides. This sequence makes it less likely that dust will be deposited onto the felt light trap as the dark slides are withdrawn.

2) Remove both dark slides and set them on a clean surface. Now, pinch the holder along its outer edge, about one inch from the top. While the holder is held vertically, tap both sides with a solid portion of the brush to dislodge any dust caught in the light trap. Dust remaining here might fall onto the film when the dark slide is moved in or out.

3) Brush out the inner area of the holder. Brush in one direction from top to bottom and then horizontally along the bottom hinge.

4) While brushing, you can aid the process by blowing out the area with your mouth.

5) Use canned air on all grooves and surfaces. Point the nozzle away from the worktable. There's no point in disturbing air in the area where you will set your holder.

6) Next, thoroughly brush off each dark slide and blast it with air. Reinsert the dark slide completely, making certain the white pull-tab indicating unexposed film faces out.

7) Finally, place the clean but empty holder in a zipper-locking bag. The one-gallon size will hold up to six holders.

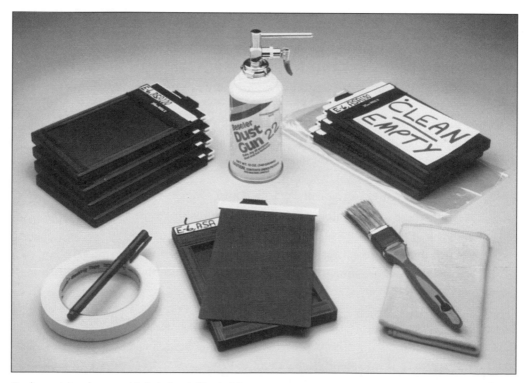

Equipment to clean and label sheet-film holders.

### Controlling Static

Some photographers use *anti-static cloths.* Static can physically damage film and also attracts dust. An anti-static cloth can be used to wipe off any of the holder's surfaces, and it's useful in removing smudge marks. When used, be on the alert for any stray lint. If static is a persistent problem in a studio, make it a practice to move the film and dark slide in and out of the holder, slowly. Anti-static bags are also available at computer stores.

### Take Your Time

Even when you're rushed, it's not prudent to cut corners in the cleaning process. In the end, the person who cleans a holder bears responsibility for any dust marks or scratches. At times, when you have many holders to clean, you can fall into a monotonous routine. You assume that just because you tapped, brushed, and used canned air that the holder is clean. *Don't forget to look,* especially when the brush has a tendency to loose its bristles. Holders must be spotless. Dust spots will appear as black marks on processed color-transparency film. When dust settles on the film, no light reaches the surface there, and that area isn't exposed.

## LOADING THE FILM HOLDER

Now that you've cleaned and labeled all holders, they can be loaded with film. But before turning out the lights, be sure you're well organized.

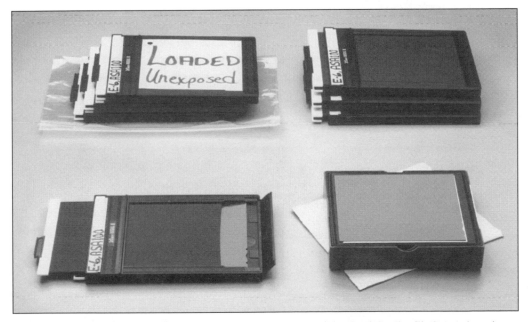

Arrangement of holders and sheet film in order to load sheet-film holders. The film's notch code must be in the lower-right corner.

### Before the Lights Go Out

1) Place all cleaning items and unneeded holders far from even the most disoriented reach.

2) Remove the holders from the plastic bag. Recheck that the dark slide's white pull-tab is facing out, denoting unexposed film.

3) Restack the holders on the table and pull both dark slides out about one-half inch. This small gap signifies that both sides remain unloaded but won't let any dust inside. When both dark slides are reinserted entirely, you'll know both sides are loaded.

4) While facing the worktable, position the stack of holders so that they are lying horizontally, with the top of each holder on the left.

5) Take the top holder and place it on the table between you and the stack. Unless space is very limited, avoid loading a holder while it's on top of the stack. If the stack is bumped and topples, it could lead to complications.

With the holders in place, turn your attention to the box of film. In this list, I'll describe a new, unopened box of film:

1) Place a rubber band around the box to make certain it only comes open when desired. Then, cut the paper bands sealing the box. To open the box further, all lights must be off.

2) But before turning off the light, be sure the door is locked. If no lock exists, make it known to everyone that you'll be in the dark and post a note on the door.

3) Make it a point to remember where the light switch is located. Hopefully, it's marked with a piece of phosphorescent tape.

If unfamiliar with a sheet-film box, visit a professional lab and ask for an empty one. Having spares is part of the lab's job. Sheet-film boxes consist of three interlocking lids, providing a reusable, lightproof arrangement. Depending on format and film type, there are ten, twenty-five, fifty, or a hundred sheets per box. New film is enclosed in a sealed, foil envelope. There are either ten or twenty-five sheets per envelope.

### Lights Out!

Now, turn off the light. Remove the rubber band and put it on your wrist. As you open the box, insert one lid inside the other, so none are misplaced. Tear open the foil envelope and remove the film. The envelope isn't needed to ensure a lightproof environment and is usually discarded.

The film is still covered top and bottom with sheets of white cardboard, the kind so useful in making the identification cards discussed earlier. These are retained with the film.

### The Notch Code

It is now critically important to properly orientate the film relative to the holders. You do so by using the film's *notch code*. The notch code consists of a series of small notches. Each film type has a unique notch code, and it's always located near the corner on one of the short sides. Besides serving as identification, the notch code is used as a reference point for loading film. It allows you to load the film correctly, with the emulsion side up.

Place the box of film parallel to the holder. Make certain that the notch code is in the lower-right corner when the holder is lying horizontally with the dark slides on the left. This placement allows the notch code to be read by your fingertip, even though the dark slide is removed only slightly.

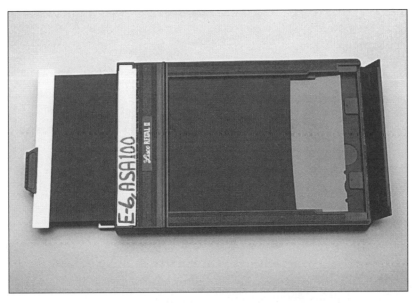

Sheet-film holder loaded with 4" × 5" sheet film. When the holder is positioned horizontally as in the above photograph, the film's notch code must be in the lower-right corner to ensure that the emulsion side faces out.

## INSERTING THE FILM

With both the holder and box of film properly oriented, the film can be inserted into the holder with a minimum of handling. Follow these guidelines:

1) With your left hand, pull out both dark slides about another inch. Then, using your left thumb and index finger, hold open the small, hinged flap found along the holder's right side.

2) Using the thumb and index finger of the right hand, grasp the film along the edge containing the notch code. Touch the film surface as little as possible.

3) Insert the film under the holder's film guides. There are two sets of guides or grooves. The top one is for the dark slide, and the bottom one is for the film. You must be certain you don't place the film in the grooves intended for the dark slide.

4) Positioning the thumb and index finger of the left hand on the very beginning of the holder's film guide facilitates the loading process.

5) Once the film is under the film guide, use only your fingertip to gently push the film in completely. Run your finger along the only edge of film remaining exposed and reconfirm that the notch code is located at the bottom right.

6) Finally, slowly reinsert the dark slide from the left. Make certain it interlocks with the hinged flap. Turn the holder over and repeat the process.

7) Position the small locking hooks so the dark slide can't inadvertently open.

8) After all the holders are loaded, rebox the unused film. Place the rubber band around it so that it can't be opened inadvertently. Now turn on the light.

**Lights On!**

With most holders, the small locking hooks are very loose, hence unreliable. If you expect an inordinate amount of handling, secure the dark slides with a rubber band fitted lengthwise around several holders. The rubber band will help when you later attach a Polaroid print. Place the holders in a clean bag and insert an identification card.

Before leaving the darkroom, write on the lid how much film remains in the box. The cleaning and loading process is complete. Now check to see if you're needed on the set.

## THE EXPOSURE PROCESS

When working in the studio, leave all film holders in the changing room until it's time to go to film. Then bring out only those holders required for that particular shot. Include the canned air, so the photographer can blow off each holder, before placing it in the camera. The following list describes the exposure process:

1) Usually the photographer operates the camera and makes the exposure.

2) The assistant is often close to the photographer, helping the exposure process go smoothly. You want to have holders readily available and be ready to write down pertinent information.

3) Once the film is exposed, it should be stored in a safe place, ideally back in the changing room.

While on location, holders are often placed in a dedicated case. Although holders containing exposed film are identified by the black pull-tab on the dark slide, they should still be kept separated from unexposed film holders. When there's a Polaroid print related to a group of holders, attach it with masking tape or a rubber band.

## WHY YOU IDENTIFY FILM

With proper preparation, you should be able to place some identification on a holder soon after it's exposed. Because each sheet of film can be processed individually, it's often essential to know what's in each holder.

One complication that can arise is shooting more variations than initially planned. This results in using more holders than anticipated and having more to keep organized. For example, the photographer could decide to bracket exposures more than usual, attach a filter for one series of exposures and remove it for others, and decide to try a variation in composition. Now you would have shot 1A and 1B, both with and without filtration, and each at several different exposures. Plus, you may have four more shots that day.

*Dynamic subjects* can often complicate matters because you never know exactly what you've got until you see the film. This might be a model in action or a freshly poured beverage. In such cases, the photographer may bracket relatively little and process only one sheet of film. The result will indicate how the other exposures will look and whether there's a need to deviate from normal processing.

Time permitting, the photographer may process the film in two separate processing runs. It's reassuring to know that if anything goes wrong with the first batch, there's a backup. Obviously, you need to know what's in each holder to do this. Don't forget, as a freelancer you might be working in another studio the next day, so the photographer had better not have any questions about how you organized the film.

## UNLOADING THE FILM HOLDER

Before any film can be taken to the lab, it needs to be removed from the holders and placed in a film box. Prepare to unload the film holder as follows:

1) You'll need an empty film box and a rubber band for securing it.
2) Clear away a work space and stack the appropriate holders next to the open box.
3) Plan to put only one type of film in a box. All film should also be processed the same way, either normal or pushed, for example.
4) Now, lock the door and turn off the light.

### Lights Out, Again!

Basically, unloading a film holder is the opposite of loading a holder. Do so as follows:

1) Slowly pull out the dark slide a couple of inches. Then remove the film by grasping its edge, making sure to pull it straight out from the holder.
2) With some holders you will find it more difficult to get hold of the film's edge than with others. You can try a fingernail under the edge, in order to lift the film. The key is to grasp only the film's edge.
3) Leave the slide partially withdrawn to verify the holder is empty.
4) After the holders are unloaded, replace the two lids and attach a rubber band around the box. Now you can turn the light on.
5) If you expect to add more film to the box, keep the rubber band on it. If not, secure the box with four short pieces of masking tape. The taped box is ready for the lab after it has a proper label.

## ENSURING PROPER PROCESSING

Just as the assistant needs to know what's in each holder, the lab must know what's in the box and what to do with it. Unlike roll film, there aren't any readily identifiable marks. Therefore, the *instruction label* must be clear and precise. Since boxes are used again and again, remove any old notes so there isn't even a hint of confusion.

Some photographers have their own labels for boxes; if your photographer doesn't, tape the white cardboard found in new boxes to the lid. At the top, write the photographer's name and phone number. This should be sufficient if the photographer has an account with the lab.

### The Different Film Types

Now note some information about the contents. Indicate the number of sheets, the format, type of film, and any specifics regarding its processing. All *E-6 processed,* color-transparency film is handled identically. These films include Ektachrome and Fujichrome, but not Kodachrome. Here, "E-6" or "E-6-processed film" will suffice.

Color-negative film is developed with a process referred to as C-41. It can be noted as "C-41," or "C-41 color negative." Black-and-white negative film must be specifically identified, because processing times differ depending on film type. The label might read, "B+W, Plus-X film."

Both black-and-white and color-negative material can be difficult to interpret, and a contact print is often requested. Here, the negative is placed directly on the photographic paper and exposed. The result is an unmanipulated print, the size of the negative. The contact prints made from a roll of film make a contact sheet. When contact prints are needed, write "Process and Contact" on the label.

Properly exposed film that is processed for the recommended time is referred to as normal processing. If this is the photographer's intent, the label should state, "Process Normal," regardless of film type. Normal film processing is also designated with a capital *N* enclosed in a circle.

As with roll film, if the development process is to be altered, the lab must know how and by how much. Film can be pushed or pulled, with the amount measured in stops for f-stops. For instance, the label might read: "Push +⅓ stop" or "Pull -½ stop." See chapter 7, "The Medium-Format Camera" and the section "Film Processing" for greater detail.

## WORKING WITH THE PHOTO LAB

You can arrive at the studio and be on your way to the lab before you even set your coat down. When sent to pick up something, know exactly what it is. Not all items are stored in the same place, and getting two out of three isn't good enough. Often times, the lab will inquire if there's more. How do you know if you don't ask?

When dropping off material, try to get all the specifics. If questions arise, call the studio. The photographer is likely to have very definite opinions about every aspect of the photographic process.

## THE CHANGING TENT

You may be called on to work with a film-changing tent or bag, especially while on location. These provide a small, lightproof environment. The standard *changing bag* looks like an oversized sweater. The waist area is opened and closed with a series of zippers. The bag's arms provide access for the user's arms. Since you can't take your arms in or out of the bag without letting in light, preparation is essential. The changing bag evolved into the *changing tent*. The tent has an internal framework that makes the bag into a small dome tent. The tent is a roomier and cleaner work environment.

The biggest problem is usually dust, no matter how clean the changing tent and how proficient your technique. Try cleaning the tent's inside by tipping it upside down and gently tapping the sides to knock the dust into the peak of the tent. Then wipe out the insides with a damp sponge.

Your basic film-loading technique is the same when using a changing tent. However, keep these points in mind:

1) It's best to be organized to minimize movement and reduce the number of times you move your arms in and out of the tent.
2) Withdraw the dark slides as little as possible and keep holders in plastic bags until needed.
3) Try to limit yourself to loading four or five holders at a time.

If you know there will be a need to change film away from the studio, it's often better to look for a small, windowless room and cover the door. When you're on the road, a motel bathroom is clean and easy to seal off. A combination of black cloth, pushpins, and gaffers tape will handle most situations. Also, see if there are any professional photo labs with a changing room available to pros.

## SUMMARY OF RESPONSIBILITIES RELATED TO CAMERA AND FILM

❏ Prepare camera by attaching to tripod or camera stand.

❏ Attach a cable release and sync cord, if necessary.

❏ Be ready to change lenses and attach filters, as needed throughout the shoot.

❏ Gain an understanding of the day's film requirements.

❏ Differentiate camera bodies, film magazines, and sheet–film holders as to film type.

❏ Load camera bodies, magazines, or holders with the appropriate film.

❏ Prepare for the inevitable accumulation of exposed film so it remains well organized.

❏ Anticipate the photographer's need for film by following the evolution of each shot and understanding the exposure sequence.

❏ Unload and reload camera bodies, film magazines, or holders as needed. Always have film immediately available during the exposure process.

❏ Annotate exposed film cartridges or holders, being sure to include a shot number and processing information. Correlate to a Polaroid print when possible.

❏ Monitor film usage to ensure an adequate supply is available at room temperature.

❏ Be prepared to remind the photographer of variations in the exposure sequence with regard to composition or filters.

❏ After the exposure process, establish which film is to be processed and how. Don't make assumptions.

❏ Review the chapter on digital backs and scanning backs for more information on digitized view cameras.

# 9

# Polaroid
# Instant Film

P OLAROID INSTANT FILM IS AN INTEGRAL PART OF PROFESSIONAL PHOTOGRAPHY, not merely a convenience. Before the advent of digital camera backs and monitors, Polaroid was the only way to make an exposure and see the results almost immediately. Even with computers and digital backs, the assistant is still going to work with Polaroid instant film. Photographers may not feel comfortable having you load sheet film holders on your first day, but Polaroid is all yours.

## WHY USE POLAROID INSTANT FILM?

Unfortunately, Murphy's Law—anything that can go wrong, will go wrong—readily applies to photography. The more variables there are in any job, the greater the likelihood that some aspect of the shoot will not proceed as planned. Most commercial jobs utilize a considerable amount of equipment, and Polaroid instant film helps confirm everything is working. A Polaroid print is often referred to as a *proof print*.

You begin with a camera, which is likely to be connected to a power supply. The power supply in turn leads to several flash heads, with each flash head having some form of light-modifying device. Then there are various fill cards to add light and perhaps black cards to control unwanted light. Every component must function as desired. No one wants a surprise.

The use of electronic-flash equipment or strobe greatly increases the need for Polaroid. Such lighting systems produce a flash of light. Because of its short duration, the effects cannot be evaluated with the unaided eye. A Polaroid print provides an instant picture and instant feedback.

Often, it's the subtle differences in lighting that really make the shot, and much time and energy is spent in its refinement. As you'll see, each Polaroid print is numbered sequentially and pertinent information noted. The resulting series of Polaroid prints is literally a documentation of the shot, a tremendous learning experience for the assistant.

## Checking Exposure

While helping the photographer evaluate the aesthetics of the lighting arrangement, Polaroid provides information on purely technical matters, such as the exposure. Photographers learn to interpret a Polaroid print in relation to the specific film they use. They determine through experience that a Polaroid that looks a certain way will translate to a good exposure on their particular film. For example, a photographer knows when to expect to retain sufficient detail in the film when there is little in the Polaroid print. Determining exposure beforehand also limits bracketing and reduces film usage.

## Checking Focus

Besides exposure, a Polaroid is used to check for focus. In other words, it shows whether the camera is holding or pulling focus at a specific aperture or f-stop. This can be done by simply evaluating the print for overall sharpness. However, there is a more critical procedure.

Some black-and-white Polaroid films, such as *Type 55* and *Type 665,* provide both a positive print and a negative. When examined with a magnifying loupe, the grain of the negative provides greater resolution, in order to evaluate sharpness. The negative also tends to retain more detail, both in the shadows and highlights, as compared to the print.

However, the Type 665 negative needs to be thoroughly washed with water before it can be viewed with a magnifying loupe. In fact, it's the backing material you removed to stop development. But before washing, it bears little resemblance to a conventional black-and-white negative.

## The Only View That Matters

In addition to the photographer, the assistant, client, model, hair stylist, or food stylist will also use the Polaroid. Objects differ in appearance depending on your position when you view them. Regarding photography, only one position or viewpoint matters, and that's the camera's.

When critically evaluating anything on the set, you must do so from the camera's position. You either look through the camera or stand directly in front of the lens. Unfortunately, either is often impractical. It may be physically impossible to squeeze between the camera and the set. And for the uninitiated, the upside down and backward image of the view camera is foreign. Besides, not everyone needs to be hanging around the camera. Again, Polaroid is indispensable.

## GENERAL CHARACTERISTICS

Although many people utilize the Polaroid print, most tasks rest with the assistant. Polaroid is used with 35mm SLRs, medium-format cameras, and large-format view cameras. But regardless of the format, the material is basically the same and shares the same general characteristics. These properties greatly influence how you handle Polaroid instant film. There are two basic kinds of Polaroid instant film: color and black-and-white. Both are available in a variety of film speeds or ASA ratings, and the specific films are designated as "types." Like other photographic materials, Polaroid must be exposed and then processed.

## Processing Polaroid Material

After the Polaroid film holder is attached to the camera, Polaroid is exposed like any film. However, processing is initiated as the Polaroid material is removed from the specialized holder. To put it simply, the removal action spreads developing chemicals over the print's surface and the developing process begins.

At the appropriate time, the development process must be stopped by peeling off either the protective envelope or the paper backing from the print. The print's image surface will be rather delicate for several minutes, but you can still annotate it before handing it to the photographer.

The print's development is temperature dependent. As ambient temperature decreases, processing time must be increased. Timing the development process ensures consistent results. This is the most important reason for always wearing a watch with a sweep hand. Color Polaroid takes longer to process than black and white, making a watch even more important.

Type 55, a commonly used black-and-white material, provides both a 4″ × 5″ positive print and a conventional negative. At seventy-five degrees Fahrenheit, processing takes twenty seconds. However, at sixty degrees Fahrenheit, development requires forty seconds. *Type 59,* a comparable color-print material, takes sixty seconds at seventy-five degrees Fahrenheit. When the temperature drops to sixty degrees Fahrenheit, development time must be increased to seventy-five seconds.

Problems usually occur when the temperature is quite cool; then you must increase development time. When underdeveloped, the print appears dull and low in contrast. Also, portions of the surface may not receive the developer and will appear white. It's harder to ruin a Polaroid by overdevelopment.

## THE ASSISTANT'S RESPONSIBILITIES

Now that you know something about Polaroid material and how useful it is, you may be asking yourself what your responsibilities are in regard to the process. In general, you must make certain it's *always available.* When taking an inventory of film, include Polaroid instant film. Many photographers refrigerate unopened boxes. Refrigerated film should be given two hours to reach room temperature, so plan ahead. While in use, the Polaroid film holder should be kept loaded, with plenty of extra film nearby. A good assistant pays close attention to the photographer's actions and to the progression of the shot. When the photographer is ready to expose a Polaroid, the assistant is normally near the camera with Polaroid ready. The assistant should also anticipate when the photographer is likely to change from Polaroid to regular film, and then possibly back to Polaroid. This can be an important time saver in fast-changing situations.

## Annotating the Polaroid Print

By annotating the print, I mean make a few pertinent notes along the print's border. Exactly what you write will depend on the individual photographer and the stage you're at in the shot. If unfamiliar with the photographer, try looking near the light box or on the set cart for some previous Polaroid prints. You might also inquire as to any preference.

Usually, the photographer shoots several Polaroids during a shot; more difficult shots require more Polaroid prints. At the very least, each Polaroid print should be numbered sequentially. It's imperative to keep track of Polaroids and embarrassing to find one unnumbered, with everyone wondering where it fits in the sequence. Numbering also helps the assistant track Polaroid usage, insuring there's always plenty available.

Other basic information to note includes the f-stop, the *power setting* for each light or flash head, and the shutter speed when appropriate. As the lighting set-up takes shape, major changes in lighting might be noted. A medium soft box may replace a smaller one, or perhaps some filtration is attached to the lens.

It's easy to note that a silver fill card was exchanged for a white one; however, a slight change in the position of a light may be difficult, if not pointless, to describe. The assistant needs to use a little discretion, along with the photographer's preferences, when annotating Polaroid prints.

The last Polaroid in any sequence is usually marked "Final." Some photographers like to annotate the final print fully and then file it with related paper work. Other times, a final Polaroid is left relatively unmarked and given to the client.

You'll find that few pens consistently write on the print's surface. A fast drying, felt-tipped pen with indelible ink works best. The Sharpie brand is a good choice. Some photographers also like to use grease pencils. In either case, the studio should supply the writing instruments.

Some types of black-and-white Polaroid prints need to be coated with preservative, to resist fading. This chore can usually wait until the Polaroid isn't being viewed. The chemical needs several minutes to dry thoroughly, and it's quite sticky in the meantime.

### *Feeling Rushed?*

Often, there's little time to annotate the print. The moment it's finished developing, everyone wants to view it. Regardless of the demand, it must be annotated sooner or later. At the very least, put a number on the print, before handing it over. Under hectic circumstances, record a few notes during the development process.

When using 4″ × 5″ Polaroid, make notes on the edge of the protective envelope. If it's a small- or medium-format Polaroid, write along the border on the back of the print. Be sure not to write or put pressure on the delicate, developing surface. When given the opportunity, transfer this information to the print.

## Annotation of the Polaroid Print

### KEY TO ABBREVIATIONS

**Shot 1:** The first of several different shots associated with a job.

**Shot 1A:** Changes in composition or filtration within a shot may be designated as Shot 1A or 1B.

**FINAL:** Denotes this as the last Polaroid of Shot 1. This is usually exposed just before going to film.

**#4:** The fourth Polaroid exposed for Shot 1.

**f32.0:** The lens's f-stop. Include shutter speed, if appropriate.

**5 secs.:** Lens open for five seconds for ambient light.

**N/F:** No filtration on the lens.

**05M:** Denotes an O5 Magenta Color Correction filter is attached to the lens.

**2400 w-s Main:** 2400 watt-seconds of power going to a main overhead light.

Annotated black-and-white Polaroid print of Cover photo.

**1600 w-s Reflector (blue):** 1600 watt-seconds of power going to a flash head, with a reflector and blue gel. Photographers may prefer "full power" or "⅔ power."

### 35MM SLR AND MEDIUM-FORMAT INSTANT-FILM BACKS

Many small- and medium-format camera systems can utilize Polaroid instant film by attaching an NPC Polaroid instant film back. NPC is the manufacturer. With most medium-format systems, the camera's film magazine is removed and the Polaroid instant-film back is attached. When an instant-film back is used with a 35mm SLR camera body, the hinged film door is removed, and the Polaroid film back is attached. Although very similar in appearance and operation, film backs are manufacturer specific.

Regardless of format, the Polaroid instant-film back is designed to hold a packet of Polaroid instant film, containing eight sheets of film. Each sheet is sequentially numbered, one through eight, both on the back of each print and on the exterior pull-tab. This arrangement aids in annotating the Polaroid print, and allows you to monitor Polaroid usage more easily.

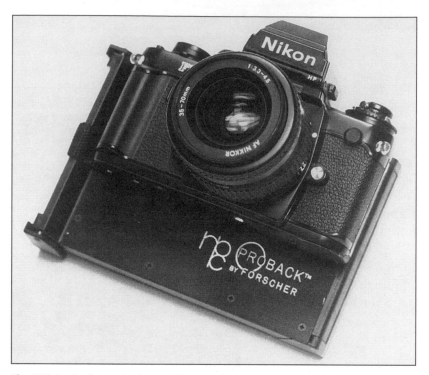

The NPC ProBack attached to a Nikon F3 35mm camera. NPC Instant Camera Backs are designed to hold an eight-sheet packet of Polaroid instant film. *Photo courtesy of NPC PhotoDivision.*

Both 35mm SLR and medium-format instant-film backs can be removed from the camera in the middle of a packet of film. This is accomplished with a stainless-steel dark slide. When fully inserted, the dark slide allows the film back to be independent of the camera. Once attached to the camera, the dark slide is pulled out and the exposure made.

Although the use of Polaroid instant film with small- and medium-format systems is very similar, there is one difference. The 35mm instant-film back lets you make two independent exposures on each Polaroid instant print. Each image measures 24mm × 36mm, and permits bracketing of exposures on the same print. Because 35mm SLR cameras utilize medium-format Polaroid instant film, this procedure allows for greater usage of a relatively large piece of film.

## Loading the Instant-Film Back

In the following description, the Polaroid instant-film holder is attached to the camera. To load the instant-film back, follow these steps:

1) Position yourself as though you are viewing through the camera. The film back is opened by releasing a latch found on the right side.
2) The hinged door swings open and the film packet readily slips into place.

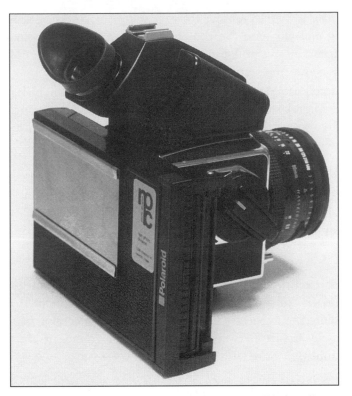

The NPC Instant Camera Back attached to a Hasselblad medium-format camera. *Photo courtesy of NPC PhotoDivision.*

3) Make certain the paper pull-tabs found on the film packet are situated on the right. Now close the door and latch it.

4) When a new film packet is placed in the holder, the top sheet of film is covered with a black piece of paper. This lightproof, protective covering must be discarded, but only after the film packet is placed in the film back. It's removed the same way an exposed sheet of Polaroid instant film is removed and developed.

## Developing the Polaroid Print

Here are a few points to keep in mind when removing either the protective paper covering or an exposed print to initiate development:

1) Position yourself behind the camera. With your left hand, place the thumb under the bottom-right corner of the film back. Next, place the left index finger on the top-right corner. You are grasping at a point where the two halves snap shut. Now make a firm pinch with these two left fingers.

2) The left hand is used to stabilize the film back and the camera. If not stabilized, the force generated from the pulling action used to remove the print will topple most tripod-mounted cameras.

3) The *right hand* is used to remove the exposed print. To do so, firmly grasp the protruding pull-tab with the thumb and index finger of your right hand. Make one continuous pull, using moderate force. The entire pulling process should last about one second.

4) Be sure to pull straight out from the holder. If you pull slightly up or down, or side to side, relative to the holder, there's a chance of tearing the protective paper cover or the print. Some paper may then remain caught in the holder, often affecting the next print.

Immediately after a print is pulled from the holder, time the development with a watch that can show seconds. The development process is stopped by peeling off the backing material. The image surface is still rather delicate, but you can write pertinent information on the print's white border.

## POLAROID FOR THE VIEW CAMERA

The general characteristics of 4″ × 5″ and 8″ × 10″ Polaroid instant films are similar. Both color and black-and-white instant films are exposed while held in a specialized Polaroid film holder, then processed following the same general principles. However, due to the disparity in size between the two formats, there are distinctly different handling procedures.

### Why Use Polaroid Instant Film?

In addition to the reasons given earlier, view cameras give several more reasons for using Polaroid instant film. One is the need to verify that you are in focus or pulling focus. Large-format view cameras provide a large image, commonly 4″ × 5″ or 8″ × 10″. Larger size means a need for lenses of longer focal length. A 50mm focal-length lens is considered normal for a 35mm camera, but a 150mm lens is normal for a 4″ × 5″ format camera. Longer focal-length lenses provide less depth of field, when set at the same f-stop. Therefore, having adequate depth of field is not a given, as is often the case with the smaller-format cameras.

The view camera moves both the film plane and the lens. Camera movements allow the photographer to position the plane of sharp focus and control perspective. This control is best utilized if the photographer can verify that everything is as it should be.

### The 4″ × 5″ Polaroid System

Let's first consider the 4″ × 5″ Polaroid instant film and the Polaroid *Model 545 film holder,* which looks like an overgrown sheet-film holder. Like the small- and medium-format systems, the Model 545 holds the film during exposure. The holder is also used to start the development process as the film is removed from the holder. But here, only one sheet of film is placed in the holder at a time.

A few notes regarding *4×5 inch Polaroid instant film.* Each individual sheet of 4″ × 5″ film is enclosed in a lightproof, paper envelope. This also contains the processing chemicals. The envelope must be handled carefully, because you can inadvertently expose the film or disrupt the pod of chemicals.

In simple terms, the envelope containing an unexposed sheet of film is inserted into the holder. The envelope protects the film from light and is moved out of the way during the exposure process. Once exposed, the envelope is slipped back over the film. Then the entire envelope is removed from the holder, which initiates development of the print. Once development is complete, the envelope is peeled away from the finished print.

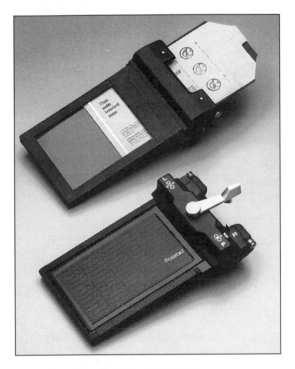

The Polaroid Model 545 instant-film holder. (Top) An individual sheet of Polaroid instant film is inserted into the holder and the protective paper envelope is partially withdrawn. (Bottom) The back of the holder showing the control arm and the Load (L) and Process (P) positions. The small film-release lever (R) is also visible.

### Loading the Model 545 Holder
1) Position the control arm found on the Model 545 holder to *L*, for "load."
2) Grasp the envelope along the edge and carefully insert it completely into the holder. Make certain the side of the envelope marked "This Side Toward Lens" faces the holder's opening. You can hear a click as the envelope locks into place.
3) The holder is then slid into the camera, like any standard sheet-film holder.

### Preparing the Lens Shutter
1) Close the shutter, stop down to the working aperture (f-stop), and reconfirm the shutter speed.
2) Cock and trigger the shutter. This *test firing* reaffirms that the lens is closed and the strobes are firing. Failure to perform this test firing often results in a ruined sheet of film.

### Exposing the Polaroid Film
1) After recocking the shutter, you are ready to proceed with the exposure.
2) Gently pull the protective envelope out from the holder until it stops, about six inches. The envelope acts as a dark slide; now the film is uncovered and ready to be exposed.

3) Make the exposure. Once exposed, slowly reinsert the envelope into the holder, so it covers the film.

### Developing the Polaroid Film

1) After the exposure is made, the film is ready to be developed. At this point, remove the holder from the camera.
2) Move the holder's control arm to *P,* for "processing."
3) Pull the envelope from the holder, using a firm, continuous pull. The ideal duration for the entire pull is ½ second. With the aid of stainless-steel rollers, the removal process spreads developer over the film.
4) Once the film envelope is removed, time the development. Development time depends on the type of Polaroid and room temperature. Development is stopped by peeling open the envelope and removing the print.

### Removing a Polaroid Print from the Envelope

1) Grasp each of the two tabs with the thumb and index finger of each hand. These tabs are found on the tapered end of the envelope, opposite the metal cap.
2) Carefully peel open the envelope, all the way down to the metal cap.
3) Remove the print, being careful to keep its delicate surface free of chemicals. The print is now ready to be annotated and given to the photographer.
4) Move the film holder's control arm back to *L* and reload the Polaroid holder.

## Removing Unexposed Film from a Holder

Photographers often standardize on either color or black-and-white Polaroid instant film. However, there are times when a change is necessary. A photographer may prefer color, then switch to black-and-white to utilize the negative. If you are quick to reload the holder, as you should be, you may need to remove an unexposed sheet and exchange it for another.

Removing an unexposed Polaroid film envelope is accomplished as follows:

1) Place the holder's control arm to *L* for "load." This relaxes the stainless-steel rollers.
2) Then depress the small film-release lever, labeled *R.* This releases the holder's grasp on the envelope's metal cap. With the film-release lever still depressed, gently remove the film envelope.
3) If the envelope's metal cap remains engaged within the holder, the film will be inadvertently exposed and must be discarded. This is avoided by placing your thumb on the envelope near the metal cap and gently pushing while the release lever is depressed.

Some color-transparency film can be used with the Model 545 holder. These E-6-processed films are available from Fuji and Kodak. Like Polaroid instant film, one sheet of film is contained in each envelope. Once exposed, the envelope is removed from the holder like an unexposed Polaroid. Later in a darkroom, the film is removed from the envelope and put in a box for processing. This film is most likely to be used while on location. It's especially useful when film usage is expected to be high and there's little opportunity to reload film holders.

### The Model 550 Film Holder
The *Model 550 film holder* is designed to hold a film packet. Each film packet contains eight sheets of 4″ × 5″ instant film. The holder functions much like the instant-film holders designed for small- and medium-format camera systems. The model 550 is held in the camera like a standard sheet-film holder and utilizes a dark slide.

## THE 8″ × 10″ POLAROID SYSTEM
The Model 545 holder and instant film are quite compact and convenient, when compared to the 8″ × 10″ system. With 4″ × 5″ Polaroid, the positive print and the negative are contained in the same envelope. Plus, both exposure and film processing are accomplished using the same holder.

The 8″ × 10″ Polaroid system is somewhat different, affecting both its loading and processing. Here, only the negative is placed into the specialized Polaroid holder. This holder resembles a sheet-film holder, and the negative is exposed like any other film.

Afterwards, the exposed negative and an unexposed positive are placed into a specialized Polaroid processor. The processor moves both the exposed negative and unexposed positive print over a set of rollers, initiating development of the print. The 8″ × 10″ processor is most commonly an electrical unit; however, a manually operated unit is also available.

To ensure customer satisfaction, Polaroid Corporation provides considerable technical support. Detailed instructions regarding a product's use are supplied with each package of film. In addition, technical assistance is available through 800-prefix phone numbers and Polaroid's Web site. Refer to the appendixes on equipment and periodicals for more contact information.

## RESPONSIBILITIES RELATED TO POLAROID INSTANT FILM
- ❏ Establish the type of Polaroid film to be used.
- ❏ Have an adequate supply of film at room temperature.
- ❏ Keep the Polaroid film holder loaded.
- ❏ Anticipate when the photographer is likely to expose Polaroid film. At these times, prepare the camera and have Polaroid film immediately available.
- ❏ Expose Polaroid instant film.
- ❏ Time the development right after the envelope is pulled from the holder.
- ❏ Immediately reload the 545 holder; recheck status of instant film backs.
- ❏ At the appropriate time, stop development by peeling off the envelope or backing material from the print.
- ❏ Annotate the Polaroid print.
- ❏ Attach an annotated print to exposed film. Record any specific processing information.

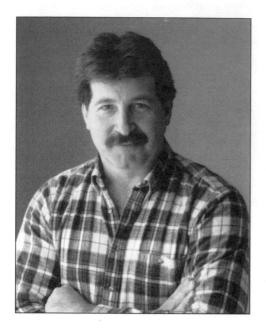

## AN INTERVIEW WITH STEVE UMLAND

Steve Umland is a commercial photographer in Minneapolis. He's known for shooting large-scale advertising campaigns both in the studio and on location.

**John Kieffer:** Can you give me a little better idea as to the kind of photography you do?

**Steve Umland:** I do large-production advertising photography; the vast majority of my clients are advertising agencies. These campaigns have included Winnebago, Polaris Snow, Watercraft, Mercury Marine, and AT&T. Most of the time, I shoot with a Linhof 4″ × 5″ view camera, but I also use Mamiya 2¼ and Nikon 35mm systems.

**J.K.:** What kind of person are you looking for in an assistant?

**S.U.:** I want somebody who's fired up and energetic about being an assistant. I want somebody who arrives in the morning with stars in their eyes—so excited to be in the studio doing photography that they want to pitch in and do whatever they can. I also need somebody who can be professional around the clients. They might ask the art director if he or she would like a cup a coffee.

I feel you can teach the assistant almost everything technical that they need to know. It's really nice if an assistant walks in and knows 4″ × 5″ cameras and strobe. I have Norman strobes, and I might ask them to set the power supply from 1200 to 800 watt-seconds. They need to know that they can't pull the flash head cable out of the pack when the power is on. But those kinds of things can be taught, so it's whether the personality fits. I spend a lot of time on the road, and I have to feel comfortable with somebody.

I believe that the assistant is another set of Umland eyes. An assistant can really save my ass because I get really focused when I'm shooting. It's like I have blinders on. A good assistant is looking out for the big picture and will tell me if there's a problem, like a reflection in the lens. The assistant also tells me so the art director can't hear. I really believe that they're an integral part of the team. Assistants work better if you make them a part of what you're doing.

**J.K.:** What technical qualifications are you after?

**S.U.:** Most assistants walk in with a portfolio, and as I look through it, I ask them which camera format they like to shoot. I tend to gravitate towards somebody who likes large format. If an assistant's portfolio is mostly 35mm editorial, I wonder why they want to work with me. Basically, I'm a large-production advertising photographer, and I use large format. I'll also ask them if they like natural light or strobes and what kind of strobe they can operate.

**J.K.:**   Do you place much importance on the assistant's portfolio?
**S.U.:**   I feel the portfolio is just something to look at while I'm talking to them. I have never hired an assistant based on whether they had a good or bad portfolio. However, I do expect assistants to work on their portfolio when they're working for me. If an assistant comes in and works for me, but doesn't work on their personal work, I question why they're assisting. I also kick my assistants out after one year.

**J.K.:**   Are most of the assistants that approach you graduates of a photography school?
**S.U.:**   I would say that most of them are graduates, maybe 60 to 70 percent.

**J.K.:**   What's the best way for an assistant to get in to see you?
**S.U.:**   They can call me. I usually won't hire anyone who I haven't talked to and seen their book (portfolio).

**J.K.:**   Upon graduation, are most of these aspiring assistants knowledgeable as far as what assisting involves?
**S.U.:**   No, absolutely not. I think most photographers coming out of school aren't taught about being a good assistant. Assisting is something that you have to have inside of you, the desire to work for someone else and do a good job for them. I think 95 percent of the schools produce such poor photographers that it's really sad. I had one assistant who worked for me for three months. Afterwards, he wrote a letter to his school saying he had spent four years at their school getting a photography degree and that he learned more in three months by assisting a photographer.

I've had lots of assistants ask me whether they should go to a photography school or assist, and it's not a question that I can answer. It's an individual decision. Some people need to be in a school environment to learn, while other people don't need school at all but just need to be exposed to the business.

**J.K.:**   Do you have any ground rules concerning to what degree you want the assistant to interact with the client?
**S.U.:**   I tell the assistant that if they have something to say and contribute, don't hold back—but talk to me. I also give a tremendous amount of responsibility to my assistants. They are responsible for exposure, and they run the front of my camera. This is because I want to be as focused as possible on producing the image. Before I go out on a shoot, I like to sit down with my assistants and look at the layout together. I draw diagrams on how I plan to do the lighting and where the camera is positioned. So when we get out there, they have an idea of what I want to do. Later, when we're on the set, I not only tell the assistant to do something, but why I'm doing it. That gets them involved in the shoot.

**J.K.:**    With all the strenuous location work you do, do you have any preference in hiring male or female assistants?

**S.U.:**    I've used both male and female assistants; however, it can enter into who I select. I don't have any problems with using a woman in the studio. On location, though, when I'm lugging sixteen cases through airports, I need someone who can really carry the load. I often use very large soft boxes, and if they caught by the wind, I need someone with strength to control them.

Another problem I run into is that clients don't want to pay extra for an additional room for a woman. On almost all my location shoots, I go with two assistants. I get one room and they share the other. This isn't feasible if I take a female assistant.

**J.K.:**    When on location, do you pay your assistants the same as in the studio?

**S.U.:**    I usually kick it up. However, if I can guarantee them six straight days of work, we may work out a flat fee. On the other side of the coin, I pay for all living expenses. I don't believe in per diems for the crew, and I feel that whatever they want they get. I feel that's compensation for being away from home and working so hard on location.

**J.K.:**    Can you recall any major mistakes caused by an assistant?

**S.U.:**    It happened when I was just out of school. At the time, I didn't trust assistants to load film. When the shot was almost where I wanted it, I went into the loading room to load film holders. When I walked out, the art director told me that my assistant had approached him. The assistant said that the next time he had a shot like this to come to him. He could do it cheaper. I almost caught the assistant before he got out the door. That is the biggest social faux pas an assistant can make, trying to take your clients away from you, right in the middle of the shoot.

As far as problems, I've had packs blow-up because assistants unplugged the flash head without powering down, but that's just life. An assistant is going to make mistakes.

**J.K.:**    Of the assistants that you work with, what percentage make a successful transition to professional photography?

**S.U.:**    I'd say maybe 10 percent. It's a tough field, no doubt about it.

**J.K.:**    Do you usually bring your assistants with you, or do you find them at the site?

**S.U.:**    I bring them with me. Every once in a while, I'll find a second assistant at the site, but I only do this if I have a lot of logistical problems.

**J.K.:**     Any parting advice for aspiring assistants?

**S.U.:**     I'd love assistants to get back into the love of photography. I got into this business because I love photography. So many of the assistants I see now don't seem to have that passion. When I got out of school I wanted to be an assistant and I didn't care how much it paid me. I would assist with somebody because I wanted to watch them shoot, and I wanted to learn. But now I meet assistants who walk in the door and ask about my pension plan and insurance coverage. It turns me off, but it's a trend I see. I'm more than happy to pay a fair price, but if 80 percent of the conversation is about money, I'm probably not going to hire them.

# 10

# Scanning Film
# and Using Digital Files

TODAY, JUST ABOUT EVERYTHING THAT IS SHOT ON FILM IS ULTIMATELY SCANNED or converted to a digital file with a *film scanner*. Most assistants would not be responsible for making quality, high-resolution scans unless they were given specific training. However, some scanning basics will come in handy when assisting, and you might use scans when making your own promotional material.

In simple terms, a scanner acts like a photocopier and converts the film image to a digital file that can be used on the computer. The best scans are made on expensive *drum scanners*. These scans have the quality and resolution for use in high-end print jobs. Working as an assistant, you're more likely to use a *flatbed scanner* or a scanner dedicated to 35mm slides. These provide sufficient quality for Web applications and some printed materials. If you don't have a scanner, the most practical way to have 35mm slides scanned is with Kodak Photo CD, available through most professional photo labs.

A common use of scans by an assistant might be to make a portfolio and place it on a CD-ROM or a Web site. You might also scan film so the photographer could e-mail it to a client for a quick review. For these uses, your main concern is that the photography looks nice on the computer monitor. Here are a few things to keep in mind when scanning for *multimedia applications* and not for four-color offset press. Because the majority of commercial assignments and stock photographs are shot with color-transparency film (slide film), that film will be emphasized when discussing the scanning process.

## GENERAL SCANNING PROCEDURES

1) Be sure your monitor is *calibrated*. Refer to its manual to see that the gamma, brightness, and contrast controls are set properly. Tape them in place when feasible. It helps to keep the light in your work area consistent. Ideally, it should be a neutral light and white walls. If the scans look good on your screen, they should look good on most other monitors.

2) Set any scanner controls to maximize *screen quality*, not print quality. Fortunately, getting scans to look good on the screen isn't difficult.

3) Gently clean off the color transparency or print and any glass surfaces on the scanner. This will save retouching time later.

4) Flatbed scanners may require a special *transparency adapter* to hold the trans-parency, while prints are laid flat on the glass platen.

5) For maximum screen quality, it's better to scan your transparency to the size the photo will appear on the screen. If you only do one scan, scan a larger size and then resize to a smaller size or "thumbnail." To maximize quality, resize a file only once, if possible. When starting with high-resolution scans, use the Image > Image Size command in Photoshop to reduce their size.

6) Set the scanner's resolution to 72 pixels per inch and the image size to the appropriate size in pixels.

7) Set the scanner to 32-bit, RGB color (red, green, blue).

8) Select what type of material is being scanned. Scanner software generally refers to slide film as transparencies, while prints are referred to as *reflective* or *flat art*.

9) Do some experimenting with your scanner's settings, so you feel you're get-ting the best possible scan.

10) It can be helpful at first to record your settings. You'll soon recognize that similar transparencies use the same settings. Recording the settings helps with rescanning and scanning similar shots.

11) Lighter transparencies scan better than denser or darker ones. I've also learned to err on the side of too light rather than too dark for the final scan.

12) When you're finished scanning, back-up your files. Place them on an exter-nal storage device, such as a Zip disk, or burn a CD-ROM.

## TIPS FOR ADJUSTING AND WORKING WITH SCANS

Throughout this book I refer to Adobe Photoshop when discussing photo-editing software. This is because it's the industry standard, and more than likely it is what you'll come in contact with as an assistant. Familiarity with Photoshop can certainly be an asset, both for assisting and working on your own scans.

1) Once the scan is complete, it can be worked on in Photoshop and saved as a Photoshop file. If you have problems with a Photoshop file responding to commands, check Image > Mode and make sure that "8-bits/Channel" and "RGB Color" are selected.

2) Keep the scan as a Photoshop file. This allows you to make changes to a high-quality file. Do not flatten; leave in layers. As with resizing files, you want to convert from Photoshop to another file format like TIFF or JPEG only once.

3) Once you have a good basic scan, you can use Photoshop to remove any spots, sharpen, or enhance color. These commands are for version 4.0. The command Filter > Sharpen > *Unsharp Mask,* set at a low level, is most use-ful to sharpen the scan. If you need more sharpening, just use Unsharp Mask again. Try these settings: Amount is 30 percent; Radius is 1.0; Threshold is 1. Try not to oversharpen, as this builds contrast.

4) To adjust *brightness,* try using Image > Adjust > Levels or Image > Adjust > Brightness/Contrast.

5) Color balance can be adjusted by using Image > Adjust > Color Balance or by using Adjust > Curves. Sometimes it can be difficult to tell just how a scan's color is off. Try Image > Adjust > Hue/Saturation. Increase the saturation levels to the max, and any color shift is evident.

6) When viewing a scan on a monitor, you often can see *bands* or *striations* in areas with a very homogenous color, such as an even blue sky. This can be mostly eliminated if you add a little "noise." Use: Filter > Noise > Add Noise. Try these settings: amount three at "uniform" distribution and "monochromatic" not checked.

**Drop Shadows** add a nice finishing touch to a photo that you intend to put on your Web page. Here's a simple way to make a drop shadow for a photo, button, or graphic element:

1) While in Photoshop, select the appropriate layer for the photo and make a copy of it. Using the Layers pull-down menu (located at the upper-right corner in the Layers palette), choose Duplicate Layer.

2) This new, duplicated layer is the same size as the original photo, but you want to fill it with black. Select the new layer and make a *Floating Selection.* Use Select > All (command A). Then "nudge" the selection by selecting the Move command in the Tool Box or by hitting the keystroke *V.* Use the arrow keys to nudge the layer up and down by one pixel. This makes a floating selection.

3) Use: Edit > Fill to fill the layer with black or any color.

4) This solid-black box can be turned to a fuzzy, drop-shadow box by using Filter > Blur > Gaussian Blur. Set at about a radius of two or three.

5) Use the arrow keys to move the drop-shadow box down and right three to four pixels.

6) The Opacity tool is found at the top of the Layers palette; it decreases the opacity of the black drop shadows to gray. Try 60 percent.

## DIFFERENT FILE FORMATS

You may start with a scan that's in one file format, such as Photoshop or Kodak Photo CD. And then you might want to change it to another file format in order to reduce file size or to make it compatible with another software application. All other things being equal, the larger the file size, the longer it takes to load on the Web or from a CD-ROM.

### JPEG File Format

Since, in this instance, we are talking about scans for multimedia use, you will probably want to save your Photoshop file in a *JPEG file format* (pronounced: jay-peg) to reduce file size and maintain a fairly high quality. Try these settings: Medium Quality (level 3–4) and Save Paths not checked.

Now you have a choice under Format Options. If you check Progressive, the image will come up rather blurry and then will refresh itself three to five times until it's sharp. Under the Scans setting, you can choose a refresh rate of three, four, or five. Progressive JPEGs are generally preferred on the Web because the viewer is quickly assured that something is loading. The second choice is Baseline Optimized. Here, the image comes up in sections or all at once, but it's sharp from the beginning. For the Web, *GIF file format* (pronounced: jif) is also common.

### Images Saved as TIFF

When the goal is to print ink on paper using a four-color offset press, digital files are usually saved as *TIFF* (Tag Image File Format). For the best final result, I suggest a drum scan from a service bureau familiar with the printing industry. Know the lines per inch the job will be printed at and get the scan a little larger than the final size of reproduction. Ideally, don't get a 250Mb file and reduce it to 10Mb. Again, convert from one file format to another only once, to retain maximum quality. TIFF images can be compressed to reduce file size by checking *LZW Compression.* This is known as lossless compression because no data is lost. JPEG, on the other hand, is known as lossy compression, which means data is lost when you JPEG a Photoshop file.

Regarding *resolution,* most good printing presses run at about 150 lines per inch (lpi) or higher. The rule of thumb to convert lines per inch to digital resolution is to double the lpi figure. For example, a press running at 150 lpi would require a resolution of 300 pixels per inch. This 300 ppi figure is the digital resolution required for the scan. If the photo is to be reproduced to 4″ × 5″, then 300 ppi times 4″ × 5″ is 1200 and 1500 pixels for each side. Multiply the two sides together to get the total area. Therefore, 1,200 times 1,500 equals 1,800,000, or 1.8Mb. This is multiplied by 4 bytes, for 32-bit color. Four times 1.8MB yields a 7.2MB file.

### KODAK PHOTO CD SCANS

Kodak Photo CD scans let you economically digitize your photography so it can be used on a Web site, sent via e-mail, or saved to another storage media so it can be sent to a client. The same scan can also be used to produce printed promotional materials of reasonable size. Kodak Photo CD makes handling scans fast and easy. Go to the Kodak Web site at *www.kodak.com* and follow the links to free software and plug-ins.

Here are some things to remember when working with Kodak Photo CD. A scan on *Kodak Master Photo CD* can be opened in five different sizes or resolutions. This is adequate for most applications and is very affordable. The *Pro Photo CD* provides an even larger, sixth-resolution file. In either case, open the file size a little larger than needed. Large files can take considerably longer to open, resize, manipulate, and save.

### Accessing Your Kodak Photo CD Files

1) The most consistently reliable way to open any file is to have the appropriate software application already open and then to use File > Open. In this case, have Photoshop open and use File > Open.

2) Open the Kodak Photo CD via your CD-ROM drive. The Kodak CD will have a name like "PCD 1234."

3) Open the folder PHOTO_CD. Don't use the "Photos" folder, which contains files with names such as 04—these are low-resolution thumbnail images.

4) Next, open the folder IMAGES.

5) Now open the appropriate image file. The file name for image 4 is "IMG0004.PCD".

Although I generally open the file from within Photoshop and do all my cropping and resizing there, you can download software from *www.Kodak.com* called *Kodak Photo CD Acquire*. This software gives you capabilities for cropping, resizing, and some rudimentary manipulation.

## WEB SITES

Perhaps the most likely use of your own scans will be for a Web site or to e-mail your photography to someone. Review the chapter on marketing your skills to get ideas as to what *content* to place on your Web site and links to possibly generate traffic. Here are a few points to keep in mind:

1) Generally the simpler your site, the less likely you are to have problems with any of a wide variety of browsers.

2) Not all photos translate equally well when placed on the Web; most photos end up being small and pixilated. Choose photos that have strong graphic elements and good colors. Don't rely on subtle details.

3) It's easier on the eyes to read black text on a white or very lightly tinted background as compared to white text on black.

4) As discussed above, the JPEG file format is the most useful. Its relatively small size helps reduce load time while still providing good quality. If you notice excessive banding or striating, go back to the Photoshop file and add some noise. Use Filter > Noise > Add Noise.

5) Progressive JPEG files are preferred for the Web. Here the image starts out fuzzy and progressively sharpens.

6) Your home page will start loading at the upper-left corner. Place your most important information at the top of the page so the viewer sees it immediately. Fit this information in an area about 600 pixels wide by 400 pixels high so that the viewer doesn't have to scroll down to see what's important.

7) Carefully consider whether you really need sophisticated graphics and other elements that increase load time, reduce reliability, and possibly subtract from your message. Are you trying to display your talents as a photographer, a Web master, or as a photographer's assistant?

8) Usually, PCs and Macs (Apple) come bundled with software that can be used for Web applications. Publisher is supplied on Windows systems. This easy-

to-use program lets you make print brochures and mailers, but you can do more. Just about anything you can create in Publisher can be readily placed on your Web site. This is a simple and economical way to get a basic Web site up and running. Macintosh has a similar program called AppleWorks. High-end software programs include Dreamweaver from Macromedia and Adobe GoLive. Less sophisticated programs are Adobe PageMill, Microsoft FrontPage, and FileMaker Home Page.

## BURNING A CD-ROM

Once film has been scanned or an image digitally captured, it usually ends up on the computer's hard drive. But sooner or later you will need to send the image to a client, or you may even run out of storage space. Archiving or *burning* files to a CD-ROM is popular because CD-ROMs are inexpensive and hold lots of data that can't be erased; further, nearly everyone has a CD drive. The following instructions are for the Macintosh-based software Adaptec Toast. Software for Windows/PCs includes HyCD Publisher by Creative Digital Research and CD Everywhere by Interactive Information R & D.

Before you burn the CD, determine whether it needs to work only on Mac computers or needs to be a *hybrid*—that is, capable of working on both Mac and Windows/PCs. If there are any time constraints—such as the CD has to make the last FedEx pick-up, or else—you had better plan your tasks accordingly. Burning CDs can take quite a bit of time if there are large files.

### Burning a Mac-only CD-ROM
Writing files to a CD that runs on Mac only is quite easy and similar to copying files to a floppy or Zip disc.

1) While in Toast software, use the Format pull-down menu and select Mac Files & Folders.
2) Now click Mac in the Toast window. This lets you select the files you want to copy to the CD. Afterwards, you'll see the file names appear in the Toast window. Proceed to step 8 in the following list for burning a hybrid disc.

### Burning a Hybrid or Dual-platform CD-ROM
Making a hybrid or dual-platform CD that can be used on both Mac and Windows/PCs requires a few more steps. The first thing you need is a special place to put the files that will ultimately be copied to CD-ROM. The storage space is most often referred to as a *Disc Image*. The Disc Image is just a part of the computer's hard drive that has been partitioned off and made available for Toast files.

When the photographer burns lots of hybrid CDs, determine if there's an existing Disk Image ready to use. If so, make it available by selecting Utilities > Mount Disc Image while in Toast. The disc image will then act like a *volume* (or a hard drive) on the desktop.

You can then go to step 5 in the following list. If the photographer doesn't have a disc image to use, you'll have to make one.

Before starting, it's important to name the files properly, so check to see if the photographer has a preference regarding file names. Generally, both Macs and PCs can read file names of any length, but under certain circumstances, problems can occur. Although it may not always be necessary, it is probably safest to use the old *eight-dot-three naming convention.* Name the individual files within the disc image using eight characters or less, followed by a period, then the appropriate suffix. For example, photo_1.psd or photo_2.tif or photo_3.jpg for Photoshop, TIFF, and JPEG files, respectively. Using the Photoshop Preferences pull-down menu, these suffixes can be added automatically. You *must* avoid using the following characters in your file names: ?, /, ", <, >, and :.

1) While in Toast, select Utilities > Create Temporary Partition. What you're doing is taking part of the computer's hard drive and partitioning it into what's called a volume, which is sometimes called a Disc Image. All files are copied into this volume. If you have more than one hard drive, select one with sufficient space to hold the volume you are creating.

2) Make the Volume or Temporary Partition on the hard drive a little larger than what you expect to use, but not larger than 650MB.

3) Name the Volume using eleven characters or less. Name the individual files using the eight-dot-three naming convention.

4) Click OK and quit Toast. You'll be asked if you want to delete the Temporary Partition or Volume that you just made. Click No. Now it's officially a Disk Image.

5) Go to the Desktop and click open the new volume. It's empty and ready to have the files copied to it.

6) Reopen Toast and select Format > Mac/ISO Hybrid.

7) The Toast window has both a Mac and an ISO button. Click Mac and select on the desktop the volume you created above. Then select ISO and add the same volume.

8) Click Search to find the CD-ROM writer.

9) Then click Write CD. You're asked the speed, such as 1×, 2×, or 4×. The 1× speed is the slowest, and the most compatible on old CD drives. Also, check Don't Copy Free Space.

10) Click Write Disc. Depending on the amount of data and the speed, burning a CD can take from five to forty-five minutes. So plan accordingly, if time is a concern.

## E-MAIL

More and more people want things immediately. Normally, e-mail is designed to handle text files. However, you can send a graphic or photo file by making it an *attached file,* which tags along with your e-mail. Opening attached files from people you don't know is a very good way to get a computer virus. Consequently, informed computer users won't open attached files unless they know the sender and are expecting something. Keep this in mind if you're considering e-mailing your promotional piece to a prospective photographer. You could instead send an e-mail that contains a hot link to your Web site. Then, if the photographer is interested, it is easy for her to visit your site.

1) Begin by writing a regular e-mail message and state that there's an attached file. In the standard Write Mail window there is a button, usually labeled Attachments.

2) Click the Attachments button; the next window provides the option Attach.

3) When you click Attach, you see the familiar Mac or PC File dialog box.

4) Open the file you want attached to your e-mail.

5) When you go back to the standard Write Mail window, you see a confirmation as to which file was attached.

6) On Macintosh systems, make sure the file name for your attached file has the proper suffix. For JPEG's, the format is *filename.JPG;* for Photoshop files, the format is *filename.PSD.*

7) You can send multiple attached files by repeating steps 2 through 6. Generally, larger attached files will take longer to arrive at their destination than smaller ones.

If a photographer requests to see some of your work, you might try e-mailing an attached file. Instead of sending five different files, place the five photos in one file. While in Photoshop, use File > New and create a new file. Have it measure about 800 pixels wide by 600 pixels high. Next, reduce each scan to about 200 by 300 pixels and drag them into the new file. After you've arranged your photos, flatten the Photoshop file and JPEG it. Then select File > Save As.

You can take the technique further. Design the 800 by 600 space as you would a nice *promo piece.* Arrange your photos and use creative crops; then, add drop shadows, a ghosted background, and some text.

## PROTECTING YOUR PHOTOGRAPHY

When your photography goes on the Web, it's available for anyone to take and use. At the very least, all photos should give the photographer's name, copyright (©) symbol, and date of the photo's creation. On a PC, you can make a copyright symbol by holding down the shift key and typing parenthesis, the capital letter c and parenthesis (C). On Macintosh it's Command G. Here's an example: © John Kieffer 2000— All Rights Reserved.

In addition, you can state that none of the photography can be used without your expressed written permission, that it is not royalty-free, and that none of the photography is in the public domain.

You can also imbed a "watermark" or any type of identifying mark into the photo. A watermark is any symbol that is laid over the photo; it is usually ghosted back (opacity is reduced). It allows someone to see the photo, but the identifying mark makes it unusuable. You can make a watermark for your photos in Photoshop. Use the Text tool and type in your initials. Place your initials over the image and reduce the opacity to the desired level. There's your custom watermark. The Layers palette has the Opacity tool located at its top.

Digimarc Corp. offers a technology that embeds into an image a digital watermark that carries information unique to you. Digimarc then uses Web "crawlers" to traverse the Internet looking for Digimarcs. When it finds one, it's recorded. You can then confirm whether that the image is a valid use of your photography. Digimarc can be applied in varying levels or strengths. The higher levels are more likely to be found by a Web crawler, but the image degradation is greater. Digimarc's Web site is *www.digimarc.com/register.*

# 11

# Capturing
# Digital Images

D IGITAL CAPTURE OF IMAGES IS GRADUALLY REPLACING THE USE OF FILM, particularly in some areas. One can debate the merits of film versus digital capture, but it's not going to change what's happening in the field of photography. Currently, photographers in several categories are more likely to use some kind of *digital camera* or a digital back that attaches to a conventional film camera than they are to use film.

The view camera has always been fairly big and cumbersome to operate, and having it tethered to a computer makes it even more so. Most people working with a digitized view camera or medium-format camera are in the studio, often doing *product photography,* especially catalog work. Here, the photographer usually shoots many similar items. The reproductions of the photos are small in size, and a consistent look is important to a product catalog. Eliminating film and Polaroid is both a time and money saver. Usually the emphasis is on getting many shots done in a day, often with relatively little change in the background and lighting arrangement.

Another area that has seen a rise in digital cameras is *editorial* or *magazine photography.* Always looking to cut costs, these areas often don't have a budget for an assistant. The digital cameras used in these areas look like traditional 35mm cameras, and digital files are usually just large enough for a full page in a magazine. A digital file can be sent electronically to the editorial offices. This can save film-transport time and also reduces prepress costs, because the photos are ready to drop directly into the magazine's computer page layout. These can be important considerations for a weekly publication.

The previous chapter, "Scanning Film and Using Digital Files," discusses many of the concepts and responsibilities pertaining to digital cameras.

## DIGITAL CAPTURE

Some of the greatest changes in photography are due to the new digital recording of images. The good news for the assistant is that everything leading up to the digital capture remains the same. Some of the specific information that follows will undoubtedly change, but hopefully the basic concepts will not.

## Charged-coupled Device (CCD)

The *charged-coupled device (CCD)* is the foundation of digital cameras and film scanners. The CCD chip accounts for much of the cost of the equipment, and increases in camera performance will be largely due to advances in CCD technology. A common specification for a CCD is its resolution, which might be 2000 × 3000 pixels. This means the image is 3000 pixels wide and 2000 pixels high, which are the proportions and approximate size of 35mm film. Such an image yields approximately an 18MB file, an adequate size for a full-page reproduction at 150-line screen on a four-color offset press.

The high-resolution image file or capture file can originate in a variety of file formats, but it's often later saved to a Photoshop, TIFF, or compressed JPEG file. (For more about file formats, see chapter 10.)

### *Single-Pass Digital Capture*

The CCD works in two basic ways—the *single-pass* (single-pop) and the *multiple-pass* (multiple-pop) *CCD.* The single-pop or single-pass CCD captures the image in an instant, like a conventional camera. The big advantage with single pass is that you can photograph moving objects and use electronic flash. This type of image capture can be found on cameras resembling traditional 35mm, medium-format, and view cameras. The quality from the smaller, 35mm-style cameras is fairly good, but there's only so much room to store data files, or photos. When shooting in the studio, the camera can be connected to a computer, eliminating the storage problem. Medium-format cameras and view cameras can also use a single-pass CCD and are always going to be connected to a computer.

When on location, the 35mm-format cameras use *removable media* or *"cards"* to store data. A couple of the more common card brands are Smart Media and Compact Flash. The latter come in storage sizes from 4MB to 128MB. Because each image may require 10MB to 15MB, this is not a lot of space. However, they can be downloaded and reused. In order to get the most out of the small memory, these cameras usually have some way to compress the file to varying degrees. Generally, the greater the compression, the smaller the file size and the lower the image quality.

### *Multiple-Pass Digital Capture*

A camera with a multiple-pass or multiple-pop CCD captures the image three separate times. Each time, a red, green, or blue filter (RGB) is used, so just one of the three primary colors is scanned. Currently, this process produces the highest-quality image, which tends to mean the largest file.

However, it's slow and imposes some shooting limitations. In essence, the camera is making three separate exposures to produce one image. Consequently, everything must be stationary. Lighting is also different. When using electronic flash, the strobes must pop three separate times, and the power supply must fully recycle each time.

Currently, a strobe yields a comparatively small file compared with a continuous light source. Only so much information can be acquired in the brief moment of an electronic flash.

Ultimately, the multiple pass design yields the best quality, but scan times become so long that you must use a continuous light source like tungsten, daylight, or HMI (metal-halogen) lights. Voltage fluctuations during the exposure process must be eliminated, and even vibrations to the camera or on the set can cause problems. Therefore, the camera should be on a sturdy camera stand. The very fact that exposure times are in minutes increases the odds that something can go wrong.

## DIGITAL CAPTURE USING MEDIUM-FORMAT AND VIEW CAMERAS

There are two basic ways to capture digital images using a traditional view camera and medium-format camera. These are the *digital back* and variations such as the *scan back*. Usually, the same digital back can be made to work on both view cameras and medium-format cameras, if you have all the adapters. It is important to remember that the *capture area* of a digital back is small, about the size of 35mm film—not 6 × 7cm, and not 4″ × 5″. So you're using a relatively small part of the camera's total image area. To compensate, photographers use wide-angle lenses because the digital back is only going to scan the center part of the traditional image area.

When using a digital back on a 4″ × 5″ view camera, the capture area is so small that wider-angle 35mm camera lenses are used in place of large-format lenses. There isn't a bellows for focusing because you focus using the lens barrel. Plus, there's less opportunity to take advantage of the view-camera movements. Consequently, if the photographer owns both a medium-format and a view camera, it's more practical to use the medium-format camera with a digital back.

The use of wider-angle lenses has other ramifications. A wider-angle lens provides greater depth of field than normal and long lenses, when set at the same aperture. Consequently, you use less power because you're shooting at f 11 versus f 32. This three-stop difference translates to one-eighth less power needed.

In chapter 12, "Artificial Lighting," carefully read the "Adjusting the Power" section under "The Electronic Flash System." This section discusses "bleeding power" to another head and other ways to reduce power output. With the minimal lighting requirements of digital capture, many 2000 and 4000 watts-per-second power supplies are overpowered.

### Medium Format

A digital back is attached to a traditional medium-format camera in the same place as the roll-film back. Because camera bodies are often modified to accept another manufacturer's equipment, the actual attachment may vary. However, it must be designed to be very secure. A digital back is bigger and heavier than the film back it's replacing, plus it can cost $25,000 or more. You don't want it to fall off the camera. Even so, they can still be hand-held when the photographer is shooting in black-and-white mode. Here, no filters are used and there's only one pass and strobe pop.

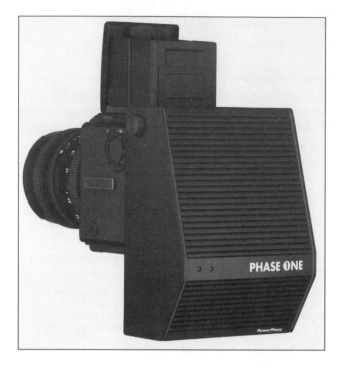

The Phase One digital scanning back attaches to the Hasselblad medium-format camera in place of the film magazine.
*Photo courtesy of Phase One.*

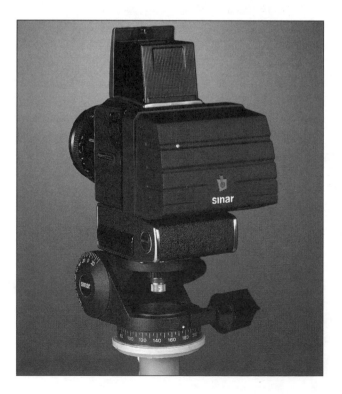

A medium-format Hasselblad with motor drive. The Sinar digital back (Sinarback) has replaced the film magazine. *Photo courtesy of Sinar Bron, Inc.*

With a Hasselblad, two new screws are likely to be added to the side to firmly attach the digital back. Hasselblad cameras must also be equipped with a motor drive, attached by a cable to the digital back. A second cable connects to the computer. One looks through the camera using the same viewfinder that attaches to the top of the camera. As mentioned, in the three-pass mode, one of three filters (RGB) is in place during each pass. With medium-format cameras, the filter attachment is placed in front of the lens. A switch on the back of the digital back changes from horizontal to vertical format.

## View Cameras

Many digital backs that are used on the medium-format camera can also be fitted to a view camera. A digital view camera looks so different because it doesn't have a bellows and uses a 35mm lens. The digital back begins where one used to find the rear standard and ground glass. The three filters (RGB) used in three-pass cameras are placed within the camera, not in front of the lens. You focus the camera by turning the lens barrel, but you look at the monitor to view the image. The "cable release" is positioned on the back of the camera, not on the lens.

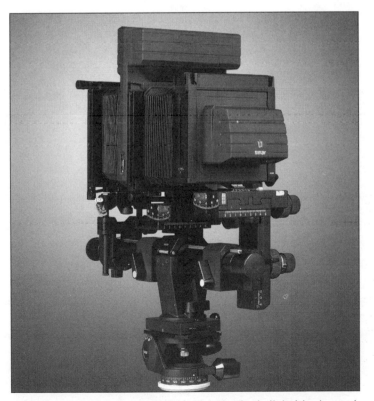

The Sinar P2 digital camera system. The Sinarback digital back attaches to the rear standard. *Photo courtesy of Sinar Bron, Inc.*

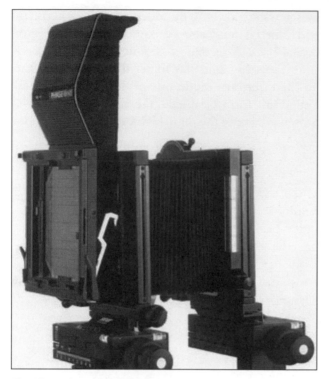

The Phase One digital scanning back slides into the Sinar 4″ × 5″ view camera like a traditional sheet-film holder. *Photo courtesy of Phase One.*

A *sliding digital back* is another digital device that makes use of a traditional view camera. It attaches to the view camera using the same mechanism that attaches the ground glass. The digital back slides out of the way, and you look through a ground glass provided on the digital back. A cable connects the digital back to the computer, possibly via a power supply. When you're ready to capture an image, the digital back slides into place.

Another digital-capture device is called the *scan back*. It looks like an oversized 4″ × 5″ sheet-film holder and is held in the view camera like a traditional film holder. It connects to the computer with a cable. Scan backs are usually of the three-pass design and can provide a very large file (250MB), often up to 8000 × 12,000 pixels. When using a multipass device and acquiring a very large file, you need to have adequate storage space and know the ramifications of a five-minute exposure.

## VIEWING THE IMAGE

Viewing the image isn't what it used to be, and that's probably a good thing. Looking through the ground glass while huddling under the dark cloth is a learned skill. The image is upside down and backwards, dark and difficult to focus.

As you'd expect, digital capture provides different ways of evaluating what the camera is seeing. One way is to capture a low-resolution image or *preview* and view it on the monitor. You can review composition and zoom in to check focus. If the assistant fails to double-check the strobes and one doesn't fire, no Polaroid film is wasted with a preview.

Digitizing cameras often provide *live video preview,* which allows you to view the monitor in real time so you can see what's happening as you arrange the set. Here the photographer might have two monitors. One is positioned right at the set so the photographer can critically position objects without moving back and forth between the camera and set.

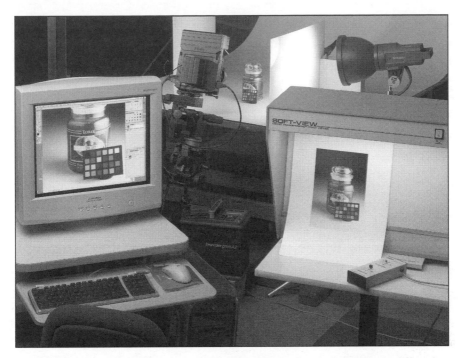

A product shot using a view camera with digital back. The strobe's light is diffused by passing through white Plexiglas. The shadows are filled by reflecting the light off a white fill card on the left. The background is swept up and the light is designed to gradually taper off. The monitor replaces the ground glass and a digital print replaces a Polaroid proof. Digital photograph © 2000 Tony Dube, Ulsaker Studio.

## COMPUTERS AND SOFTWARE

There are two choices of computers for most consumers: either a *Macintosh (Apple)* or a *PC with Windows.* In the photographic and graphic-arts industries, the Macintosh has been and still is the standard. All brands of digital-camera backs were first built to interface to the Mac but are just starting to be PC compatible. Many assistants and photographers buy a PC instead of a Mac because it saves them money on the front end and has more general software available. However, price is not the only factor.

With the Mac system, it is easier to set up and learn the basics. It's also less likely to crash. If you're a beginner with the computer, these factors should be taken into consideration. Because Macs are still the standard with graphic designers, art directors, and digitally savvy photographers, knowledge of Mac computers is a boon to the assistant.

Each manufacturer of digital-capture equipment has its own proprietary software. This means it's specific to the manufacturer, and the only way to learn it is to use it. However, after an image is captured, the file is usually imported into Photoshop, where it can be retouched, sharpened, and color corrected. Adobe's Photoshop is the industry standard. You can often get a lower-end version (the LE version) free when you buy a new scanner. Review the previous chapter, "Scanning Film and Using Digital Files," for additional information on useful Photoshop commands and saving files.

## THE ASSISTANT AND COMPUTER

The advent of the digital camera has impacted both the photographer and the assistant. In many ways, what time is saved in preproduction work (loading holders, etc.) is often spent in increased postproduction work (i.e., the work performed after the photo is taken). Here are some considerations. When a digital camera is used, an assistant isn't needed to handle regular film or Polaroid instant film. Also, there's no need for the assistant to run film to and from the lab. Eliminating these tasks can be a great time and money saver, especially when the alternative is sheet film.

It used to be that when the film came back from the lab, the photographer's job was done. You'd strike the set and get ready for the next day's shoot. With a digital camera, there's often more work to do after the image is captured. This original capture file or *raw scan* may need to be sharpened, color-corrected, and cleaned of dust spots or scratches. It may have to be reduced in size and converted to another file format. Afterwards, the file might be burned to a CD-R and sent to a client.

So assistants who are competent with Mac computers in general and with Photoshop specifically will end up with more work. The digital-camera manufacturer's proprietary software, however, presents a problem; if you don't work with the same photographer and the same system often, there may be little time to gain experience on the software. But if you're adept with Photoshop, you might get up to speed more quickly because some camera software resembles Photoshop, and many files ultimately are transferred there.

## WORKING WITH PHOTOSHOP

The amount of work performed on the raw scan or original capture file can range from minutes to hours. If the scan is to be used for a high-end print job, great care must be taken not to oversharpen and overly color-correct the file. The high-end job is best left to an experienced photographer or the designer responsible for getting the files to the printer.

The work is much less stringent when the file is being used for multimedia applications, like a Web site, kiosk, or CD-ROM. Also, the files tend to be smaller and faster to work on. The previous chapter contains many tips for working with PhotoShop, but here are a few more:

1) Save the original capture file and work on a duplicate. You can then always go back to the original at any time. Archiving data onto a CD-ROM is smart because it can't be erased.

2) Determine if the scan needs to be saved as another file format. First, open the original file and click File > Save As. At the bottom of the Save dialog box, select the appropriate format, most likely Photoshop, JPEG, GIF, or TIFF. See the previous chapter, "Scanning Film and Using Digital Files."

3) Use Image > Mode and make certain that both 8-Bits/Channel and RGB Color are selected. Now you can work on the image.

4) Save often and back-up your work when finished, especially when working on important files.

5) A *proof print* is often made for the client—ideally, on a quality desktop printer that's calibrated to the monitor. Confirm the quality of print that's needed. The final proof print is often made on a higher-quality paper at a higher resolution, which dictates more time and more expensive paper.

6) Determine how the files are to be given to the client. The file might be reduced in size and stored to a Zip disk or burned onto a CD-ROM.

## SUMMARY OF RESPONSIBILITIES RELATED TO COMPUTERS

❑ Ask the photographer about specific duties regarding the digital camera. The cameras are very expensive and not nearly as standardized in design and operation as traditional cameras.

❑ Determine whether strobe or a continuous light source is used. The deciding factor could be which type of camera—single pass or multiple pass—the photographer shoots with.

❑ Turn on the computer and digital back to allow the CCD and monitor to warm up for 30 minutes for greater color consistency.

❑ Determine how many different shots there are and the average file size, to establish how much memory is needed.

❑ Find out where the original capture files or raw scans are to be stored and if there's enough free disk space. Double-click on the hard drive icon to see the available memory along the top of the folder. A digital-image file can range from 10MB to 300MB.

❑ Ask if the photographer has a specific naming convention for the new files.

❑ Determine if the image being captured is a preview or a final capture. A preview is quicker and provides a smaller file size to review. It's analogous to shooting a Polaroid proof print.

❑ Be aware that a final capture takes longer and yields a larger file. This is especially true with a multiple-pass camera. The raw file or original capture file is often imported into Photoshop to be adjusted.

❑ Record pertinent information, just as you would do with film. You can note how one file or shot differs from the next, perhaps in variations in composition or changes in the subject.

❑ Review the discussion in the chapter "Scanning Film and Using Digital Files" on saving files to different file formats and burning to CD-R.

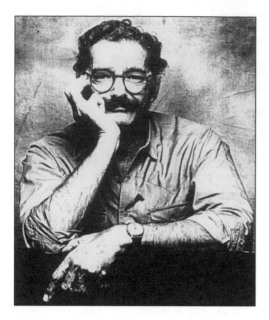

## AN INTERVIEW WITH CARL FISCHER

**John Kieffer:**  Could you give me a better idea as to the type of photography you do at your studio in New York City?
**Carl Fischer:**   Most of the work I do is advertising, and about 20 percent is editorial. Most is what's called illustration: portraits of people, scenes, sets, and still lifes. But over time, I've become interested in special effects, sometimes called concept photography. I was an art director originally, and I still become involved in the ideas behind the pictures. Overall, I could be called a generalist; I do many different things.

**J.K.:**   In general terms, what do you look for most in an assistant?
**C.F.:**   Over the years, I've had good ones and bad ones. I find it difficult to judge someone at an interview. You have to make a calculated guess. I prefer someone who has had some experience—only rarely someone just out of school.

We're looking for someone who is intelligent, diligent, a decent person. We find that techniques can be learned. We have our own system of doing things and we teach that system to assistants when they start. The best assistants have been those who have adapted to our system. Not that assistants haven't improved on it at times and made good suggestions—they have. The poorest assistants have been people who are set in their own way of doing things and won't change. I would say Horatio Alger types make the best assistants.

**J.K.:**   Do you interview assistants and look at a portfolio?
**C.F.:**   When we're looking to hire someone, yes. When we're not, we ask for résumés and keep them on file.

**J.K.:**   Do any assistants have Web sites or send you their portfolio on CD-ROM?
**C.F.:**   I know of several assistants that have Web sites, but I've never gotten anything on CD-ROM. We still get a lot of résumés.

**J.K.:**   Do you have a full-time assistant or hire freelancers?
**C.F.:**   We have both. We have assistants on staff and we hire freelance people.

**J.K.:**   What's the day rate for a freelance assistant in New York City?
**C.F.:**   Day rates in New York go around $200.

**J.K.:**   When looking for an assistant, do you put more emphasis on the individual or the fact that they graduated from a recognized photography school?
**C.F.:**   The most emphasis is put on the individual. We take it for granted that if you've graduated from a photography school, you probably know the rudiments and

we aren't too concerned about that. If someone didn't go to school, we want to make sure that he or she knows the basics.

**J.K.:** Do you still require assistants to know darkroom work?
**C.F.:** I no longer keep a darkroom, and when the need arises, I send it out.

**J.K.:** Regarding the digital revolution, what's your ratio of shooting film versus digital in your studio?
**C.F.:** Now, it's virtually 100 percent on digital.

**J.K.:** Has this change to digital been out of necessity to keep your clients?
**C.F.:** I prefer it this way. Instead of seeing Polaroids, I see the image on the computer and it's a much more accurate image. It's also quicker.

**J.K.:** What kind of equipment do you use?
**C.F.:** Right now, it's the Nikon D1. Eventually, I'll get a digital back for the Hasselblad.

**J.K.:** Do you find that because you're not shooting Polaroid and film, and then afterwards running to and from the lab, that you're using freelance assistants less?
**C.F.:** Yes, I do.

**J.K.:** When you have a "raw" or unaltered scan up on the computer screen, how much work lies ahead of you before you can give it to the client?
**C.F.:** That depends on the client. When they've chosen the final shot, I'll go over it myself. I'll sharpen it, perhaps correct color and make minor changes or major changes.

**J.K.:** What tasks do you have the assistant perform in your studio, that require the use of a computer?
**C.F.:** When I use a digital camera, like the Nikon D1, she'll make a contact print of the different exposures using a desktop printer. Afterwards, when the client selects the final shot, we'll provide a digital print and the scan on a disc. We also have a desktop scanner to scan film, but it's of limited quality.

The digital trend is certainly a major influence in how we take pictures, but a lot of things have not changed. We still make pictures, one way or the other. When I started in the business some thirty-odd years ago, view cameras were the way pictures had to be taken if you wanted to do national ads. The 35mm was out of the question. Now 35mm cameras are fine for national ads and digital is coming in. But all of this is just the mechanics of taking the picture. No matter what type of cameras we use, the problems are the same—composition, lighting. If you see an ad in a national magazine, you can't tell if it was photographed digitally or the traditional way.

Years ago I shot a shoe ad and there was a fire in the background. I wanted to use a Hasselblad because of the possible variations in the fire. However, the art director said the client insisted on 8 × 10 film for the sharpness and quality. So I shot it on two and a quarter and we picked out the best picture. We then made an 8 × 10 dupe of it. When the client saw it he said, "See, I told you. You have to shoot 8 × 10. Look at the good quality you get."

**J.K.:**     Have you had any disasters or near disasters caused by an assistant?

**C.F.:**     We count on assistants making mistakes—that's why they're assistants. We have a lot of backup procedures, so it's hard for assistants to goof—unless, they're really incompetent or lazy.

**J.K.:**     That redundancy, did it develop as your personal approach to photography or because you felt you had to do that when working with assistants and the increased chance of errors?

**C.F.:**     Both. I never had the useful experience of working as an assistant. I came from art direction directly into photography. Because of that lack, I reinvented the wheel. I invented all kinds of clever procedures that had previously been invented. I made a lot of mistakes doing my own work, and the advantage of that is that I remembered those mistakes and I developed procedures, so as not to make them the next time.

**J.K.:**     I shoot Polaroid and I still tend to be a little anxious until I see the actual film. Do you find that capturing an image digitally has reduced any anxiety?

**C.F.:**     I've always mistrusted the magic of negatives or not being able to see the transparencies until the next day. I've never liked that. I've never trusted exposure meters; I've always counted on Polaroid. So in a way, it is calmer. You see the image larger and clearer than on a Polaroid. Just make sure you back up the material at the end of the shooting.

**J.K.:**     What is your feeling regarding assisting as a way to learn photography and break into the field?

**C.F.:**     I think it's the best way to learn advertising and editorial photography. There are so many skills that have been developed over the years, from setting up lighting to working with the machinery that we have available to us. I missed being an assistant. I learned a little bit being an art director and visiting a lot of studios. I kept my eyes open and noticed the clever things that photographers did—how they stacked background paper and the like. I think being an assistant in more than one studio is a useful experience. One learns all the skills other photographers have developed over the years. I strongly recommend that when people get out of school they work as an assistant for several years.

**J.K.:**     Do you have any instances where an assistant saved the day or came up with an ingenious solution?

**C.F.:**     Assistants have frequently done that. Good assistants are invaluable on a shooting. There are times when we travel to California then drive a hundred miles and have about fifteen to twenty minutes to take a picture of some personality. Then we'll drive and fly back. So we all work for only about a half hour, while the project takes a day or so. During that fifteen minutes or half hour of a shooting, there's a lot going on and that second set of eyes can be invaluable. Assistants have a different view of what's going on than the photographer, and good assistants see things that are going wrong. A smart assistant doesn't just mechanically load the film backs and feed them to you and take meter readings. A good assistant knows what's going on and frequently makes valuable contributions.

**J.K.:** How long do your assistants tend to work with you?
**C.F.:** It varies, usually two to three years.

**J.K.:** Did most of them stay in New York and pursue the same kind of photography or did some have completely divergent views and go off and do their own thing?
**C.F.:** Over the years—and I've been in this business a long time—about everything that can happen has happened. I've had assistants from Europe, one from Italy and one from Germany. They both went back and opened their studios and both are successful. I've had assistants who went into other kinds of photography. One is working with the Metropolitan Museum of Art doing photography of artwork. Most have tried to become photographers and set up their own business, and my guess is that only about 20 percent of them have succeeded.

**J.K.:** Have you had any experiences of unethical behavior from an assistant—for instance, approaching clients that they met while assisting with you, showing their portfolio, and suggesting they could do the same job for less?
**C.F.:** I know that assistants who have worked for me have shown their work to clients that they've worked with here. I don't find that unethical, by the way. I feel that is legitimate. After all, if they are going in business on their own, who else are they going to see? After they leave the studio they are allowed to see the kind of people they've been working with as an assistant. Do they work for less? Of course they work for less. That's the free-market system.

**J.K.:** Is there anything you'd like to add regarding assistants or the field of photography in general?
**C.F.:** You have to remember that photography is not like working in a bank. It's an entrepreneurial business, and as such it's fraught with danger, but that's the kind of business it is.

You haven't asked about women versus men. There was a time when women assistants said that they were discriminated against, and I believe that was the case because some of the chores of assistants are to carry around heavy cases, climb up ladders and do physical work. However, I believe that the women that we've had on staff have all been able to do that sort of work. Yes, there are heavy cases to carry, there is physical labor involved, but nothing so horrendous that a woman can't do it. The best assistant I've ever had, by the way, was a woman. Afterwards, she went on to do still-life photography very successfully herself. And there do seem to be a lot of women assistants around now, so I presume that any discrimination that once existed is now gone.

**J.K.:** So you've seen an increase in the number of women assistants over the years?
**C.F.:** Yes, definitely. Certainly among art directors, there are as many or more women as there are men. And as far as women assistants, there are a great many more than there used to be.

# 12

# Artificial Lighting

A LARGE PROPORTION OF ASSISTING JOBS INVOLVES THE USE OF *ARTIFICIAL LIGHTING,* or lighting supplied by the photographer. By providing the light source, the photographer gains a level of control over the photographic environment. The assignment and current trends influence the choice of light source and the manner in which it's manipulated.

Artificial lighting and assistants go hand in hand. The generation of artificial light requires equipment. Most professional lighting systems consist of heavy *power supplies* and numerous *flash heads.* Devices to modify the raw light are equally important. Soft boxes, umbrellas, reflectors, and fill cards are used routinely, and they are all supported with various stands and clamps. The assistant, of course, is of great help in setting up the equipment.

And, of course, the photographer needs a continuous supply of Polaroid instant film to evaluate changes in lighting. The assistant helps here, too. The amount of lighting equipment and the time spent working with it isn't fully appreciated by those unfamiliar with professional photography.

## COMPARE AND CONTRAST

The two basic kinds of light source available to the photographer are electronic flash and a continuous light source, like tungsten. The two systems are very different in many ways and are best discussed separately. But first, to show their unique qualities, I'll compare and contrast the two.

*Electronic flash equipment* or *strobe* produces a *daylight-balanced* light. It's referred to as daylight balanced because the flash of light resembles natural daylight. Although difficult to discern with the naked eye, daylight is basically blue in color and has a color temperature of 5500 degrees Kelvin. For daylight-balanced film to reproduce daylight so it looks natural to the eye, the film needs to be fairly warm or yellow in color.

*Continuous light sources* are turned on, and the light stays constant. The best known is *tungsten lighting,* which produces a continuous light source from a quartz or incandescent lamp. It has a yellowish or warmer light, and its color temperature is 3200 degrees Kelvin. When using tungsten lights, you use a tungsten-balanced film, which has a cool or blue color to it. Using tungsten film with electronic flash results in an overly blue cast to the film. Using daylight-balanced film with tungsten lighting results in a very yellowish cast to the film.

Another continuous light source is *HMI lighting* or *quartz halogen*. HMI lights produce a daylight-balanced light and can be used with electronic flash. HMI lighting is also very popular in digital-photography studios using multi-pass cameras, which require a continuous light. Here, exposures or capture times are many minutes long.

Another basic difference between the two systems is heat. On one hand, electronic flash systems produce very little heat when they flash. Light-modifying devices can therefore be placed around the flash head and positioned close to the subject.

On the other hand, tungsten and HMI lights remain on continuously, and the lamps quickly get very hot. The heat restricts the use of light-modifying devices and limits how closely the light can be positioned to the subject. Ultimately, this influences lighting technique and styles. Regardless of light source, its control is arguably the most critical aspect of excellent photography.

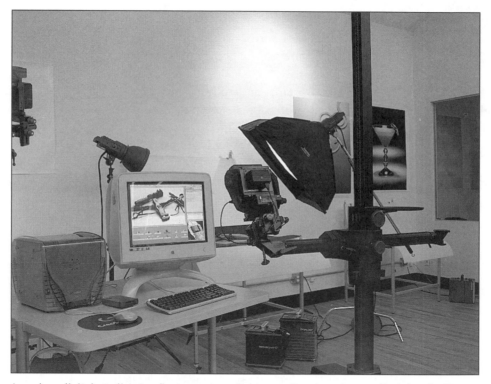

A modern digital studio. A reflector and a soft box are fitted to the two flash heads. The two power supplies are on the floor. A 4" × 5" view camera (Sinar) with a digital back is best supported by a camera stand. *Digital photo courtesy of Jeff Hirsch's Foto Care, NY, NY.*

## THE ELECTRONIC FLASH SYSTEM

Currently, electronic flash or strobe is the lighting of choice for the majority of professional photographers, even those using some form of digital capture. The electronic flash system presented here is very different from the on-camera flash unit associated with a 35mm SLR camera. Strobe is a *modular system,* consisting of a power supply, flash heads, and assorted light-modifying devices. It is an approach that provides great flexibility, allowing it to be used in almost every lighting situation.

## THE POWER SUPPLY

The heart of the system is the power supply or power pack. To the power supply, you connect one or more flash heads. Basically, the power supply is a large battery or *capacitor*. It's plugged into an electrical outlet and when switched on, the capacitor charges. After the capacitor is fully charged, it can be discharged. The stored electricity is released through the flash head in one very brief, but powerful, flash of light. The capacitor then recharges.

The amount of electrical energy or light a particular power supply can produce is designated in watt-seconds. A watt-second is the work done by one watt, acting for one second. Therefore, larger power supplies produce more watt-seconds of energy in the form of a flash than smaller power supplies.

The number of watt-seconds is the most important figure regarding power supplies. Small power supplies deliver a maximum of 800 watt-seconds per flash. Moderate units range from 1600 to 2400 watt-seconds. Power supplies producing 4000 watt-seconds are very powerful.

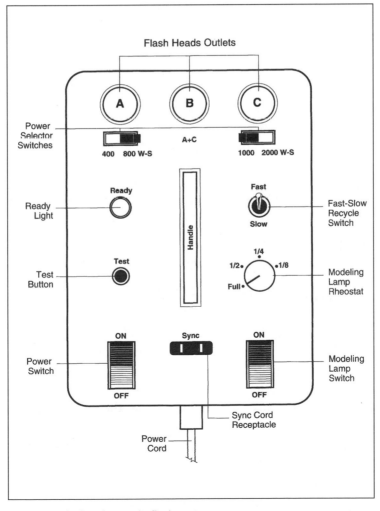

Power supply for electronic flash system.

## Operating the Power Supply

The key features regarding the operation of a power supply are quite similar among the various manufacturers. The power supply is plugged into a standard electrical outlet. All power supplies have an on/off switch, and when switched on, the capacitor charges. This takes several seconds, and the capacitor is fully charged when the ready light comes on.

For the assistant, the ready light is one of the most important items on the pack. First, it signals that the capacitor has fully charged. Second, when the capacitor discharges or fires, the ready light goes off and then comes back on when the capacitor has recharged. The time it takes to recharge is the *recycle time.*

The ready light is universal on power packs. But on some systems, audio signals are also present. In other systems, the flash head's modeling light becomes dim or flickers until the power supply has recharged.

## The Recycle Time

Tracking the recycle time is critical, especially when working with a fast-shooting photographer. If the power supply hasn't fully recharged, it will still fire. Unfortunately, the resulting flash won't be at full power. The photographer can shoot fast and furious, but the film will be underexposed.

Outpacing the power supply's recycle time is possible with most roll-film cameras and even more so when a motor drive is used. Observe the cadence at which the photographer routinely advances and exposes the film. When it becomes faster than the power supply's recycle time, the photographer must be told to slow down. During breaks in the action, the photographer will often ask whether the pack has been recycling fast enough. Be sure you know whether it has been.

Electronic flash is still compatible with most digital-camera systems, both the one-pass and the multiple-pass varieties. When using electronic flash with a multiple-pass camera, the strobes pop three separate times, so make certain the power supply fully recycles each time.

### Factors Affecting the Recycle Time

Several factors affect the length of the recycle time. Most packs have *fast* and *slow recycle switches,* often designated with the figures of a rabbit and turtle. As you'd expect, the fast recycle setting makes the pack recharge more quickly. The slow recycle setting can be useful in older buildings, because it puts less strain on the electrical system, thereby reducing the likelihood of blown fuses.

Another factor influencing the recycle time is the *power setting,* relative to the pack's total power output. For example, when a 2400 watt-second (w-s) power supply is adjusted to deliver 400 w-s to a single flash head, it will recycle almost immediately. When set to deliver a full 2400 w-s, the pack may require three to four seconds to recharge.

Finally, the use of *excessively long extension cords* can lengthen the recycle time. The extra wire causes greater resistance.

## Adjusting the Power

It's essential for the power supply to be able to deliver varying amounts of power to the flash head. Although all packs are rated in watt-seconds, determining the power setting is far from universal. A power supply can accommodate from three to six separate heads; many times, additional heads just complicate the situation.

The simplest arrangement is when one flash head is plugged into one socket, and a single switch is used to adjust the power. When set at maximum, the unit might deliver 2000 watt-seconds of power to the flash head. When switched from 2000 w-s to 1000 w-s, power is reduced by 50 percent, or one f-stop. Conversely, switching from 1000 w-s to 2000 w-s doubles the power, or increases it by one f-stop.

The assistant may need to adjust the power at any time. Reducing the output from 2000 w-s to 1000 w-s can be as easy as flipping a switch. But with some packs, you must then discharge the power supply of its 2000 w-s and let it recharge to 1000 w-s. If you don't, the first exposure will be over exposed by one f-stop. When in doubt use the test button to discharge the pack after decreasing the power. Increasing power from 1000 w-s to 2000 w-s doesn't require this step; just wait for the ready light to come back on.

The *number of flash heads* plugged into the power supply also influences the power output. Again, imagine one flash head attached to a power supply, set at full power, or 2000 w-s. However, when two heads are connected to the pack, the total power must be divided between the heads, possibly at 800 and 1200 watt-seconds. Adjusting power among several heads is accomplished by plugging the flash heads into the appropriate sockets, coupled with the use of switches.

Occasionally, a power supply can be too powerful. Perhaps 400 w-s is the lowest setting, but the shot calls for a mere 200 w-s. Oftentimes, you can decrease the power further by connecting a second flash head to the same power supply. So 200 w-s would go to each flash head. The unused flash head would be placed well off the set so it wouldn't affect the shot. Some refer to the procedure as *bleeding off power* to a second head.

Bleeding off power is becoming more necessary with the use of digital backs on view cameras. As explained in chapter 11, "Capturing Digital Images," digitized view cameras use very wide-angle lenses, which provide great depth of field, even at large apertures. Consequently, less power is needed.

The design of the power supply and the procedure used to adjust its output varies with the manufacturer. The variance can influence how the assistant annotates the Polaroid print. When working with some packs, noting that "1000 watt-seconds" is going to head number one is most logical. With others, it makes more sense to note the power relative to maximum power, such as "full power" and "half power." Still others might dictate "full power" and "full –1 stop."

## Synchronizing the Power Supply to the Camera

A power supply must be designed to discharge while the lens shutter is open. The duration of the flash is less than $\frac{1}{500}$ of a second, and the shutter might remain open $\frac{1}{60}$ of a second. These two events must be synchronized.

The most common way to synchronize the shutter and the power supply is to physically connect the two with a sync cord. The sync cord attaches to the power supply's sync-cord receptacle, using what resembles a household electrical plug. The sync cord's other end connects to a socket on either the camera body or lens. Regardless of camera format, this connection is the same.

Attach the sync cord to the camera or lens by carefully pushing the sync cord plug directly into the socket. The sync cord and this connection are one of the more fragile links in the system. To minimize the pull on the delicate connection, drape the remaining cord over a tripod handle. Or better yet, loosely tie a loop in the sync cord and suspend that from the tripod.

Once the sync cord is attached, set the lens shutter speed to the appropriate *sync speed*. A setting of one-sixtieth of a second is a safe choice. When the shutter speed is set too fast, it may not capture the entire flash. When the shutter speed is too slow, light from the strobe's modeling lamp may influence the exposure. If the shutter has an *X-M setting* or *sync terminal*, use the one designated *X*, for electronic flash.

Before leaving the camera area, position the sync cord so it's protected from traffic. In heavily congested areas, it may need to be taped to the floor. Due to the cord's fragile nature, most photographers pack a spare sync cord when going on location. It's your responsibility to make sure it's in with the gear.

## The Master and Slave Power Supply

The power supply connected to the lens shutter with a sync cord is designated the *master pack*. Oftentimes, more than one power supply is used; each additional power supply is referred to as a *slave*.

Each slave power supply must also discharge at the appropriate time; the correct discharge is accomplished with a *flash slave*. A flash slave is a small, light-sensing device that is plugged into the power supply's sync-cord receptacle. When the master power supply is triggered, the resulting flash is detected by the flash slave, and the slave power supply triggers.

## *Testing the System*

After any flash slave is plugged in, you must verify that it's working. To test, turn on both the master and slave power supplies. After their ready lights come on, find the *test button* on the master pack. It is often designated with a bolt of lightening.

Depressing the master pack's test button causes the pack to discharge and its flash head to fire. If the flash slave is detecting light, the slave power supply discharges. Monitor the ready light on the slave power supply. It should immediately go out after the master power supply discharges.

If the slave power supply fails to discharge, make certain the flash slave is receiving plenty of light from the master pack. Flash slaves are sensitive devices, but they do impose limitations on where the power supply can be placed. If the flash slave receives sufficient light but still doesn't fire, unplug the flash slave, rotate it 180 degrees, and plug it back in. It is important to understand that most flash slaves will function only when inserted into the sync-cord receptacle.

It will not always be possible to position the slave power supply in such a way that the flash slave detects sufficient light. Under these circumstances, the flash slave can be connected to the end of any extension cord and then placed in an effective location. This technique is especially useful on architectural shoots that utilize many well-hidden power supplies.

If you encounter any difficulties in getting any of the power supplies to discharge, avoid rearranging them once positioned. And *never rearrange* a power supply fitted with a flash slave just before going to film.

Flash slaves are another essential item that must make it to the location site. They are often left plugged into the sync-cord receptacle, so be careful during the transportation process.

### Radio Transmitters and Receivers

Because of the inherent limitations imposed by physically connecting the shutter to the power supply, the sync cord is often replaced. The most common means is with a radio transmitter and receiver setup, also called a *radio slave unit*. Here, the transmitter is connected to the lens shutter with a short sync cord. The transmitter then hangs from the tripod. Next, a receiver is connected to each power supply via the sync-cord receptacle. As the photographer trips the camera's shutter, a radio signal is sent from the transmitter to the receiver, and the power supply discharges.

Although radio slave units are relatively easy to operate, a few points need to be remembered. First, they require batteries, and the units must be turned on and off. Also, most radio transmitters have more than one channel. You must switch the transmitter and each receiver to the same channel.

### Safety

Keep in mind that power supplies store, and quickly release, a considerable amount of electrical energy. To state that electrical equipment should be kept clear of water is almost too obvious, but it's amazing the conditions studio photographers can conjure up and location photographers encounter.

Be aware that there are procedural differences between manufacturers, as to the exact operation of various power supplies. Before plugging in a power supply, make certain it's turned off. Do not discharge the capacitor until it has fully recharged and the ready light is on. Also, with many units it's a good idea to power down when connecting and disconnecting flash heads. When in doubt, ask.

## THE FLASH HEAD

It's time to turn our attention to the flash head. Each flash head is connected to the power supply with a cable. The connection is specific for each manufacturer, necessitating the use of the same brand of flash head and power supply. Cables are quite sturdy, but you shouldn't coil them too tightly or allow gear to be set on them. Extension cables are available, but they reduce power going to the flash head. If required, inform the photographer so the power setting can be increased accordingly.

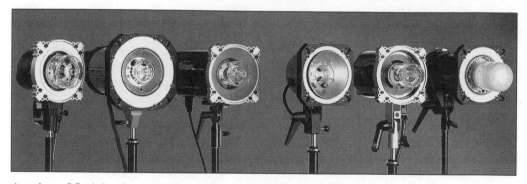

A variety of flash heads, or strobes. Visible is the flash tube, modeling light, and mounting ring (speed ring) for attaching a soft box. *Photo courtesy of Chimera Photographic Lighting.*

### The Flash Tube and Modeling Light

Each flash head consists of two different light sources, the *flash tube* and the *modeling light*. The flash tube produces the daylight-balanced flash of light that's used to expose the film. The bulk of the power supply and its adjustments are related to the flash tube. These include the capacitor, ready light, fast-slow recycle, sync cord receptacle, and power settings.

The modeling light is a tungsten lamp situated next to the flash tube; it is designed to remain on continuously. The modeling light provides a general idea as to how the flash will look on film. Most are sufficiently powerful that they're the only light needed to focus the camera and work on the set.

To be of greater value, modeling lights are often controlled with a modeling-lamp rheostat, or dimmer. Found on the power supply, the dimmer dial lets the photographer adjust the lighting ratio between two modeling lights. But more importantly, the rheostat allows the modeling lamp to be set to a very low level. While still useful, a lower setting generates less heat.

### The Cooling Fan

To dissipate heat, most flash heads have a cooling fan. Excessive heat is a potential danger when using light-modifying devices that restrict airflow. Such devices include smaller soft boxes, snoots, and reflectors with colored filters or diffusion material attached.

Don't assume the cooling fan to be completely effective. If you sense that heat may be a problem, monitor the situation. The modeling light may need to be kept very dim or off most of the time. When there isn't a cooling fan, you must be even more careful. At the end of the shoot, turn off the modeling light. Let the fan run, so as to cool down the entire flash head.

### *Care and Handling of Flash Heads*

It should be apparent that all photographic gear must be handled carefully, flash heads even more so. Though fairly rugged, they're still largely glass. A modeling lamp is expensive, but a flash tube is extremely expensive. Limit working with unprotected flash heads. At the very least, attach a small reflector.

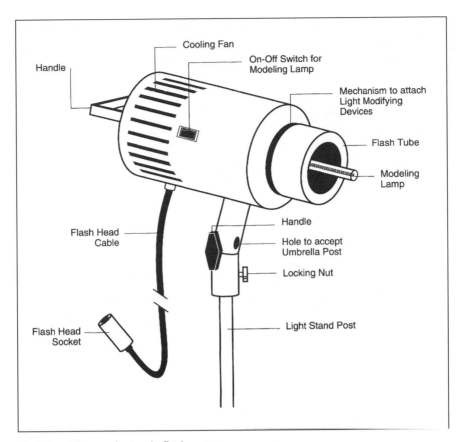

Flash head for an electronic flash system.

If a modeling lamp or flash tube fails to work, turn off the power supply and unplug it. Then, using a towel so as not to touch the glass directly, make sure the tube is firmly seated. *Using a towel is important* because oil from your fingers can become deposited on the flash tube or modeling lamp. These oils can create uneven heating and a shorter life span. It's inevitable for equipment to get bumped around, and lamps can work loose; make sure you have a towel so that you can safely check connections.

## Multiple Flashes

Under most conditions, the modeling light can remain on for the entire shot. It has no affect on the exposure, unless the photographer is using a very long shutter speed. When necessary, the modeling light can usually be switched off, either at the power supply or at the flash head.

Conditions requiring modeling lights to be turned off usually dictate that all nearby lights should also be turned off. Here, the photographer might require *multiple flashes,* or *pops,* in order to produce enough light to properly expose the film. The photographer opens the shutter and the assistant uses the test button to discharge the power supply. The assistant refires the pack only after the ready light comes back on.

The total number of flashes is critically important. With too many, the film is overexposed; too few, and the film is underexposed. When more than a couple of flashes are required, keep count aloud to help signal the photographer when to close the shutter.

### The Angling and Securing of Flash Heads

Most of the time, flash heads are inserted onto the end post of a light stand and then secured in place with a thumbscrew. A second knob tilts the head to the desired angle. When in use, the knobs must be tightened to prevent the flash head from changing position or falling off the stand.

Flash heads are designed to accept a wide range of light-modifying devices. These and related items will be discussed later.

### Monolights

The monolight electronic flash system differs from the one just presented in that the power supply and flash head are combined into one unit. Monolights resemble a standard flash head, only they are larger. Although these units have less output than systems containing separate power supplies, they can be more convenient. Adjusting the power output is simplified, and the cable connecting the power supply to the flash head is eliminated. Otherwise, the two systems are quite similar in principle and operation.

## ON-CAMERA ELECTRONIC FLASH UNITS

There's often less need for assistants on jobs in which the 35mm SLR camera is used. But one factor that can greatly increase the need is artificial lighting. The lighting may take the form of the powerful electronic flash systems just discussed, or the photographer may work with the *small flash units* that attach directly to the camera.

Due to the relationship between a camera's film size and lens focal length, small-format cameras provide more depth of field than large-format cameras, when lenses of comparable focal length are set to the same f-stop. Consequently, 35mm SLR cameras require less light to make an exposure and can utilize on-camera flash units. One reason for using smaller-format cameras is their overall portability and ease of handling. Small, on-camera flash units are designed to keep them that way.

### The Different Kinds of Flash Units

Smaller, on-camera flash units are far from universal in design and operation, due in part to the tremendous variability between different 35mm SLR cameras. There are *manual flashes,* somewhat analogous to the larger electronic flash systems, which, logically, can be manually controlled by the photographer. In contrast, automatic flash units control the flash, and hence the exposure. Still others are designed to interface only with specific cameras. These *dedicated flash units* usually have even more features.

The variety, coupled with the fact that you will probably work with the flash units less often than other forms of lighting, makes the learning process more awkward. What is presented here are the areas of operation most important to the assistant. Like any equipment, the photographer makes the decisions concerning the flash unit's setting. The assistant must know enough to make sure these settings remain as desired.

## Operating a Flash Unit

On-camera flash units can connect directly to the 35mm SLR camera's *hot shoe*. Flash units can also be supported on a handle mount or held by the assistant. Any distance is bridged with a sync cord. When more than one flash unit is incorporated into the system, several cords and adapters are needed. Be sure you understand the arrangement of all cables.

*Sync-cord connections* seem particularly vulnerable on smaller flash units. When the assignment calls for plenty of activity, sync cords and their connections need to be checked and rechecked throughout the day, especially when the assistant holds a flash unit. If necessary, loose connections can be taped down. It's also possible to tie a square knot in such a way that the connection is protected within the knot.

The assistant must track the recycle process, because the unit can flash while still recharging. Unfortunately, like strobe lighting, the flash won't have sufficient power, resulting in underexposed film. It's easy for the photographer to outpace the recycling time. It becomes even easier as the batteries begin to run down and recycling time increases. In addition to a ready light, flash units often use an audio signal. Most commonly, a buzzer remains on during the recharging process.

## Determining the Exposure

As with larger flash systems, there are ways to adjust the power output. However, smaller flash units are rated by a *guide number* (GN), not watt-seconds. The larger the guide number, the greater the power. A guide number of 70 represents a lower-powered flash, while a flash unit with a guide number of 150 is fairly powerful. By performing a calculation, the flash unit's guide number lets you determine the proper exposure.

You need to consider three variables when using on-camera flash units: *film speed, lens aperture,* and *flash-to-subject* distance. Dividing the flash unit's guide number by the desired lens aperture results in the correct flash-to-subject distance. Conversely, dividing the flash-to-subject distance into the guide number results in the correct lens-aperture setting. Exposure calculations supply basic information, but flash meters and Polaroid instant film are still necessary.

### *Automatic Flash Units*

The simplest arrangement of an automatic flash unit is when the unit has only one setting. Here, the lens aperture is determined by film speed, and faster films allow for smaller apertures. To increase versatility, some automatic units offer a choice of f-stop settings, versus one determined by film speed. Other more sophisticated units allow you to vary the power output when switched to the manual mode. The assistant should note how the controls are set and make sure they remain that way. Incorrectly set switches cause errors in exposures.

For an automatic flash unit to control the exposure, it must be able to sense the flash of light reflected off the subject. The unit then turns off the flash at the appropriate time. The process is accomplished with an exterior *photocell,* located on the front of the unit, and internal *thyristors.* The photocell must remain unobstructed and be positioned so as to detect reflected light.

The photocell is of little concern when the flash unit is attached to the camera or a handle mount. It's a different situation when held by the assistant. There are several important points to remember when hand holding a flash unit. Besides making sure that the photocell is unobstructed, the assistant must position the flash so it produces the proper lighting effect. Balancing these placements requires concentration.

## Batteries and Battery Packs

To produce light, flash units require a battery, either a disposable kind or a specialized rechargeable battery pack. Whichever is used, the flash unit must of course be switched on. When powered up, the battery charges the capacitor. Once fully charged, the ready light comes on.

Any battery-powered system can run down, quickly putting a halt to shooting. To increase capacity, rechargeable battery packs are often used with smaller flashes. *Supplemental battery packs* provide more flashes and shorter recycling times.

Some form of indicator informs the assistant how much of a charge remains on the rechargeable battery. When necessary, these units are recharged utilizing standard electrical outlets. However, specialized items are sometimes used in recharging, so inquire as to their need before leaving the studio.

During busy shoots, take advantage of opportunities to recharge. If the need arises and a suitable situation presents itself, set up quickly. Recharging might require every minute of your lunch break. If you find yourself working in a cold environment, try to keep the battery pack warm. Cold batteries are less effective. When packing up at the end of the day, tape down the on/off switches, so there's no possibility of accidentally draining the battery.

## Light-Modifying Devices

Fewer light-modifying devices are available for the small electronic flash units than for larger lighting systems. Small reflectors are sometimes used; they attach directly to the unit and bounce or direct the light more effectively. Diffusion material and colored gels can also be placed over the flash. These will soften or add color to the light. Small soft boxes and umbrellas, similar to those associated with larger systems, are also used. The smaller soft boxes are particularly useful. Remember, all light-modifying devices absorb some light; thus, they reduce a rather limited light source even further.

## SUMMARY OF RESPONSIBILITIES RELATED TO ELECTRONIC FLASH SYSTEMS

❏ Obtain a general idea of the *lighting requirements* for the shot.

❏ Position the *power supply* in an unobtrusive spot close to the set.

❏ Connect the power supply to a grounded electrical outlet, first making certain the supply is *turned off.*

❏ Put the *flash head* on a light stand and then connect it to the power supply.

❏ Attach the *light-modifying device* specified by the photographer.

❏ Place the light at the approximate position on the set.

❏ Connect the camera's shutter to the power supply's sync-cord receptacle, via the *sync cord*.

❏ Set lens shutter to the appropriate *sync speed,* usually ⅟₆₀ of a second.

❏ Switch on the power supply and modeling light, making certain the *ready light* comes on.

❏ *Test-fire* the system to be certain each flash head is firing. Observe both the flash head and ready light.

❏ When more than one power supply is being used, make certain the *flash slave* is operating and the slave power supply is discharging.

❏ Position yourself at the appropriate power supply during *the flash metering* process. Discharge the power supply using its test button.

❏ Generally, tend to film-related responsibilities during the exposure process. Occasionally reaffirm that *all flash heads are firing.*

❏ If the shutter is to remain open during the exposure process, turn off the modeling light. If *multiple pops* are required, remain near the master power supply and discharge the power supply using its test button.

❏ Throughout the day, monitor flash heads for *excessive heat.* Adjust modeling lights accordingly, using the rheostat or the on/off switch.

❏ Expect to work with lighting equipment and related hardware throughout the day.

❏ After the film is exposed, turn off the modeling light and allow the fan to *cool the flash head.*

❏ When cool, place a *flash-tube protector* on the flash head, loosely coil the cable, and store it.

## SUMMARY OF RESPONSIBILITIES RELATED TO ON-CAMERA FLASH

❏ Establish with the photographer how the flash unit is to be *adjusted* and make certain all switches remain as desired. Secure them with tape, if practical.

❏ Understand all *sync-cord connections* and monitor these throughout the day's shoot. Secure them with tape, if practical.

❏ Before going to film, turn the flash unit on and observe *the ready light.*

❏ *Monitor* the flash of light, in addition to the ready light, during the exposure process.

❏ *Hand hold* automatic flash units in a manner that you don't obstruct the photocell.

❏ Position automatic flash units so the *photocell* can detect the reflected light.

❏ Monitor the *low battery indicator.* If necessary, recharge the supplemental battery pack or replace batteries.

❏ *Turn off* the flash unit when it's not needed.

❏ *Tape down* any on/off switch on flash units and battery packs to prevent inadvertently running down the batteries, especially before packing away.

## CONTINUOUS LIGHT SOURCES (TUNGSTEN AND HMI)

The second basic type of artificial light source is a continuous light source, like tungsten and HMI lights (metal halogen). The fact that the light remains on continuously influences how it's used and the assistant's responsibilities. Using a continuous light source hasn't been nearly as popular among still photographers as electronic flash, but the use of the digital camera is changing that. Because some multiple-pass digital cameras cannot use strobe, they require a continuous light source. At present, the best digital quality is achieved by using a multiple pass digital back with long scan times.

In many ways, continuous lighting is easier to operate than strobe. Basically, the light consists of a light bulb enclosed in a metal housing. Tungsten units plug into a standard electrical outlet and don't have a separate power supply. Few if any adjustments are required. What adjustments are required, involve the light bulb. HMI lights are a little more complicated. They have what looks like a power supply, but it's called a *ballast*. A ballast is rated in watts, with 1200w a standard size. Unlike tungsten but like strobe, HMI lights are daylight balanced. The ballast provides a more constant voltage, which is very important during long digital exposures.

Besides being simpler to operate than electronic flash, there are other advantages to continuous light. A continuous light source makes it easier to evaluate the lighting arrangement. What you see is what you get. Even so, the assistant should expect to use Polaroid instant film. The constant light also eliminates the need for a sync cord and flash slaves for additional power supplies. With fewer components, less can go wrong, and less equipment needs to be transported to a location site. Just remember to bring spare light bulbs and plenty of extension cords. Whereas tungsten lighting is much less expensive than an electronic flash system, an HMI lighting system is more comparably priced.

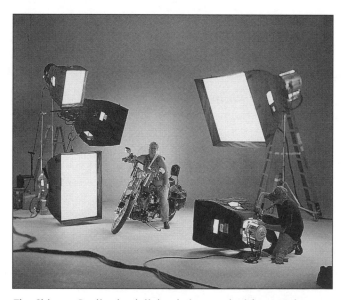

The Chimera Daylite bank lights being used with a continuous light source. Large soft boxes are very useful when photographing reflective surfaces like chrome and glass. © 2000 Brian Mark Photography.

### Tungsten and HMI Lamps

There are two basic kinds of tungsten lamps, *halogen* and *incandescent*. Both produce a warm, yellowish light and have a color temperature of 3200 degrees Kelvin. Like most household light bulbs, tungsten lights are rated in watts. However, photographic lights are much more powerful, usually ranging from 250 watts to 1000 watts.

HMI lamps can be even brighter than tungsten, but they are daylight balanced (5500K) and have a bluish color. This makes them useful with strobe systems and some digital cameras. The lamp head has a fan for cooling, allowing a greater diversity of light-modifying devices to be used.

The fact that both kinds of high-wattage lamps remain on for long periods has several implications. The most important is heat. These lights get hot; hence the common name *hot lights*. Heat influences how they're handled, the availability of light-modifying devices, and what can be photographed.

### Using Continuous Light Sources

A tungsten light is fairly easy to operate. Usually, a switch located at the head turns the unit on and off. HMI lighting is turned on at the ballast. To handle either light safely, you must take a few precautions. Before turning it on, connect it to a stand. The light gets hot almost immediately and can be difficult to handle or safely set down.

These lights are also very bright, and 1000 watts becomes an instant intrusion on the set. So have it properly positioned, making sure it's kept well away from flammable materials. A pair of leather work gloves can be indispensable. Being able to clip the gloves to your belt is another plus.

### Controlling a Continuous Light Source

The overall shape of the tungsten unit does much to control the light. Those designed to illuminate a large area are referred to as *flood lights* or *broad lights*. Those with a concentrated beam are *spot lights*. Lights capable of adjusting from a flood to a spot are called *focusing lights*. To control the light further, various styles of *barn doors* and *leafs* are available. To decrease the light output, it's generally best to change the bulb, use a filter, or move the light further from the set.

Most of the light-modifying devices used with electronic flash can't be used with tungsten lighting. It could be disastrous to enclose a 1000-watt lamp within most soft boxes or tape a colored filter over it. Although some soft boxes are specifically designed for continuous lights, they still require adequate ventilation. Diffusion material and colored filters must be positioned well in front of the light source, often supported in a filter frame.

HMI lights are generally made of a better quality than tungsten, plus they're designed much like a flash head. They are usually fitted with a cooling fan and timer, which affords some protection. So a greater variety of light modifiers can be used. Placing a filter in front of the light is the best way to decrease light output.

### Applications

Although most photographers have their preference, the specific assignment can dictate whether electronic flash or a continuous light source is used. Due to the relatively long shutter speeds associated with tungsten and HMI lighting, you can't freeze motion. However, this can be an advantage. Whereas the brief duration of a flash freezes movement, a continuous light source can be used to convey a sense of motion when movement is combined with a long exposure and constant light.

Digital capture is another reason a continuous light source is being used more frequently. Some multiple-pass digital cameras require the light to be on during the entire exposure process, and electronic flash can't be used.

Architectural photographers often employ tungsten and HMI lighting. They may not have any control over the lighting found at a site, or the shoot may involve a very large area. Under these circumstances, it can be more practical to add more of the same kind of light, rather than trying to integrate several different kinds. A combination of color-compensating filters is routinely part of the solution, but it requires still longer exposures.

Although tungsten might not be incorporated into the lighting arrangement, it's still used in the studio. Tungsten lights can aid in focusing, especially of view cameras. The light produced by a strobe's modeling light isn't always sufficiently bright to critically focus the camera. In addition, surfaces lacking texture or sharp edges often require even more care when focusing.

Lens selection can also add to focusing problems. A 300mm, f9, large-format lens lets in less light and is more difficult to view than a wider-angle 150mm, f5.6 lens. To aid in focusing, position the light in front of the camera, so it doesn't interfere with viewing the ground glass. Once the light is on, remain near it. It'll probably need to be turned off soon afterwards.

Finally, the heat produced from tungsten lights can speed the drying process of paints and glues. However, don't place it too close to the treated surface and change its position frequently.

# 13

# Working with Light

LIGHTING IS SO CRITICAL TO GOOD PHOTOGRAPHY THAT IT'S DIFFICULT TO OVER-
state its importance. While assisting, you'll be exposed to a diversity of lighting
styles and equipment. However, to best work with light, it's important to have a
good understanding about how light behaves. The proper use of the light meter is one
part of the process, and another is the choice of light modifying devices.

## QUALITIES OF LIGHT

The photographer is responsible for the exact positioning of a light modifier, but the
assistant is often involved with its placement. To help understand the photographer's
intent and why something is being positioned a certain way, it's important to be
familiar with an important law governing light: *The angle of incidence equals the angle of
reflectance.*

In simple terms, light hitting a surface at a certain angle will be reflected from
that surface at the same angle. For example, a billiard ball striking the cushion at forty-
five degrees will bounce off at forty-five degrees. To most accurately review the
results, position your eyes as near to the camera lens as possible.

There are two important terms referring to the quality of light. These are
*specular* and *diffuse.* The size of the light source, relative to what is being lit, controls
these qualities. The smaller the light source, the more *specular* the resulting light.
Conversely, the larger the light source, the more *diffuse* the light.

Specular light tends to yield very sharp shadows and is sometimes referred to
as hard or harsh. The light from the midday sun on a cloudless day is very specular.
The opposite of specular is diffuse light. Here the light source is very large, and the
resulting shadows are less well defined. The quality of light might be described as soft.
The sun hidden behind a homogenous cloud cover produces very diffuse light.

## LIGHT-MODIFYING DEVICES

The ability to control light is often the photographer's most valuable asset. In an
attempt to control and modify light, a photographer employs many different techniques. One way is through various light-modifying devices, such as reflectors,
umbrellas, soft boxes, and fill cards.

If you're not familiar with the more common light modifiers, I suggest you browse through an assortment of professional equipment catalogs and manufacturer Web sites. These showcase a tremendous array of equipment and information related to lighting. Few photographers utilize all the equipment. Most develop a certain style or area within photography that's best served by certain equipment.

There are several categories of light modifying devices. Almost all can be used with professional electronic flash systems, but only to a limited extent with tungsten lighting. Tungsten lighting doesn't provide the same degree of flexibility, especially when it comes to attaching accessories to the light itself.

HMI lights also provide a continuous light source, like tungsten, but it's daylight balanced. Like tungsten lights, HMI lights get very hot. However, many have a cooling fan and timer. These provisions increase the variety of standard light modifiers available. Regardless of the light source, most basic assisting responsibilities are the same.

## Reflectors

The most basic light-modifying device is the *reflector*, a bowl-shaped accessory that comes in various sizes. With electronic flash systems, reflectors are designed to be interchangeable. They attach directly to the flash head, using some form of bayonet-style or latching device. The exact mechanism is specific to each manufacturer, necessitating that the reflector and flash head be from the same manufacturer.

Most tungsten lights are not designed to allow interchangeable reflectors. You instead purchase a light that provides the desired angle of coverage. This is a viable approach because tungsten lighting is much less expensive than an electronic flash system.

Reflectors are so fundamental that they're found in every studio. An unaltered reflector helps contain the light and redirects it in the form of a broad circle, usually fifty to one hundred degrees wide. When only a reflector is attached, the resulting light is very specular in nature.

Photographers are always altering the bare flash tube, a *point source,* in order to produce a more diffuse light. Therefore, reflectors are often used in association with some other light-modifying device. Reflectors are also placed on the flash head to protect the flash tube and modeling lamp. If flash-tube protectors are available, reflectors can be hung on a wall or stacked on a shelf.

## Umbrellas

*Umbrellas* produce a more diffuse light compared to a flash head with a reflector. Umbrellas are inexpensive, are very effective at lighting large areas, and vary in size, shape, and material. Most, though, are octagonal in shape, with a reflective white or silver interior surface. Some umbrellas are made with a translucent white material. The light, instead of being reflected, passes through the material, in a somewhat similar manner as with a soft box.

### Using an Umbrella

Regardless of the exact configuration, all umbrellas are attached to the light the same way. To use an umbrella, place a flash head with a medium-size reflector on a light stand. The flash head faces toward the inside of the umbrella, and the light is reflected or bounced back out, and in the process becomes more diffuse.

The umbrella is opened up like an umbrella used for rain. It's then attached directly to the flash head. A hole is provided on the flash head, just above the point where it connects to the stand. The umbrella's shaft is slid through the hole and secured in place using a thumb screw. It's important not to overtighten this screw, as the shaft is easily dented.

To find the point along the shaft at which to attach the umbrella to the flash head, locate the largest grouping of dents along the shaft. Or, turn on the flash head's modeling light and position the umbrella so that light fills the umbrella's dome, but little escapes beyond the its edges.

The modeling lamp can remain on while using an umbrella. However, excessive heat usually limits the umbrella's use with tungsten. When not needed, the umbrella is collapsed and stored in a protective sleeve to keep it clean, tear-free, and able to be hung up for storage.

## Diffusion Material/Colored Filters

*Diffusion material* is translucent white in color but varies widely in type of material. Most often, it's a flexible plastic sheet coming in long rolls about one yard wide. Diffusion material can also be nylon fabric or even something as simple as a bed sheet or tissue paper. The amount of diffusion material needed depends on the photographer's solution. *Colored filters* are made from a transparent, flexible plastic material. They come in a wide variety of colors and are generally used in smaller pieces. However, both materials are handled the same way.

### *Using These Materials*

Diffusion material and colored filters can be held in a filter frame or, more simply, taped directly over the reflector's opening. When attaching either material over the reflector, make sure it covers the entire reflector. It must yield an even effect across the entire angle of coverage. To ensure adequate ventilation, it shouldn't be a tight fit. When practical, leave gaps between the material and the reflector to assist in cooling.

Once the material is attached, it's important to monitor the flash head for excessive heat. These materials will melt. If the modeling lamp can be controlled with a rheostat, it's often best to keep the modeling lamp at a lower setting. Otherwise, you can turn off the lamp when it is not needed. Be especially concerned about heat when using a flash head without a cooling fan. When monitoring for heat, check the adhesive tape—it can fail at the worst time.

At times, a small reflector called a *snoot* is used. It has a very small opening, which emits a form of spot light. Due to its restrictive design, overheating is a real problem and almost guaranteed if diffusion material or a colored filter is taped over its small opening. Here, the modeling lamp should remain on only when the light is being positioned.

At the other end of the size spectrum, a large *light bank* can be quickly and inexpensively fabricated from diffusion material. You simply suspend a large piece of diffusion material from a cross bar supported by two heavy stands. Lights with

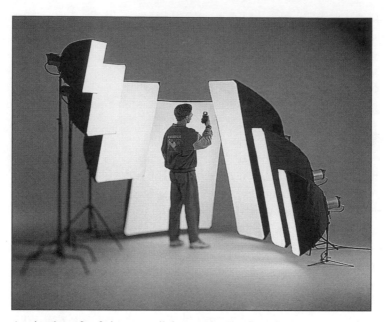

A selection of soft boxes on light stands. The flash heads are connected to power supplies. *Photo courtesy of Chimera Photographic Lighting.*

reflectors are then placed behind the material. This arrangement produces a fairly diffuse light.

Diffusion material and colored filters are also used with tungsten lights. But due to the heat, the material is placed well in front of the reflector, held in a metal filter frame or supported by a light stand. Because of this increased distance, larger pieces of material are required to ensure adequate coverage. Most diffusion material and filters are quite flexible. They are easily rolled up and then placed in a cardboard mailing tube for storing. Unlike lens filters, diffusion material can become quite ragged and yet still be functional.

## The Soft Box

The *soft box* is one of the most popular lighting tools, and it's found in one form or another on strobe, HMI, and on-camera flash units. It's designed to produce a very large and evenly distributed light source that's diffuse in nature. A soft box resembles a dome-shaped tent. The flash head is positioned at the soft box's apex and is direct-ed inside. The tent's interior walls are made from a reflective material, usually silver. The exterior walls are of black fabric. What would be the tent's floor is made from white diffusion material. Whereas an umbrella bounces light, you direct the light through the diffusion material when using a soft box.

A soft box can be square, rectangular, or circular in shape. The translucent, light-emitting area measures approximately one by two feet in a smaller box, and four by six feet in a larger one. A long, narrow soft box is often called a *strip bank*.

A soft box can be a permanently constructed unit, either professionally manufactured or built by the photographer from foamboard, diffusion material, and tape. However, the most common soft box is the collapsible unit. It's light weight, quickly assembled, very transportable, and fairly inexpensive.

### Assembling a Soft Box

A collapsible soft box consists of the fabric tent portion, four flexible *wands,* and a *mounting ring.* To assemble, work at the small opening where the flash head will be positioned. First, slide each wand into the sleeve found along the inside corner of the soft box. Then, the free end of each wand is inserted into one of the four holes in the mounting ring, often referred to as a *speed ring.*

When finished, the soft box is quite rigid. The mounting ring is now attached to the flash head by using the same type of mechanism used to attach a reflector. When possible, build the soft box first and then attach it to the flash head. It's always possible for a wand to slip while you're inserting it into the mounting ring. A mishap could easily break a modeling lamp or flash tube. Before you begin to break down a soft box, remove it from the flash head. Pull the four wands out of the mounting ring and leave the wands in the fabric sleeves. Now, wrap the fabric around the wands, positioning the white diffusion material in such a way that it remains clean. The soft box is stored in a long, narrow stuff sack. When space permits, soft boxes often remain assembled.

### Mounting Rings

Here are a few additional notes about mounting rings or speed rings. Some mounting rings rotate; others are stationary. *Rotating mounting rings* allow the box to rotate 360 degrees around the flash head, while *stationary mounting rings* hold a soft box in a fairly fixed position. It is important to understand that when using a stationary ring, a rectangular soft box must be assembled in either the horizontal or vertical orientation, as viewed after it's placed on the light stand or boom. You can't simply rotate the box if it's built horizontally instead of vertically. See the photo of flash heads with mounting rings in chapter 12.

Some bigger soft boxes accommodate more than one flash head. Hence, there are mounting rings that hold two or three flash heads. Although such large soft boxes are used in a manner quite similar to the smaller soft boxes, they do become rather heavy and very cumbersome. A sturdy light stand or boom is mandatory, possibly reinforced with a shot bag.

### Filters and Soft Boxes

Colored filters can be used with soft boxes. The filter is positioned fairly close to the flash tube and then taped to the flash head. The filter must be positioned far enough from the modeling lamp so heat can dissipate, yet close enough so that an even color is produced. A distance of five inches from the flash tube is about right.

## Fill Cards

Some of the simplest light-modifying devices are fill cards, which work by modifying and redirecting light. Although fill cards are usually fashioned from inexpensive cardboard, they prove invaluable, regardless of the light source or the type of photography. The assistant should expect to handle all shapes and sizes of fill cards.

Most fill cards are made from some form of mat board. An advantage to using mat board is that fill cards can be cut to the necessary size. Foamboard, such as the brand name Foam-Cor, is another material used to make fill cards. Foamboard is a rigid, lightweight product made of foam backed by white cardboard. Its properties make it ideal for large fill cards.

### Choosing the Correct Fill Card

The following basics will help you to work with fill cards more effectively. Generally, a larger card reflects more light. So to direct more light to a larger area, use a larger card. In an architectural application or a shot of a large product, a fill card might measure a full $4' \times 8'$. A small still life, however, may require a card measured in inches.

It takes a certain rapport to know exactly what a photographer wants when all you hear is, "Get me a fill card." By observing the evolution of the set and lighting arrangement, you should have an idea where the fill card is needed. If not, ask. Then look for a card the same general shape as, but somewhat larger than, the area you wish to fill with light.

For example, to add fill light on a long, narrow object, plan on using a long, narrow fill card, perhaps about 50 percent larger than the area to be lit. Keep in mind, this is a starting point. Because you can never be exactly sure what the photographer wants, return to the set with a couple of logical choices.

In addition to size and shape, color is important. White is the most common, as it accurately reflects the color of the light source. Other common colors include gold and silver. Shades of gold are used to add warmth to the reflected light, possibly to enhance the appearance of a certain food or a person's complexion.

A silver card produces a more brilliant and specular fill light, and mirrors even more so. A silver card can be used to place silver-colored highlights on silverware or chrome objects, compared to the white highlights produced by a white soft box or a white fill card. When fill cards are used with highly reflective surfaces, they need to be clean.

Most studios accumulate an assortment of fill cards. These are often stored vertically in boxes or on shelves. Larger ones are commonly found leaning up along the wall. New fill cards are cut from mat board using a straight edge and utility knife. A clean cut makes for easier positioning.

### Positioning the Fill Card

Every fill card must be precisely positioned. The photographer determines its placement, but it's often the assistant's responsibility to position it. Before returning to the set with a fill card, think about how you intend to finish the job and grab the required hardware.

The photographer will work with the card until it's positioned as desired. Then, you want to quickly slide in the appropriate support. Moderate-size cards and larger are usually connected to a light stand with one or two spring clamps. Smaller cards can be propped up against a small stand, block of wood, or a can of spray paint.

Remember, fill cards are usually positioned very precisely, and considerable ingenuity can be required to secure the card in place. When there's a lot of activity around the set, an extra clamp or masking tape is prudent. Use masking tape sparingly, especially when it's going to be attached to the card's good surface. Fill cards are meant to be reused.

Use discretion when securing a card in place. A card's position is often refined as the lighting arrangement evolves, so wait until you think the card isn't likely to be moved or replaced. An assistant needs to be efficient. One way is not to do more things than necessary.

## Light-Absorbing Devices

The opposite of a white fill card is a black card. Whereas a white surface reflects light, black absorbs light and acts like a light sponge. A photographer must often keep stray light from falling onto the set or the lens. Here, a black card or *flag* is positioned to block unwanted light.

When lens flair is a problem, you can see the light's reflection on the outside lens element. Clamp a black card to a lightweight stand. Now position the black card between the lens and the problem light, keeping it about six inches from the lens. Move the card until the light's reflection is gone. Then look through the camera to confirm the card isn't visible in the frame.

When flagging stray light to keep it from reaching the set, position the black card close to the light source. Black seamless paper is also a useful way to control unwanted light. Due to its size, it can be a practical solution when large areas are involved.

### Black Velvet

At times, areas in the camera frame need to go completely black. This can be accomplished by using black velvet, the ultimate light absorber. Black velvet can control light, but it can just as easily be considered a background material. This cloth reveals no surface at all, and creates the illusion of a black void.

Black velvet is most effective when it's free of wrinkles and lint. A perfectly flat surface can be made by stretching the material across a piece of plywood and securing it with pushpins. Lint can be removed using the sticky side of masking tape. To ensure a wrinkle-free material, black velvet is best stored hanging in loose folds or rolled up, not folded flat. If wrinkles persist, try a humidifier. Don't iron it.

## LIGHT METERS

Light meters aid in determining the proper exposure. To do so, there are two ways a light meter can measure brightness. The *reflective light meter* measures the light reflected off the subject. Here, the meter is pointed at the *subject* when measuring. A camera's built-in meter is of the reflective type.

An *incident light meter* measures the illumination falling on the meter itself. The meter receives the same light that falls on the subject. The meter's photocell is fitted with a translucent diffusion dome and then pointed toward the camera when measuring. Most hand-held meters take both reflective and incident readings.

Although meters are often thought of as being either the reflective or incident type, another type of meter measures a more or less constant light source. Often referred to as an *ambient light meter,* it can be used to measure natural light and artificial sources, such as tungsten. With this meter, you dial in the film speed, take either an incident or reflective measurement, and get a combination of shutter speed and f-stop for a proper exposure. Unfortunately, this kind of meter can't measure electronic flash.

## The Flash Meter

To measure the illumination produced from electronic flash equipment, you need a *flash meter.* Most flash meters can measure both flash and continuous light.

### Operating the Flash Meter

A hand–held flash meter is usually used as an incident meter. The meter's light sensor is covered with a diffusion dome, providing a fairly wide angle of view. When the photographer positions the flash meter, it's worth noting the meter's position, not only to learn—you may need to replicate it. When called on to take a meter reading, the assistant must place the meter as the photographer had it. If not, it's very difficult to compare results.

The incident flash meter is usually placed close to the subject's surface, with the diffuser pointed toward the camera lens. For example, when metering for a head-and-shoulders shot, position the meter close to the model's nose.

All flash meters need to be turned on, using either an on/off switch or by depressing the measuring button. Then you must dial in the film's ASA number and the camera's shutter speed. The only remaining variable is the lens aperture or f-stop, which is displayed after the metering process.

Unless the exposure integrates both flash and a constant light source, such as daylight, the exact shutter speed is not that important. It must not exceed the shutter's sync speed, yet it should be fast enough so ambient light isn't recorded on film. One-sixtieth of a second is a commonly used sync speed.

### The Cord and Non-Cord Modes

There are two ways to set the meter when measuring a flash. These are designated as the cord and non–cord modes. When switched to the *cord mode,* a sync cord connects the flash meter to the power supply. Depressing the meter's measuring button causes the power supply to discharge. Soon afterwards, the measurement is displayed in f-stops. The cord mode is also used when a radio transmitter is connected to the meter.

In the *non-cord mode,* the meter isn't connected to the power supply. You depress the measuring button, and the flash meter is made ready to measure the next flash. At this point, taking a meter reading usually becomes a two–person operation. The photographer positions the meter, and the assistant goes to the appropriate power supply.

The assistant goes to the master power supply when every flash head should fire. If only one of several flash heads is to be metered, unwanted heads and power supplies must be turned off. Remember, turning off the modeling light doesn't turn off the flash tube. At the photographer's signal, the assistant discharges the power supply, and the meter displays its measurement.

The non-cord mode has an advantage over the cord mode, especially when an assistant is on the set. The sync cord doesn't need to be removed from the camera in order to take a meter reading. Often, it's more efficient for the assistant to walk from pack to pack than to constantly rearrange sync cords during the metering process.

## The Assistant's Responsibilities

When it's likely you'll be using a flash meter throughout the day, try to *anticipate* when the photographer is about to take another reading. If you sense that a meter reading is imminent, keep close to the set. When the photographer grabs the meter, head to the appropriate power supply. Many times, the photographer will take several measurements, perhaps to determine the amount of light fall-off across the background. Observe the photographer's subtle cues that indicate it's time to pop the strobes again.

It's not uncommon to work with photographers who rarely use a flash meter while in the studio. They've become familiar with their specific lighting system and how it performs under more common lighting conditions. However, few have such confidence while on location. Therefore, you need to make certain the light meter is in the camera case.

## SUMMARY OF RESPONSIBILITIES RELATED TO LIGHT-MODIFYING DEVICES

❑ Obtain the light-modifying device specified by the photographer from the storage area.

❑ Select the appropriate hardware—such as mounting rings, stands, blocks, tape, and clamps—to position the device.

❑ Monitor heat generated by the modeling lamp or the tungsten or HMI lighting, especially when using small soft boxes, snoots, and reflectors covered with diffusion material or colored filters.

❑ Periodically, reconfirm that the adhesive tape is still securing filters and diffusion material.

❑ Follow the evolution of the set and the lighting arrangement to better understand the photographer's needs with regard to light-modifying devices.

❑ Expect to be involved with all aspects of lighting throughout the day.

❑ Be careful not to disrupt any light-modifying device.

❑ When light-modifying devices are not used, attach a flash tube protector to the flash head.

## SUMMARY OF RESPONSIBILITIES RELATED TO LIGHT METERS

❑ Confirm that the light meter is set properly. Check *ASA* and *shutter speed* settings.

❑ Determine whether the flash meter will be used in the cord or non-cord mode.

❑ When in the *cord mode,* attach the flash meter to the master power supply with a sync cord.

❑ When in the *non-cord mode,* plan to be positioned at the appropriate power supply during the metering process.

❑ *Anticipate* when the photographer is about to take a meter reading and react accordingly.

❑ Make certain only those lights to be metered will fire.

❑ *Observe* how the photographer positions the meter.

❑ When in *non-cord mode,* wait for the photographer's signal before discharging the power supply.

❑ When in *cord mode,* reattach sync cord to the camera after metering.

❑ Regardless of mode, remember the meter reading.

❑ Turn off the meter when finished.

## AN INTERVIEW WITH CHIP SIMONS

Chip Simons lives just south of Albuquerque, New Mexico. His editorial and advertising assignments have him regularly shooting on location and in his studio.

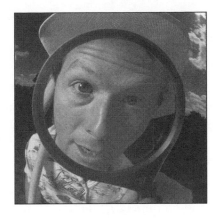

**John Kieffer:** Can you give me an idea as to the kind of photography you shoot most often?
**Chip Simons:** I guess you could say I'm more of a photo illustrator. I like my jobs to reflect my own personality, which might be best described as the original alternative to mainstream. I've pretty much shot some for every magazine there is. My work is such that whenever they feel it's time to punch up their magazine, they use me—like a spice.

**J.K.:** Much of your work that I've seen has lots of color, strong perspective, and very unusual lighting. What kind of lighting equipment do you use?
**C.S.:** As far as conventional equipment, I use Comet and Dyna-Lite strobes, along with Metz. But I also use whatever I can find, like at the auto parts store, sporting goods stores—really anything that makes light.

**J.K.:** What kind of cameras do you use?
**C.S.:** When I'm on the road, it's 99 percent Hasselblad. In the studio, it's about 50:50, between Hasselblad and Mamiya. I shoot 35mm about three jobs a year.

**J.K.:** Since you're located south of Albuquerque, how do you find assistants?
**C.S.:** My main assistant has recently left me to turn professional, so we've just run an ad in *PDN (Photo District News),* and we got about thirty-five responses. I had requested a photo, but afterwards I didn't think there were many that I could hang with. There's also the problem of getting them out here to see how I like working with them. If I take only one short road trip with them, I'll know if I can work with them.

**J.K.:** From the responses you received, did you find that most went to a photo school or did they learn on their own?
**C.S.:** I found that many had learned on their own, and they had done some small photography jobs here and there. But there are assistants at the other end. They've been assisting for perhaps five or six years, and their work is fine enough that they should be out there on their own. Perhaps it's insecurity that they're not.

**J.K.:** How did these assistants send their photography to you for review?
**C.S.** Most of it was e-mailed to me.

**J.K.:** What do you look for most in an assistant regarding his or her personal attributes?
**C.S.** I like someone with an energetic personality who's there to help me. An assistant should be like a headwaiter; they have to know when it's time to get busy and

what's the most efficient way to do things. I need to be sure that all the strobes are firing and not find out that one's not firing only after I get three rolls back from the lab. Or, if I'm in New York City, an assistant needs to have some cash and credit cards so that things can be done if there's an emergency. They'll be paid back, but you can't go to NYC without these things.

I also need someone who can think. I used an assistant recently who had worked for a well-known photographer. I showed him how some lighting was to be attached to the stand, and he could never get it right. After five major jobs in a row, he's still not getting it right. Finally, all I could say was, "What are you thinking?" At that point, it was easier for me to do his job, and he's actually in the way.

Going on the road is hard, and it's a good test for an assistant because everything is different, from the location to the car you drive, and you have to plan for that.

**J.K.:**     How do you handle stress when you find that an assistant has forgotten something or a piece of equipment fails?
**C.S.:**     I just try and be flexible and try something else. I try not to go on location and bring every piece of equipment with me.

**J.K.:**     What percentage of your photography is on location versus in your studio?
**C.S.:**     I probably shoot 75 percent on location and about a third of that is out of town.

**J.K.:**     Do you ever use women assistants?
**C.S.:**     I have, but they've all been too weak. When I go out on the road, I don't really want to carry all the stuff, and guys can carry more.

**J.K.:**     What do you pay an assistant?
**C.S.:**     I pay $175 a day, unless it's a major day, and it might go to $200.

**J.K.:**     Do you scan your film and manipulate your photos?
**C.S.:**     I started a couple of years ago. I got a magazine job about exercising in the winter; unfortunately it was July. It was pretty difficult to get good scans locally, so I bought a nice Imacon scanner and combined several photos I already had. We do scan film here and send it out, but not everyone has it together yet. When I send files out to a magazine, I tell them to have their digital person go over it, especially for color.

**J.K.:**     Do you shoot with a digital camera?
**C.S.:**     I've shot with a consumer-orientated digital camera, and the files might work for a full-page photo in *People* magazine. It doesn't look any worse than what they've done to the rest of my stuff.

**J.K.:**     Have you considered a digital back for your Hasselblad?
**C.S.:**     So far, I haven't liked what I've seen. They can't deal with the highlights, and they add noise. Plus, you spend so much time correcting the files. You also don't get the full frame when you attach a digital back to a Hasselblad. Therefore, your wide-angle lenses become doubled in focal length. When you think about it, a piece of medium-format film is still very cheap and the best scanner in the world isn't going to get all the information out of it. Under many conditions, it doesn't really matter, like with weekly magazines that just get cranked out. Sometimes I think that you might just as well throw your film to the wind.

# 14

# Photographic Hardware

UCH OF THE TIME, A SET IS BUILT, OR THE SHOOTING ENVIRONMENT IS modified, for a specific shot or series of shots. The speed in which something must be constructed and its inherent lack of permanence profoundly affects how tasks are accomplished. Many tasks are painstakingly done to perfection, only to be undone shortly afterwards. Not having the luxury of time, you're more likely to build something utilizing stands and clamps, than from wood, nails, and glue. The proper and often ingenious use of photographic hardware is an integral part of assisting.

## STANDS

The most fundamental piece of photographic hardware is the stand. Stands come in various shapes and sizes, in order to serve many functions. You'd expect to use a stand to support a flash head, but stands are used to hold almost anything. You'll find that stands quickly become an integral part of virtually every set.

### Selecting the Proper Stand

When the photographer asks you to get a stand, your choice depends on its intended use. How heavy is the object that needs to be supported? Stands range from small and light to big and heavy. Lightweight stands are easy to handle, but are restricted to lighter tasks. They tend to be more compact, which is an advantage in confined working conditions. The medium-weight light stand is considered the most typical. As the name suggests, it's ideal for supporting a flash head, but it's also used for countless other tasks. As objects get larger and tasks more demanding, still heavier stands are available.

After establishing the size and weight of whatever is to be supported, you should know where it needs to be positioned. First, how high or low does the stand need to go? A *back-light stand* is designed to provide support at ground level. Whereas a medium-weight stand might not go any lower than three feet, it may extend to eight feet or more. When something such as a soft box needs to be positioned well over the set, a boom supported on a sturdy stand is required.

Realize that sets quickly become crowded and access restricted. When trying to sneak in a small fill card, even the smallest stand may be too large. Be creative. Look for a can of spray paint or block of wood from the workshop. Photographers always have an odd assortment of such things.

Finally, your choice might depend on what's left. As the set comes together, more and more stands tend to be used. Most photographers don't have an endless supply of stands, so use discretion by not taking the last medium-weight stand for a simple fill card. Once something is in place, it can be difficult to make exchanges. This strategy is particularly important on location. You can't always bring everything from the studio, though many photographers try.

## The Proper Use of Stands

Stands extend in height through some form of telescoping action. After a section is extended, it's secured by tightening a *locking knob.* Most photographers don't like you to overtighten these knobs, and they'll let you know about it if you do. The assistant is thus in a difficult position. You certainly don't want a stand to slip, but you don't want to overtighten the knob, either. Most locking knobs hold quite effectively. However, be leery of older stands, especially small ones. These often require more force to tighten securely.

When not needed, a stand can be collapsed and hung for storage. When hanging a stand from a hook, do so by utilizing the bottom-most locking knob. The other knobs can thus be loose without causing a mishap. Most stands have several telescoping sections and an equal number of locking knobs. Stands suspended using the top locking knob can fall if any of the lower knobs become loose.

Stands require few accessories. However, the stand's *end post* or *stud* where the light attaches can be of several different diameters. Both the ⅜-inch and the larger

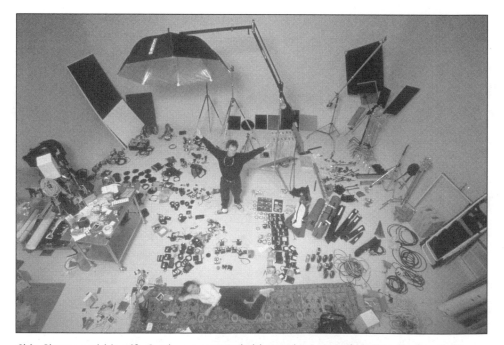

Chip Simons and his wife Cyndy are surrounded by equipment at their New Mexico studio. Seen are reflectors, a large umbrella, stands, and booms. One of the assistant's responsibilities is making sure everything needed makes it to the shoot and back. © 2000 Chip Simons.

⅜-inch end posts are common. When a stand's end post measures ⅜ inches and a flash head has a ⅝-inch diameter opening, an adapter is required. Establishing the need for various adapters is particularly critical before heading out on location.

### Additional Support

Sometimes, a stand might benefit from some added support. Compact stands are often utilized on cramped sets. Here, even a slight bump can dramatically reposition whatever the stand is holding. After a small stand is put in place, secure it. Use *gaffers tape* to attach a couple of the stand's legs to the floor.

When more clout is needed, as with larger stands, use a *shot bag*. These nylon bags are filled with either lead shot or sand and weigh from five to twenty-five pounds. When practical, position the shot bag well down on the stand's center post to lower the center of gravity. If you can't, the bag's malleable nature allows it to be draped over the stand's leg.

A pair of stands is often used to support a crossbar that holds various background materials. Under these circumstances, the stands are extended quite high, and additional support is prudent.

## BOOMS

When something needs to be suspended over the set, a *boom* is used. A boom is a metal pole that attaches to the top of a stand. The connection allows for a sort of teeter-totter action, providing easier positioning. A flash head is commonly connected to one end of the boom. At the opposite end is a counterweight to keep the flash head in position.

### Working with Booms

You need to be very careful when working with a boom. When you either attach or remove the counterweight or the flash head, you can't work with one without considering the other. The connection used to attach the boom to the stand controls the pivoting motion. Loosening a lever allows the boom to swing freely. Tightening it locks the boom at the desired angle.

Before attaching the flash head, position the boom horizontally and lock it in place. Now secure the counterweight to the boom, so the weight is very close to the stand's center post. Counterweights are very heavy, and attaching fifteen pounds to the end of an eight-foot boom produces tremendous leverage. If the counterweight is moved to one end of the boom before the flash head is attached to the other, the unbalanced stand will most likely fall over.

Next, insert the flash head onto the end of the boom and secure it by tightening the light's locking knob. Once the flash head is attached, don't let go of the boom until it's evenly balanced. To balance the boom, slowly move the counterweight toward the opposite end of the boom.

To fine-tune the weight's position, loosen the lever used to lock the boom in place. Slowly move the counterweight until the free swinging boom rests horizontally and then retighten the lever.

A properly balanced boom is much easier to handle. Finally, a counterweight also serves as an excellent substitute for a shot bag. They readily attach to the base of a stand's center post and certainly weigh enough.

### Extension Arms

Smaller versions of booms are known as *extension arms*. Some have joints or elbows for even greater functionality and are referred to as *articulated arms*. Both are used for smaller objects, perhaps to support a prop or fill card or to help position a model's hand.

Smaller booms and articulated arms are usually extended somewhat horizontally when in use. They're secured in position with locking knobs. As gravity pulls the arm downward, the locking joints can have a tendency to either tighten up, or loosen up. Be sure to place the arm in a self-tightening position.

### Safety Precautions

The boom necessitates a lead counterweight suspended on the end of a long metal pole. In addition, it's black, held at eye level, and is in a dark environment. So a few precautions are in order. First, try to position the stand and boom so they are out of the main traffic pattern. Usually, one side of the set has less activity. When a boom must be in the middle, try to make the counterweight more visible. Taping a white paper towel to it should suffice. It's expected that the photographer and assistant will be careful while working on a dark set, but don't assume the client has such awareness.

## CLAMPS

Clamps serve so many functions that it's impossible to construct a set or lighting arrangement without using them. They range from small, clothespin-sized clamps to powerful devices requiring both hands to open. Some are general purpose, whereas others serve specific functions. There are far too many different styles to mention them all.

Some of the most useful general-purpose clamps are commonly referred to as *A-clamps, spring clamps,* or *pony clamps*. When closed, these spring-loaded clamps form the shape of an A. They're routinely used to secure fill cards to stands and background materials to either a cross bar or a sheet of plywood. Other clamps might be fitted with an adapter on its end, in order to support a light or attach an articulated arm.

### Using Clamps

Generally, larger clamps can hold larger and heavier objects. Many clamps exert considerable pressure, so make certain they won't damage anything important when put to use. Most clamps have rubber-protected ends to reduce this problem. If not, a piece of cardboard can be placed between the clamp and surface. When you intend to put up a background or the photographer requests a fill card, make it a habit to grab a couple of the appropriate clamps on your way back to the set. If you find yourself working on a ladder or requiring the use of both hands, clamps can be attached to your clothes until needed.

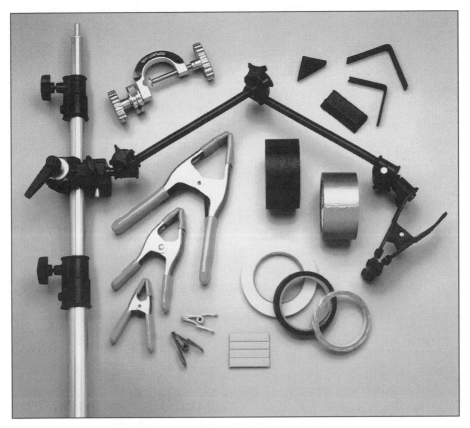

Photographic hardware, including a light stand, articulated arm, tape, temporary adhesive, clamps, and items to position objects on the set.

## ADHESIVES

Adhesives are indispensable, especially adhesive tapes. They're fast and easy, and there are many different kinds. The choice depends on the application. The most common is *masking tape*. It holds just well enough and can usually be removed without disrupting the surface. It is inexpensive, and you can also write notes on it.

*Photographic tape* is very similar to masking tape, except that it's opaque black. Its flat-black surface is ideal when the tape must appear black on film. It's also the tape of choice for many portfolio materials. However, photographic tape is fairly expensive, and it should be used when specifically required. Similar to photographic tape is white artists tape, which is ideal for labeling sheet-film holders.

*Gaffers tape,* not to be confused with photographic tape, is a two-inch-wide, cloth tape, usually black. It's very strong, yet it can be removed from most surfaces without leaving any sticky residue. Because it's a fairly expensive, use only when necessary.

A lesser-quality, but still very useful, tape is gray *duct tape.* Because it's inexpensive, it can be used in large quantities. Unfortunately, it does leave some gummy adhesive after it's removed. Even with this drawback, duct tape is ideal for quick fixes or taping extension cords to the floor in congested locations.

*Double-stick tape* is of value, especially for studio product photography. It resembles cellophane tape, but has adhesive on both sides. It's particularly useful in positioning lightweight objects. Also of value in such situations is a temporary adhesive that's clay-like or waxy; it is commonly referred to as *fun-tack* or *tacky-wax*.

An excellent adhesive that's gained wide acceptance is the *hot glue gun*. A plastic adhesive resembling a candle is placed in the glue gun. The gun heats the "candle" until it melts. You then use the gun to apply the melted plastic to the appropriate surface. As the plastic hardens, it acts like glue. The keys are to let the glue gun become very hot and not to touch the melted plastic until it has cooled, usually after a couple of minutes. It's smart to have a glass of water nearby for when you inevitably get some hot glue on your hand.

Assistants often find themselves in situations requiring three hands. If you know you'll need tape, tear it off beforehand and stick it to a nearby light stand or your pant leg. Most rolls of tape can be fitted over your wrist.

## MISCELLANEOUS HARDWARE

The following items are most likely to be used by studio photographers. These are nonphotographic items, but invaluable none the less.

A sheet of plywood commonly forms the platform, onto which many background materials are placed. The plywood shooting table is often supported by sawhorses or milk crates.

Very often, the product, a prop, or a fill card needs to be tilted at a specific angle. At the studio, you can expect to find an odd assortment of items that can help, like wood blocks in an array of sizes and shapes or a few tape-covered bricks.

## SUMMARY OF RESPONSIBILITIES RELATED TO PHOTOGRAPHIC HARDWARE

❑ Select the *appropriate stand* for the task. Consider the how much the object to be supported weighs and where it must be positioned.

❑ To minimize trips to and from the set, *establish exactly what's needed* to complete the job. Consider stands, booms, clamps, tape, and ingenuity.

❑ Remember easy-to-overlook photographic hardware required for location shoots. *Adapters* to connect flash heads to stands are especially critical.

❑ If conditions warrant, utilize *tape* or *shot bags* to add support to stands.

❑ Alert clients to the boom's *counterweight* by attaching a white paper towel.

❑ Consider photographic hardware when trying to *anticipate the photographer's needs*.

# 15

# Surface Preparation

ASSISTANTS ARE ACTIVELY INVOLVED WITH THE PREPARATION OF A WIDE RANGE of surfaces found on the subject, props, and background. They might need to be cleaned or altered to reproduce most favorably on film. Whatever the surface, you should evaluate several factors to do the job right. Remember, an assistant must balance many responsibilities. Consequently, it's imperative to work at being efficient without cutting corners.

## PRIMARY CONSIDERATIONS

Today, just about everything that is photographed on film will ultimately be scanned or converted to a digital format. In some ways, this lowers the pressure to be perfect because there's always the option to clean it up in Photoshop. Even so, I wouldn't suggest relying on this approach. Working with Photoshop adds both time and money to the shoot.

Before you begin to prepare a surface, you should determine the *level of perfection required*. This depends on a couple of aspects, one being camera format. Generally, as film size increases, the tolerance level decreases. Also, how close to the subject are you working? The closer the camera, the more apparent any imperfections.

It's also useful to know the final *size of the reproduction*. As a piece of film is enlarged, so are imperfections.

These factors help explain why product photography requires such meticulous surface preparation. Large-format view cameras are used to photograph relatively small objects.

In addition, the assistant needs to know what will be *in frame* and the approximate *camera angle*. Ask the photographer or review the layout. When photographing a box-shaped object, only three of six sides can ever show. You've already cut your work in half. Once you've established which surfaces are to be prepared, proceed with caution. This holds true for both easily replaced items and a one-of-a-kind prototype. Your efforts must not adversely alter the object's surface.

Whether working in the studio or on location, the entire set must be clean. While on location, you must tread lightly, as you're more than likely an intruder. When at someone's workplace or on private property, ask permission before moving objects. Being considerate from the beginning ultimately makes your job easier.

## CLEANING

The most common way to prepare a surface is to clean it. To be safe, keep these points in mind. Select a part of the surface well out of frame, a *test area*. Begin any cleaning process by using the least strong means, whether it's a solvent or an abrasive. Carefully change to a stronger approach as needed. Clean an area that extends beyond the edges of the frame. Finally, monitor the area during the exposure process.

### Preliminary Stages

When practical, do most of the cleaning off the set. You want to ensure that any mishap doesn't damage a prop or the background. If the object must be kept on the set, consider placing a drop cloth or a soon-to-be-discarded fill card around the object's base. One misplaced drop of fluid can ruin some materials.

Some solvents have noxious fumes, so working well away from the set makes the shooting area a healthier environment. With strong solvents, try to work in a ventilated area and use gloves. Unfortunately, ventilation can be hard to come by. Studios are often built with a certain degree of security, which translates to a lack of windows. To reduce fumes, use small amounts of fluids and recap the container immediately. Also, place saturated rags in a plastic bag. You might consider using the darkroom; it has a sink, an exhaust fan, and a door to contain fumes.

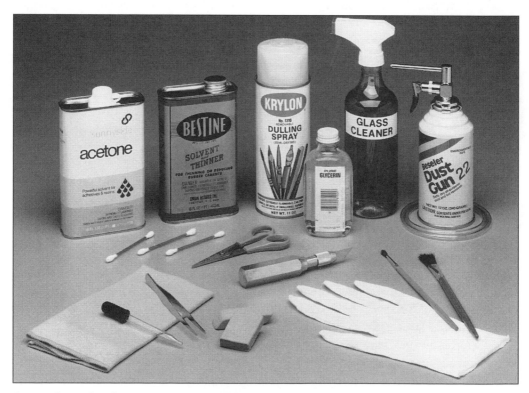

Commonly used surface-preparation materials.

You don't want to clean more than necessary. However, you must clean an area larger than what's expected to be in frame. It's not uncommon for the initial crop to expand, so give yourself a *buffer zone*. In addition, when photographing a relatively small area, a clean buffer lessens the chance of dust resetting onto the subject area.

Obviously, you don't want to disrupt something on the set. Be particularly leery of electronic equipment, like computer keyboards. It's a good idea to clean keyboards thoroughly very early on. Often, a specific display is needed for the monitor. Unfortunately, touching any key with reasonable pressure can change the display. Most likely, there will be someone on the set operating the software. When that person leaves the studio, stay away from the keyboard. As a side note, don't unplug the computer for any reason without permission. The display and who knows what will be lost.

## Liquid Cleaners

Before using any liquid cleaner, examine the surface. Liquids can dramatically alter some surfaces and should be applied cautiously to porous materials, such as wood, fabric, and paper. As a precaution, start by using the cleaner of least strength and in a test area well out of frame.

Generally, the safest liquid cleaner is water, closely followed by glass cleaner, then the brand-name household products, such as Fantastik or Formula 409. All of these are likely to be kept in a spray bottle. Near the cleaning products, you can expect to find paper towels or lint-free cotton cloths. For cleaning smaller surfaces, cotton swabs are ideal.

When water, glass cleaner, and the common household products don't do the job, it's time for another change. For persistent marks, try rubbing alcohol. If not successful, switch to the stronger solvent *Bestine,* a rubber cement solvent. Both rubbing alcohol and Bestine are fairly odorless, and readily evaporate.

Next in strength comes *acetone,* or nail-polish remover. Acetone is a powerful solvent and evaporates even more quickly than rubbing alcohol and Bestine, but it has extremely strong fumes. If using acetone and its stronger relative *phenol,* be very careful when applying them to untested surfaces. Both solvents can readily dissolve some plastics. Again, use small quantities and in well-ventilated areas.

### *Review Your Work*

In addition to removing dirt, you need to produce a surface free of any streaks. As simple as this sounds, it can take considerable expertise. High-gloss surfaces are particularly prone to streaks. Once the high-gloss surface is clean, get a paper towel or cotton cloth. Apply a small amount of cleaner to the towel and then gently buff the surface. Carefully review your efforts from several angles, particularly the *camera angle.* Make sure the surface is free of streaks, lint, and scratches. If you find scratches or imperfections that you can't remove, tell the photographer. You might be shown an ingenious solution. Regardless, the sooner you can deal with a cleaning problem, the better.

## COMMONLY ENCOUNTERED SURFACES

Your surface-preparation skills will be put to the test on a wide range of materials. The most common surface types are plastic laminates, seamless paper, assorted metals, vinyl, and fabrics.

### Plastic Laminates

Some of the most popular surfaces are the plastic laminates, such as Formica-brand materials. Often thought of as something for counter tops, these laminates come in hundreds of colors, patterns, and textures. The 4′ × 8′ sheets are an ideally sized background material for small-product photography.

Plastic laminates are readily cleaned with glass cleaner and a paper towel. Waxy or gummy residue can be safely removed with rubbing alcohol or Bestine. When cleaning, examine the surface for scratches. While working with it and storing it, be particularly careful not to scratch it.

### Seamless Background Paper

Seamless background paper is a heavyweight paper that comes in long rolls, usually measuring nine feet wide. Although sturdy, the surface to be photographed must be handled with extreme care. Once marks and imperfections occur, they are difficult, if not impossible, to remove.

It's best to remove dust from seamless paper using canned air. Attempts to wipe the dust off will cause the paper to smear. When canned air is ineffective, try using a small paintbrush while blowing gently. Next, try a gum eraser, using very gentle strokes. Because of its delicate nature, seamless paper is often discarded after one or two uses. It's a good idea to save some of it, as it makes a good drop cloth.

When an object must be cleaned while resting on seamless paper, be careful, especially if the cleanup involves liquids. Place something along the object's base to catch any drops, as they will inevitably discolor the paper's surface.

Seamless paper has the advantage of being able to cover large areas, large enough that you may need to walk on its surface while working on the set. If this surface will be in the shot, remove your shoes. In addition, clean fill cards can be placed over the paper as a protective layer. When photographing a model's entire figure, it's helpful to place masking tape on the bottom of the shoes to keep the paper clean longer. The storage and handling of both Formica and seamless paper will be discussed in the next chapter.

### Metallic Surfaces

The assistant also works with a variety of metallic surfaces, such as chrome, aluminum, and stainless steel. There are specific metal polishes on the market, but these tend to leave a filmy residue that often predisposes the surface to streaks and smudges. Try rubbing alcohol or Bestine to remove these oils. Then buff the surface with a very absorbent, lint-free cloth.

After cleaning, handle metal objects while wearing white, *cotton gloves.* If a metallic surface is too shiny or reflective, it can be further treated with *dulling spray,* which imparts a somewhat matte finish.

## Rubber and Vinyl Surfaces

Rubber and vinyl surfaces can be treated with specific conditioners, such as Armor-All. Although effective, the conditioners often leave a shiny or glossy sheen to the surface. Mild soap and water is an effective combination, and produces a less reflective matte finish. The choice is the photographer's. As you'll see shortly, several aerosol sprays can be used to place a highlight on black surfaces.

## Fabric and Carpet

Because cleaning fabric often involves removing any loose threads, a small pair of scissors is a necessary tool. Lint can be removed with a special lint brush, the sticky side of tape, or even tweezers.

A small *fabric steamer* is often used to eliminate wrinkles. Steamers should be held fairly vertically while in use to keep drops of water from hitting the fabric. The smaller units take a while to produce steam. So during busy days keep the unit plugged in and filled with water and ready to go. This helps eliminate inconvenient down time.

One commonplace fabric is *carpet*. To clean it, an obvious choice is a vacuum cleaner. Unfortunately, you may not always have access to one. If you don't, you might have to resort to using the sticky surface of masking tape. You can create a photogenic surface by raking the carpet with a stiff piece of cardboard. The raking action readily removes irregularities, such as footprints, and yields a smooth surface. During the process of rearranging furniture, little divots can be left in the carpet. These are made less pronounced by raking them with a plastic fork.

## The Other Extreme

Yes, you may actually be called on to dirty an object. As with cleaning, proceed with caution. It's better to slowly build a layer than to overdo it and have to remove some. Here are a few substances to keep in mind. Generic dirt can be made by rubbing pencil shavings onto clothing. Also, the fine dirt that collects in parking lots is very effective. A heavier grime can be found on any car engine, but first give a grease pencil a try. The pencils come in various colors.

## MONITORING THE EXPOSURE PROCESS

Even during the short time it takes to expose the film, it's critical to monitor the set for dust. At this late stage, canned-air is very effective, but it mustn't disrupt anything. For situations requiring a more controlled blast of air, check the set cart for a piece of flexible tubing for the nozzle. Once attached, this tubing allows for exact placement of the air. When extra caution is in order, try using a small artist's paintbrush or tweezers.

The worst time to bump something is partway through the process of exposing film. Working on the set at this time takes real concentration, coupled with an awareness of where you are relative to everything involved. You must avoid lights, fill cards, stands, and props as you weave in and out.

## PAINTING

Most studios have a few shelves in the workshop dedicated to paint. Over time, an assistant will apply paint to a whole range of surfaces. But regardless of the type of paint, how it's applied, and the kind of surface, perfection is the overriding word. This means no streaks and no irregularities. Applying paint requires skill and patience.

### General Guidelines

When practical, work in an out-of-the-way place to reduce the chance of dust falling on the wet surface and minimize fumes on the set. Next, prepare the surface so it's clean and dry. Paint can be applied several ways; however, once you begin, there's no turning back.

Usually, it's best to start at one end of the surface and work your way to the other. This lets you paint along a *wet edge,* thereby producing a more homogenous surface. Painting from top to bottom is also preferred, so that any drops of paint fall on the unpainted surface. Once paint begins to dry, don't touch it with anything, including the paintbrush. You'll invariably leave marks.

Many times, an object is painted away from the set and must be returned to the set before it's dry. Here is where some preplanning pays dividends. Determine how you'll get the item back to the set without disturbing the nearly dry surface. This is one reason to paint an area only slightly larger than required.

You can quicken the drying process by placing a tungsten light about four feet from the surface. Monitor it and occasionally change the light's position to ensure uniform drying. Don't get impatient, as placing the light to close can generate excessive heat and ruin the surface. You can also use fans and hair dryers, but the paint should be nearly dry first so dust doesn't stick to the surface.

### Kinds of Paint

You're likely to work with two basic kinds of paints: latex paints, such as those covering most household walls, and aerosol spray paints. Both have their unique characteristics. These traits strongly influence how each is handled and to what surfaces paint is to be applied applied.

### *Latex Paint*

Latex paint must be stirred before use and is applied with either a brush or roller. Before prying the lid off the can, find a cardboard box, one large enough to hold both the paint can and brush. The box will catch most drips and makes the painting process more portable. When applying paint with a brush, use back and forth strokes. Keep the brush strokes on top of, and parallel to, one another. If it's a wood surface, paint parallel to the grain.

Rollers are an advantage when large surfaces must be painted. Because rollers tend to drip paint, some sort of drop cloth is mandatory. When using a roller on rough or porous surfaces, take extra care to ensure the paint is covering completely. Try working in small sections, moving the roller in various directions, as if drawing a star. Then, immediately finish with long parallel strokes to create a smooth surface.

Latex paint is cleaned from rollers and brushes with warm, soapy water. If you need to keep a wet brush or roller on standby, wrap it in aluminum foil and then place it in a plastic bag. This will keep a brush serviceable for several days.

### Aerosol Spray Paint

Aerosol spray paints tend to be quicker to use and faster drying than latex paints. *Be careful when selecting a work area.* Due to the aerosol nature of spray paints, there can be some drift. Prepare the surface as you would for any paint. Prior to spraying, shake the can vigorously for about one minute. Then direct the nozzle away from the surface and begin to spray. If there's any inconsistency in the spray paint, it's usually at the beginning.

When the paint is flowing well, direct the spray onto the desired surface. Hold the can *vertically,* about eight to ten inches from the surface. It's best to apply spray paint using a broad, sweeping motion. Don't apply too much at any one time. If the paint begins to run, you've applied too much and lost your chance for a perfect surface. Thin layers dry quickly, so be patient. Spray paints usually need to be reshaken during the application process. When finished, hold the can upside down and spray a moment to purge the nozzle with clean air, so it won't become clogged.

## MISCELLANEOUS AEROSOL SPRAYS

There are a variety of aerosol products used to alter surfaces. Although they aren't spray paints, they're applied in much the same manner. A common product is *dulling spray* or *matte spray,* which is sprayed on highly reflective surfaces, such as aluminum, chrome, or glass. It reduces glare by producing a matte-like sheen. Here, an even surface is essential. Therefore, apply very light layers and slowly build the level of dulling spray. If you apply too much, it has to be completely removed, and the process must be started over.

At times, only part of the surface needs to be treated—perhaps the chrome label found on a product. Here, you need to cut a *mask.* To do so, get a large sheet of paper and cut a piece from its center, the size and shape of the chrome label. Placing the mask over the label protects those surfaces not requiring dulling spray. When surfaces permit, attach masking tape along the edges of the object to be sprayed. The tape provides some leeway when cutting the mask and makes for a better application.

*Spray adhesives* are used on a variety of photographic materials. On the set, spray adhesives are helpful in attaching backing material to flimsy items for added rigidity. They are handled like other aerosols. However, once applied, the surface becomes a magnet for dust and fingerprints.

There are aerosol sprays, including some antiperspirants, which produce a fine, white powder. These products can be used to place a highlight on black surfaces. Even talcum powder can be applied with a brush. More exotic aerosols include artificial snow and green foliage.

## SUMMARY OF RESPONSIBILITIES RELATED TO SURFACE PREPARATION

❏ Discuss with the photographer *which surfaces* need to be prepared and how. Surfaces may be cleaned, painted or otherwise treated.

❏ Establish the *level of perfection* required. Consider camera format, image size, and final size of reproduction.

❏ Try to accomplish most surface preparation *away from the set,* especially when noxious fumes are present or there's the potential to disrupt other surfaces.

❏ When using a solvent, abrasive, or paint, begin with a *test area* and start with the *safest* method.

❏ Prepare an area larger than required, to provide a buffer zone.

❏ While preparing surfaces, look for any *imperfections* that may be potential problems. Notify the photographer.

❏ Critically review your efforts, especially from *camera angle.*

❏ Recheck all surfaces immediately before *exposing film* and during the film-exposure process.

❏ If you must work on the set between exposures, be extremely careful not to disrupt anything.

# 16

# Background Materials

A<sup></sup>S YOU SHOULD HAVE SENSED BY NOW, THE WORD BACKGROUND IS REALLY A misnomer. The background can be as important as anything else. Its cleaning was discussed in the last chapter, "Surface Preparation." But the background must also be properly positioned and treated carefully throughout the shot. Afterwards, it must be removed from the shooting area and stored.

Generally, the photographer, art director, or client selects the background or *backdrop,* the choice being dictated by the parameters of the shot. After that, it's usually the assistant's responsibility to position it appropriately. Before rushing in, think. Here are some important considerations and basic handling procedures regarding the more common background materials.

## GENERAL GUIDELINES

At the studio, a likely start to the day's activities is to set up the background. Often, the pace is such that questions seem out of place. When the background material requires the efforts of two people, just follow the photographer's lead. If you're on your own, a basic understanding of the shot is essential. Review the *layout* for the day's shot or ask the photographer. It's impossible to make proper decisions without some information.

### Understanding Your Objective

The photographer may ask you to set up a 4′ × 8′ sheet of black Plexiglas. Before you can begin, you must have a basic understanding of what needs to be accomplished. For example, if you're photographing a product, how big is it? Does it require the use of the entire surface or should you find one small section that's perfectly free of scratches?

When viewing the layout, determine whether the background needs to be positioned horizontally or vertically. Don't forget the camera angle. This determines the height the background must be supported off the floor in order to place the camera at a comfortable working position.

Just as likely, you may be asked to suspend a piece of painted canvas for a portrait. Again, some basic information is a must. There's a difference in background requirements when photographing a person's entire figure, as compared to a head-and-shoulders shot. Once a background is in place, the set evolves on it and around it. Mistakes with the background can place limitations on the rest of the shot.

## Preparation
After gaining some sense of your objective, preparation is in order. First, clear away the main shooting area. Next, make certain the required tools are immediately available, because many commonly used materials are heavy or very awkward. When mishandled, they can be ruined or damage other equipment.

If you get in over your head when working with a background material, don't hesitate to call for help. This slight embarrassment is nothing compared to falling off a ladder or dropping a delicate background. Remember, handling full sheets of plywood and Plexiglas is difficult for everyone.

## PLASTIC LAMINATES
Plastic laminates such as Formica-brand materials are some of the most common background materials. Review the chapter on surface preparation for additional information regarding the care and handling of many materials. Briefly, plastic laminates are easily cleaned using a paper towel and window cleaner, taking special care to insure no streaks remain. Also, it's easily scratched, so handle carefully.

### Handling Plastic Laminates
Plastic laminates are most often available in 4′ × 8′ sheets. Even though a full-size sheet isn't all that heavy, don't be deceived. Plastic laminates and related materials like Plexiglas are very unwieldy, and their sharp corners can easily tear a soft box. Before removing it from storage, determine how and where it's to be used.

A plastic laminate is usually placed on top of a plywood table for added rigidity and clamped in place. The plywood rests on saw horses or crates, whichever provides the desired working height. Make sure these supports are correctly positioned and several A-clamps are at hand.

Slide the material out from storage, keeping other objects from touching its good surface. After placing it on the plywood, clamp the edges to the plywood. Clamps help flatten the surface and the plywood adds considerable stability.

### *A Common Application*
Formica-like materials are often lifted or swept upward at the back to form a concave surface often referred to as a *sweep*. If this is your intent, first secure the front edge of the Formica to the plywood surface using several strong A-clamps, the front edge being the one closest to the camera.

Next, you need to elevate the opposite end to a height of several feet so that a concave surface is formed. Do so by clamping the end to a crossbar supported by two heavy stands. Medium-weight stands should be stabilized with shot bags. There's considerable stored energy in Formica, much like a compressed spring. If a clamp slips or a stand moves, watch out.

## Storing Plastic Laminates

Full-size sheets of plastic laminate are stored one of two ways. One way is to roll it up widthwise, and secure it with a rope. Photographers store it this way when studio space permits. This procedure does reduce scratching, but may affect the flatness of the surface. A more common method is to store it unrolled. The flat sheets are placed one next to the other like a deck of cards. This stack is then positioned upright, as if in a bookcase. Plexiglas, foam board, large fill cards, even plywood, might be found interspersed between laminate sheets. The trick is getting the material in and out of this stack safely, while not damaging its surface. Here, discarded seamless paper, taped over the surface, alleviates the problem.

## SEAMLESS PAPER

Seamless paper is as common a background material as the plastic laminates. It's available in a variety of colors with white, black, and shades of gray serving the widest range of uses. A roll measuring nine feet wide by twelve yards long is standard. The paper is wound onto a cardboard core, similar to a roll of paper towels. To use, a crossbar is slid through the core and is supported horizontally between two stands. In some studios, a crossbar is suspended from the ceiling by an arrangement of ropes and pulleys.

## Hanging Seamless Paper

When hanging seamless paper, you must handle it with extreme care at all times. It's particularly vulnerable to creases and dirt, and once damaged it's rarely salvageable. When you retrieve a roll of seamless paper from storage, it's likely to be taped shut to prevent it from unraveling. Leave it that way. On your way back to the set, grab a couple of A-clamps and a roll of masking tape. To keep your hands free, clamps can be attached to your pant leg or a stand. The roll of masking tape can be worn as a bracelet. Better yet, small pieces can be taped to your clothing or a stand, ready for immediate use.

After laying the seamless paper on the floor, thread the crossbar through the paper's core. Now position the two medium-weight stands, so the crossbar can be readily attached. There's a hole at each end of the crossbar; insert the holes over the top of each stand.

Once the crossbar is attached, alternately raise the stands to a height several feet above the top of the subject. Before untaping the seamless paper, check to see that the *crossbar is level*. This ensures that the seamless paper unravels properly and doesn't develop creases.

Carefully remove the tape securing the paper. Then position yourself near one end of the roll, and slowly unravel the paper. Being close to one end lets you clamp the roll of paper to the crossbar, so it can't unravel further than desired.

## Applications

When the seamless paper is used for a head-and-shoulders shot, the free end needn't reach the floor. Instead, place a few small A-clamps on the paper's free end to minimize any movement and produce an even surface.

At other times, the paper is suspended vertically, then swept out onto a ply-wood table or the floor. The idea is to produce a smooth sloping surface or sweep. To do so, the paper must lie evenly from side to side. Once positioned, tape down the edges of the paper or use some weights. The more traffic around the set, the greater the need for tape. If people must walk on the paper, have them work in their socks or put tape on the bottoms of their shoes. An alternative is to lay clean sheets of card-board over the paper.

After the shoot, seamless paper may or may not be rerolled. Regardless, tape down the free end and then remove the roll from the crossbar. Seamless paper must be stored vertically. If not, it tends to develop flat spots, a condition that can ruin the surface.

## PLEXIGLAS

In most respects, Plexiglas is stored and handled like the plastic laminates. However, Plexiglas is usually translucent white or, less commonly, black. This means light can be directed through the Plexiglas, much like diffusion material. Yet it's much more rigid, so objects can rest on its surface.

### Handling Plexiglas

Plexiglas is often swept into a *scoop,* and a product is placed on its surface. Then a flash head is positioned underneath, so the light is directed through the Plexiglas. In order to produce an evenly lit background, the Plexiglas must only be supported along its edges. Under these circumstances, some sort of metal framework holds the Plexiglas.

If the Plexiglas begins to sag, additional support can be obtained by first plac-ing a small stand under the material and then extending the stand until a level sur-face is obtained. This Plexiglas support can be difficult to construct, and premade equipment, commonly referred to as *shooting tables,* is available.

## ADDITIONAL MATERIALS

Other materials serve dual functions and consequently are discussed elsewhere. Black velvet cloth and diffusion material can be used as a background, but because they both function as light-modifying devices, they're discussed in that section. Fabric, including carpet, might serve as a background, but it is discussed in the chapter on surface preparation.

## SUMMARY OF RESPONSIBILITIES RELATED TO BACKGROUND MATERIALS

- ❑ Understand the basic requirements for the shot in order to position the background material correctly. Look at the *layout*.

- ❑ When working with heavy or awkward materials, have the required *hardware* immediately available. This includes tape, clamps, shot bags, and stands.

- ❑ Make certain there is adequate space on the set so you minimize the chance of damage to the material and other equipment.

- ❑ Position the *supports* for the background material, including sawhorses, crates, stands and crossbars.

- ❑ Remove the *background* from storage and position it on the supports.

- ❑ Properly prepare the background material's *surface*.

- ❑ Be careful of the background material when positioning props and the subject on its surface.

- ❑ After the shoot, remove the background and return it to storage.

- ❑ Return all related hardware to its proper place.

# 17

# The Photographic Studio

PHOTOGRAPHERS WORK IN WHAT IS COMMONLY REFERRED TO AS A STUDIO. Whereas studio photographers are more dependent on the studio, location photographers also benefit from having one. There's a considerable amount of equipment and preparation for almost any photographic assignment. Studios vary in size and sophistication, but there's a common theme. Photographers need to construct a shooting environment, prepare the subject and props, set up artificial lighting, position the camera and expose film, tear down or strike the set, and store all the material.

The hypothetical studio presented here is divided into different areas or departments that can be found in some form or another in most studios. Categorizing the studio into departments here helps in discussing what devices are used in the studio, how they're used, and where they might be found.

## LEARNING THE STUDIO

A freelance assistant must become familiar with a new studio very quickly. One of the best starting points is to pay attention to the studio's layout during the *interview*. Then upon arriving for work, find the basic departments discussed here. You'll end up asking fewer questions and be in a better position to respond to the photographer.

I'm not suggesting you locate these departments by roaming through the studio, opening closed doors. Most can be found by simply standing in the studio's main shooting area and *observing* what surrounds you. Also, when you're sent to fetch something, make a concerted effort to remember what else you come across. It might be the very next item needed. This kind of learning takes effort but ultimately makes your job easier.

After you've found something, you must remember where it belongs because you'll be responsible for putting it away. This is even more important to photographers who call on the services of several freelance assistants. Here, a lack of organization would soon lead to chaos; the assistant who cleaned up yesterday evening may not be around the next morning to help find something. When photographers spend time looking for misplaced equipment, their last thoughts about you are negative.

When you first work with someone, it's expected you'll need more direction. Learning the studio quickly is one way of taking the initiative, with little chance for negative consequences. You might feel it's much easier to just wait to be told, but the

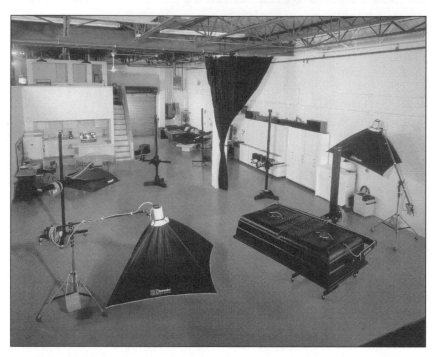

A well-equipped rental studio, featuring a kitchen, drive-in entrance, workshop, and lounge area. Standard equipment includes soft boxes, bank lights, power supplies, and view cameras on camera stands. © 2000 Pro 1st. Stamford, CT.

photographer won't think so. Photographers rehire those assistants they feel work well with them. Being efficient and not requiring constant direction is important to a good working relationship.

## THE SHOOTING AREA

A large, open section in the studio functions as a shooting area. The set, consisting of a background, lighting, props, and subject, is painstakingly assembled and positioned here. Shortly after assembly, it's taken down and removed. Although almost everything is stored somewhere else, most of it makes its way out onto the shooting-area floor at one time or another.

Even with all this activity, studios remain well organized because everything has its place. When not in use, the main shooting area remains relatively free of equipment. What you're likely to find are permanently constructed soft boxes, a camera stand, large booms, and the *set cart*.

### The Set Cart

It's useful to have a workplace close to the camera or set so that commonly used items are readily available. In the studio, these items are likely to be kept on the studio cart or set cart. Exactly what's kept here depends on the photographer and the nature of the work. A set cart usually has a small working surface, assorted drawers, shelves, and hooks. It's also built on casters so it can be positioned where needed.

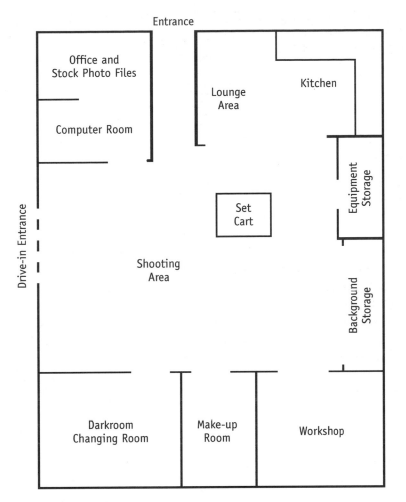

Studio Departments.

The set cart is often wheeled close to the camera because it may hold related items, such as a cable release, flash slave, and sync cord. It's also a logical place to set the Polaroid instant film, its holder, and possibly a pair of L-shaped croppers. In addition, view cameras require a focusing loupe and dark cloth.

When it's time to go to film, the set cart is a good place to keep film magazines, sheet-film holders, and canned air. If changing lens filters is part of the exposure sequence, the photographer is less apt to forget if you place them on top of the set cart.

While working with background materials, remember the set cart. Assorted clamps, miscellaneous adapters, and a whole range of adhesive tapes can be found here. As work progresses, more tools are needed. Everyone has scissors, a utility knife, and a straight edge. You might need to trim a fill card or remove an errant thread.

## Preparing and Positioning Objects

You can also expect to find plenty of items related to surface preparation, including small paintbrushes, cotton swabs, erasers, and paper towels. Once clean, objects are often handled with white, lint-free gloves.

Besides preparing an object's surface, the assistant is often responsible for positioning it on the set. Again, expect to find an assortment of tape, small blocks, tweezers, and maybe a hot-glue gun. But, one of the most useful materials is a waxy or clay-like substance, commonly referred to as tacky-wax or fun-tack. This temporary adhesive is both pliable and sticky and is very useful in positioning lighter objects.

### *Bring It with You*

Before leaving for a location shoot, many photographers transfer items into a multidrawer case or tackle box. To help make certain the photographer is prepared, it's necessary to know what is scheduled for the day. With this information, check the set cart for necessary odds and ends.

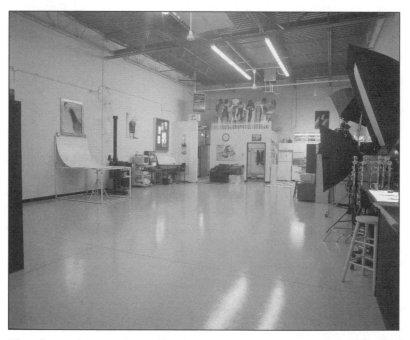

When first arriving at the studio, the assistant often encounters a large open space just waiting to be filled. After the job is complete, equipment is returned to its place, ready for the next shoot. A shooting table is visible on left, with soft boxes on the right. © 2000 Rick Souders and Sidelight Studios. Denver, CO.

## THE WORKSHOP

One of the most important areas is the workshop. The space allotted and the materials found here are determined by the type of work performed in the studio. For example, a large drive-in studio provides the photographer with the opportunity to shoot almost anything. However, to realize the potential requires a considerable investment in support material.

On the other hand, a photographer situated in a small, second-floor walk-up requires a relatively modest workshop, primarily due to the inherent limitations imposed by a lack of accessibility and space. Finally, a photographer specializing in food will be best served by committing more resources to the kitchen area.

Many of the items found in the workshop are the same ones used to maintain a home. Yet they are indispensable in creating the illusions found in photography. When in the hands of a set builder, photographer, or skilled assistant, the results on film can be amazing. You'll find hand and power tools, assorted paints and cleaners, building supplies, and items specific to photography.

## THE KITCHEN

Photographing food is a skill all its own. To prepare an appetizing food dish is one thing; to prepare one that looks equally delicious on film is quite different. In larger markets, photographers can specialize in food photography, and these studios have more elaborate kitchens. However, food photographers often call upon the services of another specialist, a *food stylist*.

The food stylist is responsible for the selection, preparation, and arrangement of the food or beverage. To this end, stylists utilize an array of small tools and other aids not found in most studios. Under these circumstances, the assistant might help carry in the stylist's equipment, but food-related responsibilities are left to the stylist.

When a stylist isn't present for a food shot, you'll most likely find necessary food-preparation items in the kitchen. Besides basic cooking and eating utensils, you might find an atomizer to mist food or an eyedropper to position beads of water. More robust water drops are made by mixing glycerin in water to the desired consistency. Colored dyes can be used to enhance or concoct a beverage.

Of course, there are acrylic ice cubes and artificial snow. But there are also granules that, when mixed with water, resemble crushed ice. Still other granules produce steam to enhance the appearance of a hot cup of coffee. After a food shot, copious amounts of food are often left over. However, before you dig in, find out what's in it, on it, and holding it together. It may look great, but it might be inedible.

### The Assistant and the Kitchen

Most likely, the assistant will use the kitchen in a more utilitarian manner. You might make coffee in the morning or get together a few items to go with a take-out lunch. Photographic shoots are usually full-day affairs. In addition to you and the photographer, an art director or stylist might be on the set. It's not uncommon for the studio to provide some sort of refreshment.

At some point in the day, the assistant may be called on to straighten up the studio. A kitchen is a logical place to look for general-purpose cleaners and trash bags. But straightening up is secondary to tasks directly related to photography. You don't want your hands in dishwater when the photographer is ready to shoot film. Prioritize.

## THE LOUNGE AREA

Many studios have a sort of lounge area that can keep people entertained and away from the set or allow clients to get some work done while out of the office. I mention this area because it usually has a telephone. The assistant may or may not be responsible for answering the phone. This task might fall on the studio manager or the photographer's representative, if there is one.

However, when it's just the photographer and the assistant, answering the phone is the assistant's responsibility. Callers and visitors consider freelance assistants as employees, and your overall demeanor reflects on the photographer. Therefore, try to sound professional over the telephone.

Unless directed otherwise, when answering the phone, state the studio's name and then your first name. It's customary to give the business name, and by stating your name, no one will mistake you for the photographer. Also, ask who's calling. Asking is an effective screening tool for unsolicited sales calls.

At times, there can be many people on the set, and you should try to learn their names. Besides allowing you to be more effective on the set, you'll know who gets the phone after you've answered it. The photographer may opt for you to take a message. Always get at least a name and phone number, write it down, and make certain the photographer knows where to find it.

Commercial studios try to maintain a low profile, and you should help keep it that way. When people unrelated to the studio come to the door or call on the phone, be discrete by not volunteering unnecessary details. In fact, it's even a good idea to dispose of trash in opaque plastic garbage bags. Studios have much expensive equipment, and they're often located in the lower-rent districts. In short, most photographers are justifiably paranoid about being burglarized.

## THE COMPUTER

All photographers will have a computer, but how it's put to use varies widely. When the computer is mostly used for bookkeeping, it is often in an office, and you may not see much of it. The computer could just as likely be connected to a film scanner or used in association with a stock-photo library. When the computer is used to capture digital images, it's positioned close to the camera on a movable cart. Here, you'll also find storage media such as blank CD-Rs and Zip disks.

## THE MAKE-UP ROOM

When the photographer photographs people, there's likely to be a make-up room. This is usually reserved for the stylist, and unless you're changing careers from cosmetology to photography, you have little need to be there.

When all that's available is a bathroom or an out-of-the-way corner, make sure it's clean. Since stylists transport several cases of equipment, remove unnecessary items and replace them with a chair, table, and ample lighting. It's a good idea to introduce yourself to the stylist as the assistant; you might be needed to find something. Keep in mind, however, you're the photographer's assistant, not the stylist's.

## THE DARKROOM

Except for the camera, few things are associated with photography more than the dark-room. Usually, a darkroom is for processing film, but it might also be a smaller changing room—that is, a room dedicated to handling sheet-film holders. The use of a darkroom to load and unload sheet film is presented in the chapter on view cameras.

But here, I'll discuss the darkroom as it relates to film processing. Most commonly, processing will involve making black-and-white prints from black-and-white negative material. These particular skills may not be put to use, at least not as much as you might imagine. You will even less often encounter E-6 film processors and the need to print color negatives. If you lack familiarity with either of these procedures, it's not much of a handicap.

### The Freelance and Full-Time Assistant

As a freelance assistant, you can get by without spending much time in the darkroom. In fact, you may prefer it that way because working the occasional darkroom job can be frustrating. First, it takes time to become familiar with the equipment and its arrangement in a new darkroom. You can find some pretty confusing arrangements of the enlarger light, timers, safe lights, and overhead lights. In addition, different papers and developers have their own characteristics. Besides the equipment, subjective decisions are required concerning cropping, dodging, and burning. Unfortunately, when questions arise, you're all alone and in the dark.

When it's all said and done, it's less expensive to send it to a custom black-and-white lab. If the lab can't satisfy the photographer, it's doubtful the freelance assistant can.

You're more likely to work in the darkroom if you're a full-time assistant. More time can then be spent instructing you as to the photographer's preferences and standards.

Again, don't say you can do something if you can't. This is especially important concerning film processing. You can't recover incorrectly processed negative or color-transparency material.

### Acquiring Darkroom Skills

There's been no attempt here to instruct you in any aspect of film processing. You can learn basic black-and-white processing and printing from books, rental darkrooms, photographic workshops, community colleges, and continuing-education programs. Used enlargers, capable of printing 35mm negatives, are readily available at very reasonable prices.

## EQUIPMENT AND BACKGROUND STORAGE

As demonstrated, photographers utilize a considerable amount of photographic equipment, and all of it needs to be well organized while remaining readily accessible. Assorted hooks, like those used on pegboards, are often located on the walls bordering the shooting area. Hooks are ideal for holding lighting hardware, such as flash heads, reflectors, mounting rings, and stands. More expensive items, like power supplies and cameras, are best stored in locked cabinets. Camera stands, large soft boxes, and booms are often set in an unused corner.

Every background material needs to be properly stored in order to remain serviceable. Large items, including $4' \times 8'$ sheets of Plexiglas, foam board, and plastic laminates, are commonly stored together in vertical stacks, much like books. Rolls of seamless paper must be stored vertically and are often in the same general vicinity.

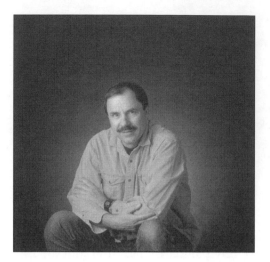

## AN INTERVIEW WITH PETE SALOUTOS

Pete Saloutos is a commercial photographer based just outside Seattle.

**John Kieffer:**      What kind of photography do you do?

**Pete Saloutos:**   I do lots of stuff: corporate annual reports, high tech, and medical technology. I also shoot sports and lifestyles. I do this for both assignment and stock. I have a studio, but about 80 percent of my work is on location.

**J.K.:**   What are you looking for in an assistant?

**P.S.:**   I think foremost they have to be committed to being a photographer and someone that's hungry to learn. They don't have to be good photographers yet, but they have to show they're interested, and one way they show that is by shoving new photography in my face. I've had assistants from the Art Center, and often they've added very little; in fact, they've been prima donnas.

**J.K.:**   Do you use a full-time assistant or freelancers?

**P.S.:**   I use freelancers. I might guarantee an assistant a certain numbers of hours a week, but I don't have anyone full time.

**J.K.:**   What do you pay an assistant?

**P.S.:**   You have to realize that I work out of both Seattle and Los Angeles, and L.A. assistants make a lot more. In L.A., I pay $175 for a ten-hour day. In Seattle I pay up to $125 per day.

**J.K.:**   When you go on location, do you bring an assistant with you?

**P.S.:**   That depends. If it's an assignment job, I'll bring an assistant with me. That assistant may come out of Seattle or Los Angeles. Regardless, I'll take care of all expenses.

**J.K.:**   How do most assistants find you?

**P.S.:**   I run ads in the *Workbook* and *Single Image,* plus I have a Web site *(www.petesaloutos.com),* so people call me from all over.

**J.K.:**   Do you interview assistants and look at portfolios?

**P.S.:**   Often, what happens is that one of my assistants gets sick, and someone has just called me, and it's test by fire. I'm in a position where I need someone, and this person sounds like they know what they're doing. I just throw them in with the wolves and see what happens. I usually can tell during a conversation if they're ready to shoot with me. People locally, I work with much more slowly. I bring them into my studio, and they might help with a stock-photo shoot.

**J.K.:**     What kind of equipment do you use?

**P.S.:**     I use Norman strobe, 35mm Nikons, and medium-format Hasselblads, both two-and-a-quarter and panoramic. I also shoot a little with the view camera.

**J.K.:**     Do you use male and female assistants?

**P.S.:**     In L.A., my assistant is a male, and in Bainbridge it's a female. I moved up here in 1990, and it was difficult to get assistants, and most of my assistants in Bainbridge have been women.

**J.K.:**     When you're on location, does your assistant have the responsibility of loading your cameras?

**P.S.:**     When I'm on location, I have to trust them to do their job. However, as I'm shooting, I'll note that film is going through the camera.

**J.K.:**     Do you shoot any digital cameras?

**P.S.:**     I have shot digital camera, but at the present, they don't give me a large-enough file quick enough. When I go on location, I'll shoot 100 rolls of film. There's no digital camera that has that capacity.

**J.K.:**     Do you have any advice for assistants that might help them transition into professional photography?

**P.S.:**     I would have to say that only about one out of a hundred truly make it. Perhaps I'm raising the bar too high, but it's a tough world. I like to be positive, but I hate to tell people there's a pot of gold at the end of the rainbow. I don't like to be misleading.

**J.K.:**     Do you set any ground rules regarding an assistant's behavior or how you want them to interact when a client is present?

**P.S.:**     I'm a pretty powerful personality, so generally that's not a problem. It's happened on rare occasions, and it doesn't take much from me to let them know they've crossed the line.

**J.K.:**     You mentioned that you shoot stock photography. What advice do you give assistants regarding the stock-photo industry?

**P.S.:**     I tell them right from the get-go that they need to consider stock, and I'm happy to answer questions. However, I am concerned when they want to contact models that I use, and they have to realize that my ideas are my ideas. Also, I'm not comfortable with my assistants contacting my clients.

**J.K.:**     Is stock photography difficult to get into?

**P.S.:**     I think stock is getting more difficult—just like assignment. However, if someone has a unique slant and good ideas, I think there's room for them. I think the competition is getting even greater as we go into digital. There're more people that think they can do it.

**J.K.:**     Currently the economy is very healthy. Have you seen a decrease in the number of people who want to go into photography?

**P.S.:**     No. I think there's more than ever because I think it's getting even more accessible in the digital world. I've been in this business thirty-five years, and I can't tell you how many people say, "Oh, I was a photographer once." Exactly what they mean as far as being a photographer, I don't know. Maybe they had a picture published in a magazine. Suffice it to say, it's a competitive world and getting more so.

**J.K.:**     Do you work with a computer and PhotoShop?

**P.S.:**     I go analog to digital all the time. On location, a reason I don't use a digital camera is the storage problem. I may shoot a thousand frames of something, and I'll put a hundred on Kodak Photo CD.

**J.K.:**     Does your assistant work on the computer, using programs such as PhotoShop?

**P.S.:**     I have three people in my studio, I have someone who works on the computer, and I have an office manager. My assistant deals with the analog side.

**J.K.:**     Do you sell stock through your studio?

**P.S.:**     Yes, some, but I really don't like being an agent. What I like is creating images, and whatever allows me to create the most images is the best for me.

# 18

# Photographic Specialties

A S THE PHOTOGRAPHER'S ASSISTANT, YOU HAVE THE UNIQUE OPPORTUNITY TO BE introduced to a wide range of photographic experiences. Many of your responsibilities remain unchanged, regardless of the exact type of photography. However, others need to be tailored to the specific assignment. The following highlights how different assignments might influence your work.

## PRODUCT PHOTOGRAPHY

Much of commercial photography can be viewed as photographing a product. A building or even a person can be considered a product. But here, I will address some specifics regarding studio product photography, where the emphasis is on a stricter definition of "product." Someone specializing in small products is often referred to as a tabletop or still-life photographer. A person might be in a product shot, but usually not as the focus of attention.

Commonly, relatively small objects are photographed using a view camera. To the uninitiated, it will seem as though an inordinate amount of time is dedicated to preparation, but this kind of work requires precision and perfection. Therefore, much is to be done by the assistant. Plus, there's usually a budget to hire one.

For the assistant, product photography requires knowledge of sheet-film-handling responsibilities, including Polaroid instant film. The chapters on surface preparation and background materials are equally essential. Of course, expect to spend considerable time with every aspect of lighting.

### Working in the Set

As any shot develops, the shooting area tends to get more crowded. Place a view camera close to the set and the congestion just gets worse. Yet at the same time, the need to be more precise increases dramatically during development of the shot, both in the placement of objects and your movements.

First let's talk about you, the assistant. Be careful. Be aware of what's on the set, your body position, and that your actions can destroy a considerable amount of effort. If you must bump something, do so in the first ten minutes. As the set evolves, any disruption becomes potentially disastrous.

You can find yourself working with any number of people while on the set. When practical, avoid handling objects directly over a small set. A still–life arrangement is often held together with little more than tape, and dropping something might compromise the shot. This is especially true when handing something to someone. Regardless of who drops it, it's your fault. Who's the photographer going to look at, you or the client who's paying for the day's shoot?

## Communicating with the Photographer

Under the photographer's direction, the assistant often positions various objects. The photographer might tell you how to alter the orientation of the product, the placement of a fill card, or the location of the soft box. To be most effective, you must understand the photographer's instructions.

Understanding requires a common basis of communication. Misunderstandings can be compounded because the photographer is often situated behind the camera, viewing an image that is upside down and backward. In addition, as placement becomes more critical, only the slightest movement may be adequate. You must sense what is meant by "a little." It may be an inch or a millimeter. If unsure, proceed slowly.

You might find the photographer's phraseology confusing. If so, try to phrase your questions in the following manner. When a photographer asks you to move something to the right, assume it's to the photographer's right. Or ask, "Do you mean, *camera right?*" The expression specifies to the right as viewed from the camera. You can also use "camera left," "away from camera," and "toward camera."

Other terms you're likely to hear are *in frame* and *out of frame.* To move something out of frame means to move it toward the closest edge, but not completely out of the frame. Conversely, moving a product in frame tells you to move it toward the center. You're more likely to respond correctly to the photographer's intent if you pay attention to what's taking place on the set.

## PEOPLE PHOTOGRAPHY

Many professional photographers prefer to photograph people. Examples are a conventional portrait of a business executive and a picture of a worker on the production floor. Both photographs might also be for the same annual report and shot on the same day.

The photographer is just as likely to utilize the services of professional models. They may be modeling clothes in what's commonly thought of as a fashion shoot. However, many other photographic jobs require professional models. Although not glamorous, they are demanding. A model is often positioned with a product, possibly using it. Even with few props, a model can be used to convey an image or attitude about a product or service.

The selection of the appropriate model is an important aspect of the photographic message. Photographers and advertising agencies often work through modeling agencies to meet with potential models in what's called a *casting call.* During the casting call, the photographer reviews the model's portfolio and possibly takes a Polaroid print. Afterwards, a selection is made.

## General Considerations

When photographing people, the assistant's responsibilities can vary widely. So expect to adjust your interactions, depending on the circumstances. Early on, establish whether there's a stylist on the set. If there is, your involvement with the person to be photographed is limited.

*Stylists* are responsible for the model's hair, make-up, and clothing. The stylist should arrive on the set virtually self-sufficient. However, you should be more familiar with the studio, and an offer to find an appropriate chair or extension cord is not out of line.

Generally, let the photographer direct the action, followed by the art director, client, or stylist. In other words, keep quiet. After two or three individuals lend their expert opinions, additional comments can be counterproductive. But don't assume you're not involved and you shouldn't be concerned; just keep in mind that it's often best to address your concerns directly to the photographer.

Regardless of who's on the set, you can keep a few points in mind. Refrain from offering the model anything to eat or drink. Models are there for their appearance, and even a slight mishap with a beverage or food caught between their teeth could be disastrous.

Once the model is in position, look closely for loose threads or hairs. Also, see if everything looks right. Are there any prominent, misplaced creases? Clothing, such as a business suit, is best positioned after the individual sits down.

## Nonprofessional Models

You'll be involved with photographing people who aren't professional models. These individuals usually require more direction. At the same time, any advice needs to be given tactfully. Most people become very self-conscious in front of the camera, so let the photographer do most of the talking.

There are several areas where the assistant can be helpful. You'll often stand in as the model while the lighting arrangement evolves. If a Polaroid print is available, show it to the model. Nonprofessional models usually don't realize what's really important to the shot.

Inexperienced people commonly strike a pose, then relax after the photographer makes each exposure. To alleviate the need to continually reposition the person, let the individual know approximately how much film will be exposed. Most can't imagine why a photographer would ever shoot a dozen exposures. Also, suggest that the model find a way to remember his position. Masking tape placed on the floor makes a good reference point, but it really comes down to making a concerted effort to remember how and where the body is positioned. Unfortunately, until now the person has never had a reason to think about it.

## Hand Models

At times, only a part of the body is in the shot. Generally, the tighter the crop and the closer in you're photographing, the greater the need to return to an exact position. In many of these shots, the emphasis is on the hands. Because hand photography is difficult work and photogenic hands are not commonplace, specialized hand models are frequently hired.

When the shot calls for the use of a nonprofessional's hand, like the assistant's, remember these points. Pronounced veins become even more so on film. When possible, keep the arm elevated to reduce blood flow to the hand and allow the veins to appear more normal. When circumstances permit, try to have the hand model remain seated, as it's easier to stay relaxed.

Consider constructing some form of *support* for the arm, like a short boom fitted to a light stand. The support helps position the hand, and the pose can be sustained with less effort. You can't have the hand sweat or shake. So for those really close shots, refrain from offering or imbibing coffee.

## Model Releases

When the photographer finishes exposing film, have the model sign a model-release form. This one-page form outlines the conditions under which the photograph can be used. It applies to both professional and nonprofessional models who appear in any photograph intended for commercial use. If the photographer is covering a public event, an editorial situation, or a wedding, model releases are not required.

## Exposing Film

The photographer often selects a medium-format camera to photograph people because the format provides a large film size and allows the photographer to shoot at a fairly fast pace. With much of product or architectural photography, exposing film is anticlimactic. However, this isn't the case when a person is in the frame.

People move and have innumerable facial expressions. Not knowing exactly what's on film until it's processed makes exposing film inherently exciting. It also means the photographer shoots more film, just to eliminate any nagging doubt about not having the shot.

When the photographer finally goes to film, the assistant has sole responsibility for many tasks. Therefore, the assistant's role regarding the model is probably secondary. As the assistant, you need to be very familiar with film-handling responsibilities regarding small and medium-format cameras.

Having film ready for the photographer at all times is of primary importance. Tasks include loading and unloading film magazines and informing the photographer when nearing the end of a roll. Due to the fast-paced shooting, it's equally critical to monitor the ready light found on each power supply. The photographer can't be permitted to shoot faster than the power supply can recharge.

## WEDDING PHOTOGRAPHY

I'll address wedding photography briefly. Wedding photographers utilize a 35mm SLR or medium-format camera. Lighting is likely to be either on-camera flash units or electronic flash systems utilizing umbrellas. Wedding photographers hire assistants far less frequently than commercial photographers because of lower budgets. If you wish to pursue this area of photography, contact the best and most expensive wedding photographers in your area. They're the ones who can afford assistants. Expect to work weekends, especially during the nicest time of the year. Remember, you're at the wedding to work, not to eat or socialize.

## LOCATION PHOTOGRAPHY

If you're not shooting in the studio, you're on location. The phrase "location shoot" can be correctly applied to many different kinds of photography. It might resemble a studio shoot, except the shoot takes place across town at the manufacturing site. It can also mean traveling to a unique locale, living out of a suitcase, and working out of equipment cases. The hectic schedule is dictated by the assignment, possibly a once-in-a-lifetime event.

The specific assignment and the photographer's general specialty influence what equipment is required. When the photographer is primarily a studio photographer, you're likely to take whatever might conceivably be needed, basically transferring the studio and the control it affords to a different location.

But location photographers tend to carry only what they really need and what can be packed into sturdy cases. Steady location work puts a premium on being resourceful and on the ability to improvise.

There's no getting around it; location work is tiring for both the photographer and the assistant. Besides completing the shot to everyone's satisfaction, they must select the appropriate equipment, pack it into cases, and then load it into a vehicle. Everything must be taken to the site, unpacked, and then set up. After the photograph is taken, everything must be taken down, more or less packed up, and moved to another site. Now you get to start the whole process over again. It's obvious that efficiency and doing everything right the first time pay even greater dividends on location.

### Background Information

When you book a location job, find out a few specifics about the day's work. Primarily, where will you be shooting—indoors or outdoors? Working at corporate headquarters is a little different than at an industrial site in winter. You need to be appropriately dressed.

When you get to the studio, some additional background information allows you to function more effectively. Insight as to the day's photography and the camera format to be used lets you think about what's needed to do the job. Such mental preparation is important whether you do most of the packing or the photographer is largely ready upon your arrival. Hopefully, two heads are better than one. Many photographers have equipment lists for various types of location shoots. Inquire about one or use the one at the end of this chapter.

The photographer can have half-a-dozen cases or more, and most items belong in a specific case. When packing equipment cases, make it a point to remember what goes where. Knowing where everything is kept lets you work quickly. Because you'll be working out of these cases throughout the day, it's the only way to keep organized.

Load the vehicle so that the most-needed items are readily accessible. Getting to the site and having to unload half the van just to find the camera and tripod isn't the best way to start the day. Before closing the doors, check to see if a handcart is available.

## Working on Site

Upon arriving at the site, remember that your actions influence how professional both you and the photographer appear to be. You're also likely to be intruding on someone's property or workplace, so show respect. While on location, you'll often need or benefit from someone's help, and starting off on the right foot makes your job easier. For most people, a commercial photography shoot is quite different than first imagined. They're often very intrigued and willing to lend a hand by rounding up a ladder or some props.

## Surveying the Site

Before unpacking, survey the work area. Try to find a lesser-used corner to place equipment, as opposed to the hallway. While working, keep unneeded equipment confined to cases or to a limited area. It doesn't take long to have valuable equipment spread everywhere, which increases the chance of breakage or theft and makes moving to another site difficult. If there's public access to the work site, you must take even greater care to watch equipment, especially recognizable items like cameras and lenses.

Soon upon arriving, you need to locate an electrical outlet to supply power for artificial lighting. Hopefully, you brought plenty of extension cords. They're essential on most location shoots. If you find yourself in a crowded area, position equipment and their various electrical cords away from the main flow of traffic.

In heavily trafficked areas tape extension cords to the floor with duct tape. Also, booms and their counterweights should be positioned and marked for everyone's safety. When working in older buildings, try using the power supply's slow recycle setting. If the longer recycle time isn't a hindrance, the slow recycle time reduces the chance of blowing a fuse.

When the photographer is combining electronic flash and other artificial lights in one exposure, the shutter often remains open for a relatively long period. Extraneous lights therefore need to be turned off. In new office buildings, one switch often controls many lights, particularly with fluorescent lighting. Individual fluorescent lights can be turned off by rotating the tube about one-fourth of a revolution. If you rotate it further, it's likely to fall out, so be careful.

## Leaving the Site

As the shot winds down, you literally have to undo everything you've done. Now comes the test as to whether you know which case holds what photographic equipment. Once packed, you're still not done—you've got to return the work area to its original condition. So you must remove tape and replace furniture, while taking one last look for equipment. During a multiday shoot, inquire about a secure room in which to store some gear overnight. Storing the gear can save valuable time and energy the following morning.

As you throw everything back into the vehicle, keep the *exposed film* accessible. Your first stop on the way back to the studio may be to the processing lab. If the photographer exposed sheet film, your first responsibility once in the studio may be to unload a few film holders.

## AUDIO-VISUAL ASSIGNMENTS

One assisting job that's usually done on location is producing an audio-visual presentation, or slide show. Such an assignment requires a 35mm SLR camera, a tape recorder, and possibly artificial lighting. If sound isn't being recorded, the assistant's responsibilities resemble any shoot. However, when both the visual and audio portions are being produced, extra care must be taken to control noise.

Often, the production of the audio and visual segments must be completed sequentially, because the sound of the camera and the strobes is quite intrusive. When the shooting stops, taping the audio portion can begin. Unfortunately, the time when you must be absolutely quiet is the only time you have to deal with reloading and reorganization.

This concern also applies when working on a film set. Here, the photographer and assistant are often shooting *production stills,* and both of you are a secondary part of the activity. If you foresee being restricted in your actions, look for an isolated spot to regroup. The ability to keep a low profile while still performing all tasks is essential in many assisting jobs.

## OVERNIGHT ASSIGNMENTS

A location assignment can involve overnight travel. It might be to any kind of destination, but whether commonplace or exotic, it's usually all work. As you might expect, with overnight assignments it's even more important to have a good rapport with the photographer.

One way to maintain a good working relationship is to discuss a few details when booking the job. As with any location shoot, get enough background information to pack the appropriate attire, especially when working outdoors. Also, clarify your rates and how travel expenses will be handled. It's reasonable to expect all expenses for transportation, lodging, and meals to be paid by the photographer when incurred. Still, carry some cash and a major credit card.

## ACQUIRING LOCATION WORK

If you have a real interest in location work, particularly overnight travel, pursue it. You might take several approaches. One is to find established local photographers who receive assignments from national magazines or out-of-town clients. Also, review the creative directories and Web sites for photographers who emphasize location work.

Another way to acquire location work is to advertise your services to out-of-town photographers who might travel to your region. It helps to keep a high profile and to be listed on any assistants list circulated in your area. Consider becoming a member of the American Society of Media Photographers (ASMP) or Advertising Photographers of America (APA). You might also try running a classified ad in the magazine *Photo District News.*

## ARCHITECTURAL WORK

Architectural photography involves photographing the exteriors and interiors of architectural structures. The photographer uses a view camera to control perspective and must often integrate different light sources, such as natural daylight, electronic flash, tungsten, fluorescent, or sodium vapor. Balancing multiple light sources is accomplished through the selection of film type, filters, and artificial light sources. In architectural photography, tungsten-balanced film and tungsten lighting is used to complement existing light sources.

Whatever the light source, the photographer is often confronted with the problem of lighting large areas, which necessitates much power and many lights. Lights are commonly fitted with reflectors, and the light is bounced off a wall, the ceiling, a large fill card, or an umbrella. A more diffuse light source is obtained by taping diffusion material over the flash head's reflector, in preference to using a bulky soft box.

The many lights and power supplies must be concealed from the camera's view. Therefore, radio transmitters are an excellent replacement for sync cords and flash slaves to ensure every power supply discharges.

When radio transmitters aren't available, it's helpful to attach the power supply's flash slave to an extension cord. The flash slave is then discreetly positioned to receive sufficient light, while remaining hidden from view. If using tape, attach it to the extension cord, not to the flash slave.

### Working Hours

For a variety of reasons, architectural photographers work odd hours. Many locations, both public and private, simply aren't available to the photographer during traditional business hours. For other jobs, such as photographing a building's exterior, it might be important to integrate natural daylight with the structure's artificial lights. This is accomplished best closer to sunrise and sunset. Consequently, the assistant should expect to work unconventional hours.

### A Giant Still Life

In some ways, it's useful to view an architectural shot as a product shot, only bigger. This is particularly true for interiors. Therefore, be familiar with the chapter on surface preparation, especially for carpet. Glass cleaner and paper towels are probably the best choices to handle the range of surfaces encountered on an architectural shoot.

In addition to surface preparation, objects need to be correctly oriented. Besides an object's location in the frame, it's important that horizontal surfaces appear horizontal and vertical lines, vertical. Remember, look through the camera or stand in front of the lens. Check to make certain that lamp shades, table tops, and picture frames look level and that drapes hang vertically. Due to an architectural project's size, a ladder can be essential.

Fabrics found on furniture, pillows, and bedspreads must be free of wrinkles. Lamp and telephone cords should be hidden from view. When that's not possible, wires should be positioned to be least obtrusive.

Reflective surfaces, like mirrors and glass, can cause problems. They must not reflect the camera, lighting, or the assistant. Oftentimes, objects like picture frames can be tilted from behind by using small pieces of cardboard. When you feel the problem is alleviated, check the result from behind the camera.

## STOCK PHOTOGRAPHY

Many photographers are involved with the stock-photo industry. It's likely that their work is represented by a stock agency or two, but they'll also sell stock themselves when the opportunity presents itself. What I'd like to discuss here are things to consider when handling a stock photo request. Read chapter 20 regarding my transition to professional photographer for more insight into the stock-photo industry. When you are called on to assist in a stock-photo shoot, your responsibilities are like other assisting jobs.

### Stock-Photo Requests

Most stock-photo requests begin with a phone call. Unless you're trained in the photographer's stock business, hand the call over. When the photographer is unavailable, here are some things to keep in mind. Most people requesting stock photography are in a hurry. Usually, they want film or a digital file sent out that day and via an overnight courier like Federal Express. Therefore, getting sufficient information on the initial phone call can be a big help.

Often, a photo buyer wants the exact photo he saw advertised in a stock-photo directory or had used before. Besides a description, it's critical to get a photo ID number, caption, and where the photo was seen. On the delivery memo, include the shipping address (no P.O. Boxes for Fed Ex), phone number, and a company/individual's name. Most film is sent out using the caller's Fed Ex or similar account number. Determine exactly when they want to receive the film.

You might also get what's called a *general request.* Here, rather than requesting a specific photo, photo buyers describe their needs. What they're looking for can range from very broad and undefined to extremely precise. At Kieffer Nature Stock, a general request might be for a great fall shot that suggests Colorado. Now the job is to select or pull film, which can easily take several hours. So the more descriptive information you can get, the better. Now you have to think like both a designer and a photographer. Ask if they can fax or e-mail a layout. After listening to their needs, hopefully you will know if it's a vertical or horizontal format, a certain color theme, or certain season. Shipping the film out is a fairly cut-and-dry task; unless you are very familiar with the stock files or library, finding and choosing the film is a much more difficult matter.

### Pricing Photography

Most of the time, the photographer charges a *usage fee;* the amount depends on how the photo is used. Leave the pricing up the photographer but get some information as to what the customer intends to do with the photo. Asking these questions is not prying, but standard operating procedure. Will the photo be used on the cover or inside a brochure? How big will it be reproduced? How large is the brochure's print run or the magazine's circulation? How long will they use the photo on a Web site? This information will give the photographer something to think about before calling back and discussing fees.

## Shipping Film

Be careful when handling and shipping film. It may be difficult to determine if a piece of film is an original or a duplicate ("dupe"). So don't scrimp on shipping material. Ideally, the film should have a return address and copyright notice already in place. Include a *delivery memo* that states exactly how much film is enclosed. Most film is sent and returned using a secure courier like FedEx or Airborne Express, so *get the client's account number*. Also, use the shipping company's labels and packaging materials. These companies will pickup packages at the studio if you call early enough in the afternoon. Otherwise, drop off at a drop box or the shipper's office.

# SUMMARY OF RESPONSIBILITIES RELATED TO PHOTOGRAPHIC SPECIALTIES

## Product Photography
❏ Expect to be involved with many *set-building* tasks.
❏ Remember that *surface preparation* is especially critical.
❏ Keep in mind that you may be required to *position* objects precisely.
❏ Be prepared to dedicate much time to the *lighting* arrangement.
❏ Remember that tasks related to *sheet film* are integrated throughout the day.

## People Photography
❏ Let the photographer, art director, or stylist direct the model.
❏ If a stylist isn't available, inform *nonprofessional models* of the number of exposures to be made; relay what's important to the shot by showing them a Polaroid print.
❏ Remember, the assistant has sole responsibility for specific tasks. However, when conditions dictate, look for *fatal flaws,* such as errant hairs or awkward creases in clothing.
❏ Monitor the *film-exposure process* closely. Keep the photographer supplied with film.
❏ Monitor the *power supply's ready light* under fast shooting conditions.

## Location Photography
❏ Understand the job so you can *dress appropriately*. Consider bringing a fanny pack.
❏ *Determine* the camera format and *general requirements* for the day's shoot in order to pack most effectively.
❏ Load the vehicle, with the most needed items readily accessible. Check for a *hand-cart.*
❏ Remember what equipment goes in each case.
❏ Keep close tabs on all equipment when on site, especially cameras and lenses.
❏ Watch for everyone's *safety*. Tape down electrical cords and flag the boom's counterweight.
❏ Realize you're intruding on someone's work place or property and act accordingly.
❏ After the shot, return the site to its original condition.
❏ Keep *exposed film* readily accessible when returning to the studio.

## Architectural Photography
❏ Treat an architectural shot, particularly interiors, as a *giant still life.*
❏ Expect to work with a variety of *light* sources.
❏ Pack cleaning items, a ladder, and plenty of extension cords.
❏ Be prepared to act quickly, especially under fast-changing lighting conditions.
❏ It's important that horizontal surfaces appear horizontal and vertical lines, vertical. Check picture frames, table tops and drapes.
❏ Be watchful of *reflective surfaces,* such as mirrors and glass.
❏ Expect to work unconventional hours.

## Stock Photography
❏ Ask if the photographer sells stock and if you'll be involved.
❏ When an *exact photo* is requested, get caption and photo ID number.
❏ For *general requests,* get as much background information as possible.
❏ Determine when *the customer* needs to have film or digital file.
❏ Try to understand how the photo will be used, to aid in pricing.
❏ Send film via a secure carrier and with a delivery memo.

## LOCATION EQUIPMENT CHECK LIST

❏ **View Camera with standard and wide angle (bag) bellows**
  - ❏ Lenses, cable release, and sync cords
  - ❏ Dark cloth and focusing loupe
  - ❏ Compendium, filter frame, and filters
  - ❏ Polaroid film holder and Polaroid instant film
  - ❏ Loaded sheet-film holders
  - ❏ Changing tent or bag
  - ❏ Tripod and possibly ⅜"-to-¼" reducing bushing

❏ **Small- and medium-format camera bodies**
  - ❏ Film magazines
  - ❏ Lenses, cable release, and two sync cords
  - ❏ Lens shade, filter frame and filters
  - ❏ Polaroid film holder and Polaroid instant film packets
  - ❏ Roll film and storage bags
  - ❏ Spare batteries for the camera and motor drive
  - ❏ Tripod and possibly ⅜" to ¼" reducing bushing
  - ❏ Power supplies, power cords, and extension cords
  - ❏ Sync cord and flash slaves or radio transmitter/receivers with batteries.

❏ **Artificial lighting, such as flash heads with flash-tube protectors**
  - ❏ Inserts/adapters to fit flash heads to light stands
  - ❏ Flash meter with batteries
  - ❏ On-camera flash unit and sync cord
  - ❏ Battery pack and battery pack recharger
  - ❏ Reflectors for flash heads
  - ❏ Soft boxes and mounting (speed) rings
  - ❏ Diffusion material and colored gels
  - ❏ Fill cards, especially white and black; black-velvet cloth

❏ **Stands of all sizes**
  - ❏ Boom and counterweight
  - ❏ Crossbar for background materials
  - ❏ Shot bags
  - ❏ Clamps of all sizes
  - ❏ Tape: gaffers, black photographic, white artists, duct, double-stick, and masking

❏ **Background material and specific cleaning materials**
  - ❏ Background supports
  - ❏ Surface-preparation material, including window cleaner, paper towels, dull spray, temporary adhesive, erasers, and white gloves
  - ❏ Canned air
  - ❏ Scissors, straight edge, and utility knife
  - ❏ L-shaped croppers and proportion wheel
  - ❏ Ladder and hand cart
  - ❏ Directions
  - ❏ Model- and property-release forms
  - ❏ Spare batteries for camera, motor drive, light meter, flash units, and radio transmitters
  - ❏ Fanny pack, pocket knife, flashlight, and indelible pen

## AN INTERVIEW WITH NANCY BROWN

Nancy Brown is based in New York City and is primarily involved with photographing people, both for assignment and stock.

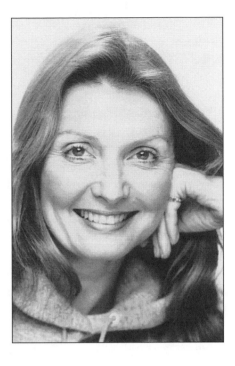

**John Kieffer:** What photographic skills do you feel are most important for a photographic assistant?

**Nancy Brown:** Technically, assistants have to know strobes and cameras, especially how to load cameras. For me, it's 35mm and medium format; I don't use 4″ × 5″ or 8″ × 10″. In addition, assistants must have knowledge of different kinds of strobes. For me, it's just one; I use Dyna-Lite.

For the most part, I hire assistants because of their personality. I've found many assistants either at workshops or seminars that I've held. Consequently, I've had a chance to work with them and get to know them. I know if their personalities are good, that's the main thing. I also get résumés mailed or faxed to me. I won't use anyone that I haven't seen, so I tell them to call me when they are in the area, and maybe they can drop by.

**J.K.:** Could you be more specific as to the personal attributes do you feel are most important?

**N.B.:** Assistants have to talk, have opinions, be alive. I want to hear what they have to say. Some photographers want assistants to blend into the woodwork. I like assistants to be very equal with me. I want them to be able to take over. They're part of my team. Assistants are not like employees in that sense. When we are going to do something, they should start to do it before I tell them. That happens after being with me for a while and they know how I work.

I have a different arrangement than a lot of people; I don't have all the rules. If I like someone's personality and I know they like this business, they can learn very quickly. Some kids come from these big schools, but could never work for me because their personalities are not what I need.

**J.K.:** Do you shoot with a digital camera?

**N.B.:** No, not at all. I believe you still have to create your images, and I think a lot of people aren't doing that. You still have to go for emotional pictures, and sometimes I think that's getting lost with all the computer work. I still believe people need to shoot base, emotional photographs; that can't be created on the computer. That's the kind of photography I've always done.

**J.K.:**    Do you find that most of the assistants you take on have formal photographic training?

**N.B.:**    Most have at least gone to a two-year school, although not all. Regarding the
assistants I work with presently, it's a combination of schooling and on-the-job training.

**J.K.:**    When you're photographing people and using a stylist, do you want the assistant to interact with the model?

**N.B.:**    We always work with a stylist. The make-up and hair is the stylist's responsibility. I don't mind people talking to the model, but when we start shooting, I'm the
only one who is communicating with the model. But the atmosphere is not rigid and
not so structured that no one can move. That's not the way I work. Working with
children is different. They have to know that I'm the one who is giving the orders.
So we let the mothers and other people be a little quieter. I want their attention on
me, and kids get distracted more easily.

**J.K.:**    Do you have a full-time assistant, or do you use freelancers?

**N.B.:**    I have a full-time assistant, and I'll hire freelancers.

**J.K.:**    What do you pay freelance assistants in New York City?

**N.B.:**    The day rate is $175 to $200 per day.

**J.K.:**    Do you have any preference for male or female assistants? Does that ever
enter into it?

**N.B.:**    No. However, I've had only a couple of female assistants. There are certainly
more women assistants than ten years ago, judging from who comes in to see us.

**J.K.:**    Do you think strength plays a role in assisting?

**N.B.:**    Oh, definitely. I've had female assistants who could pick up anything a guy
could, while others can't lift anything, and I tell them to go to the gym. When you're
trying to load a van, you need some physical strength. You need people who can carry
the load.

**J.K.:**    When you go on location overnight, do you take assistants with you?

**N.B.:**    Yes, I take my full-time assistant and freelancers if they're needed.

**J.K.:**    Can you recall any disasters that were caused by assistants?

**N.B.:**    Not really. One time, the assistant plugged my flash meter's cord into the wall
socket instead of into the strobe's power supply and blew the thing right up. Luckily,
the Minolta meters are circuited so we only blew out half the circuits, and we had it
fixed. And I've had assistants knock things over or hit the tripod after it's all set up.
But we all do that; I've done that myself.

We've also had situations when the strobes were left back in the studio. Those
mistakes can be costly. Fortunately, we were able to have them delivered across town.
There were all kinds of excuses as to why the strobes weren't in the van. That's caused
by not thinking, their hearts not being in their job, and you can't be that way in pho-

tography. You've really got to like what you're doing, and assistants have got to put your interest ahead of theirs. All the good ones do that. Your job, your pictures, your interests are first and foremost when they're with you, and that's hard for people. You have to be natural at that. That's why some assistants are so good.

**J.K.:**   Do you think that most assistants who go to a photography school and then work as a full-time or freelance assistant for a couple of years make a successful transition to professional photography?

**N.B.:**   Art directors are always looking for that new creative talent. If you're creative and if you have a viewpoint or style, I think you can have a career in photography. But, I think it takes a long time. Maybe years ago it was easier. Now it's so costly to get into this business. With the overhead of running a studio, it's hard even for the people who are already in it. However, the ones who are really good and really want to be photographers will stay in it, but those who are even borderline aren't going to make it.

**J.K.:**   Do you have a Web site, and how do you get people to visit it?

**N.B.:**   We advertise our Web site by putting our address on every promo piece we mail out. We still do three or four promos a year. We also refer people to the site who want to review my work right away.

**J.K.:**   You've been involved with stock for many years. Do you have any advice for assistants regarding the stock-photo industry?

**N.B.:**   I think it's very difficult. The big companies want to own the image or copyright and pay the photographer relatively little. I think the big money in the print-stock business has been made. This is one reason I've moved into stock film footage, because it's a growth area.

**J.K.:**   Have you experienced any instances when the assistant performed above the call of duty?

**N.B.:**   I think most of mine have over the years, especially the ones who have stayed with me a long time. We've had to move and build studios and all kinds of things. Believe me, if they didn't have my interests as a priority, it would never have been done as smoothly. When I look back, I've been very, very lucky with the people I've had to work with.

# 19

# Getting the Most from Assisting

THE KNOWLEDGE AND SKILLS THAT THE PHOTOGRAPHER'S ASSISTANT NEEDS TO bring to the job have been presented on almost every page of this book. However, besides providing a service, assisting is the best opportunity to learn about all aspects of photography. However, little can be gained by passively observing what's happening on the set. Certainly, you'll learn which processing labs are best and the preferred types of equipment. But there's much more. To realize this potential takes a conscious and directed effort.

## BE A GOOD ASSISTANT

One of the most basic ways to learn is to work hard at being a good assistant. By concentrating on the photographer and the progress of the shot, you not only sense the photographer's needs, you begin to think like a professional photographer.

In addition, the repetition of basic photographic tasks is a tremendous benefit to learning. Eventually, you become proficient at the many photographic processes that, if not done correctly, can subtract from the final image. With consistency comes the ability to improvise and create new solutions.

It's important to remember that assisting isn't one continuous question-and-answer session. Rather than asking numerous questions, try to think of the answer yourself. If you remain perplexed, approach the photographer at a less hectic moment or at the end of the day.

Lighting is one of the most critical aspects of good photography. Here, much can be learned by following the evolution of the lighting arrangement and reviewing the resulting series of Polaroid prints. Since these prints are sequentially numbered, they can be examined later in the day.

On your way home from the job, reflect on the day's activities. This will make you a better assistant, and technical or creative aspects of the shot will more likely be remembered. Consider keeping a notebook. In it you can record information, such as filter combinations for mixed lighting conditions or perhaps a unique light-modifying device.

Review the discussion on freelance versus full-time assisting. Your decision, and how you market your services, can profoundly influence who you work for and the type of photography you encounter. Ultimately, this affects what you learn.

## KEEP SHOOTING

Assisting is so beneficial because you learn by doing. You'll find too that your own photography will progress at a faster rate if you continue to shoot frequently while assisting. This is partly because you can employ recently learned techniques, but you'll also become more critical of your own work and consequently become more demanding.

Unfortunately, your progress can be hindered by a lack of equipment or studio space. If this is the case, review the section on establishing your rates and consider trading your services for the use of these items. With time, you'll know which photographers might be receptive to your proposal, and they'll know they can trust you with their equipment. If they don't, they won't continue to hire you.

## THINK BEYOND PHOTOGRAPHY

When you're first learning photography and assisting, it's easy to get too focused on photography. I feel that even though you're a photographer first, its essential to keep an open mind—not only to grow artistically but also to take advantage of new opportunities.

1) Keep up with *business* and *current events* so that you can get the broader picture. You need to know where the world is going and how your industry fits into it. It's the only way to keep ahead of the curve.

   When I began assisting, most photographers had never thought of their images as "content." The Web as we know of it today was virtually nonexistent. And, who'd of thought that a couple of corporations could end up controlling so much of the fragmented stock industry in just a matter of five years?

2) Acquire *computer skills.* Although I'm best described as a landscape photographer and stock-agency owner, it's the computer that has really allowed me to do much of what I want, which is take pictures. That's because it has allowed me to market my photography using CD-ROMs. Without it, I'd surely be out of business, considering the stock industry today. Besides being necessary, computer skills have a much higher perceived value.

3) Develop graphic design skills. Because so much can be done on the Web, it pays to know the basics. The skills can not only save you money but can also make you a better photographer. The more design work I do, the more I learn why some photos are easier to work with than others.

4) Write down your ideas into what's traditionally called a *business plan* and edit it until you feel it can be presented to someone. This is a great way to consolidate your ideas, but even more importantly, the very process of writing opens you up to new ideas.

## TAKE ADVANTAGE OF WHAT'S AVAILABLE

Many photographers continue to learn and build valuable business relationships by being involved with *professional organizations*. Local branches of the ASMP and APA have regular meetings, which are open to nonmembers for a small charge. The meetings expose you to a variety of topics while introducing you to the local photographic community. Try volunteering.

Courses, workshops, and seminars are also available. These cover many aspects of photography, but don't limit yourself. Consider gaining more expertise on computers, multimedia, graphic design, and business. Finally, immerse yourself into the stream of *information* that's readily available, including books, professional magazines, Web sites, galleries, and equipment catalogs. Many of these resources are listed in the appendixes and provide a good starting point.

# 20

# My Transition into Being a Photographer

WHEN I BEGAN ASSISTING, ALL I REALLY KNEW WAS THAT I WANTED TO BE A nature photographer. In all honesty I didn't know how to go about it, so I just took it one step at a time. I'm going to let you know where I've succeeded and struggled and give you an idea of where I am today as a photographer and businessperson. Also, I'll relate where I think our company, Kieffer Nature Stock, is headed as well as the photo industry as a whole. In the process, I'll point out some of the things that influenced me and decisions that ultimately sent me down a particular path.

I began my photographic career in earnest in 1987, when I started assisting in Denver. Until then, I had had no formal photographic training. When the first edition of *The Photographer's Assistant* was published in 1992, I had spent only a year or so transitioning from assisting by doing assignment work and stock photography. As I look back, one point stands out—we really do have control of our dreams. However, to a large extent, our business decisions dictate our success or failure as much as do our photographic skills. I've thought about why my wife and I have made a pretty good go at this rather difficult profession, and in this chapter I've consolidated my thoughts about our process and our success.

## ME, A SALESMAN?

I always loved Colorado and the outdoors, so after college graduation I was determined to live there. Not being independently wealthy, I needed a job and money. Because of my science background, I ended up in the sales and marketing of research and medical equipment for the next seven years. Having just graduated with a master's degree in entomology, I must say I found it pretty hard to think of myself as a salesman, but the experience turned out to be a real blessing in disguise. I really don't believe that I'd have made it without some very practical business and sales experience.

I remember driving to work with the book *The Photographer's Marketplace,* but I really didn't have a clue as to how to start. Over the years, I had taken a bunch of photos, done some writing, and taken some photo courses. I had vague dreams of being a writer/photographer or perhaps the next Ansel Adams or David Muench. Just when I was beginning to seriously think of changing careers, I was laid off. It was 1986, and I was among the first wave let go in the downsizing craze of corporate restructuring. The local economy was also depressed, a far cry from what we have today.

So all of a sudden I was out of work, and I had to figure out how to do what I wanted. The first six months, I wrote some magazine articles that eventually got published. I was also smart enough to do the math and could see that combining writing and photography to make a living would be difficult. At this time, I concluded that some form of commercial photography might be a better alternative.

## ASSISTING SAVES THE DAY

I still hadn't figured out how to make a living, but I wasn't ready to give up. I was always dreaming of shooting a view camera, so I decided to buy one. Figuring it could be used for both commercial and landscape photography, I was convinced it was a logical decision. At that time, I had the good fortune to meet Erwin Bunzli, who sold Sinar view cameras. After listening to my ideas, he suggested I consider assisting. I had never heard of assisting, but it really seemed like a perfect opportunity—and it was. You learned by working with the better photographers and you got paid for it. My first assisting experience was with a food photographer, and it took about five minutes to realize I knew absolutely nothing about the real world of photography. But I could also see that I could ultimately make a living at it.

## TRY SOMETHING DIFFERENT

In the mid-to-late eighties, the local economy was so poor that many photographers were heading to greener pastures, which at the time was just about anywhere. When a photographer would announce his departure, I would often propose trading my assisting services, which were really moving services, for anything they wouldn't move. I ended up with a garage full of ladders, lighting equipment, backgrounds, lumber, and stands, which I still use and stumble over to this day.

I was very excited about the opportunities assisting could bring. However, after quite a bit of looking, I could hardly find a word about assistants in photo magazines or books. I had always been interested in combining writing and photography, and it struck me that by creating a book about assisting I could use my interest to produce something unique. While assisting, I took considerable notes, which eventually became the first edition of *The Photographer's Assistant*. Because there was (and is) so little written about the subject, the book found its audience.

## NETWORKING

There's a saying that the best jobs never make it into the Sunday want ads. That's because they are filled through some form of business or personal relationship—in other words, through networking. When the new workers arrive for work on their first day, they further benefit through networking at the company. This ranges from building friendships to receiving medical benefits.

We as photographers and assistants are basically small-business owners and entrepreneurs. For the most part, we must do everything ourselves, and believe me it can get old. Unfortunately, even in today's fast-paced times, relationships or "connections" tend to be developed over time. One of the best ways to begin building a network is by going to professional meetings, such as those hosted by the American Society of Media Photographers (ASMP) or Advertising Photographers of America (APA). Try volunteering your help as a way to become comfortable with the group.

Several years ago, I was attending the annual ASMP party, and I was speaking to someone with whom I'd assisted. I always found him to be pretty smart and a very nice person. To make a short story shorter, we were talking about the digital future that has now arrived in full force. The discussion took place before hardly anyone even had a CD-ROM drive and before you could actually get "flamed" for trying to sell something on the Web—imagine that. Even though he remained quite calm and collected, I left the meeting feeling he had grabbed me by the shoulders and shaken me, saying, "This world is going digital, and opportunity is there for the taking!"

That evening I told my wife Beth that we had to get into digital full time. We purchased a new Mac and multimedia-development software within about three months. Where would I be now if I spent most of my time sheltered at home or in the studio instead of networking? I'd be out of business.

Here are three principles of networking that worked for me:

1) Network with *noncompetitive* photographers. Let's face it, if you're a studio shooter and you know mostly studio shooters, they aren't likely to pass any work your way or give tips about a potential client. A lot of people still ask for a referral.

2) When you think of approaching someone with an idea or bartering, think of what you can bring to the table so that both of you benefit. Take chances.

3) Network with *nonphotographic organizations.* Most of your business is not going to come via other photographers. Consider networking and socializing with local marketing and advertising groups. It would be far better to get your name in an art director's club newsletter than the local ASMP newsletter. If you have a specialization such as architecture, related trade associations and their newsletters are a good networking source.

## STOCK PHOTOGRAPHY: TIMING WAS EVERYTHING

I'm discussing stock photography because it's how I make most of my income and because, whether you shoot stock or not, your photography business will feel its effects. Stock photography is an integral part of the photo industry and can be a substantial part of a photographer's business. The term *stock photo* refers to a photo that already exists, as opposed to a photo produced on assignment for a predetermined use. Today, most successful stock photos are still produced and financed up front by the photographer and then offered to the marketplace. Traditionally, a photographer retains copyright ownership and *usage rights* are sold. The more a photo is used, the more is charged for usage rights. With *royalty-free photography,* the image is in the form of a digital file, and the purchaser can use the photo for just about anything, although some specific uses are restricted.

When I was assisting in the late 1980s, stock photography was relatively new and offered great opportunity. It seemed like a perfect match for me because little opportunity existed to get an assignment to shoot landscape photography. Back then, I would regularly get referrals just because large-format landscape photography was hard to come by. I learned that assignment photographers would send their clients my way not just because they knew what I shot, but because they knew I had no interest in stealing their clients. This was one of my first opportunities to benefit from networking with fellow, but noncompetitive photographers.

The success or direction of a business is rarely based on a single decision. Here are some of the factors that I weighed, and the decisions I came to in building my company. Remember, the choices I made weren't necessarily the only viable options, but they made sense to me, at that point in my life, and under that era's economy. Were I starting out today, I would make different choices.

Although stock offered opportunity, I felt it wouldn't take long to saturate the market, particularly in nature. Besides the personal satisfaction, this was one reason I kept shooting with the view camera—to offer something better and different. Also, I always shot with the idea that it was better to come back from a shooting trip with a handful of really good images than with many mediocre or average shots.

I also photographed in my own backyard, Colorado, which let me sell to the *local market*. Selling locally is easier than trying to branch out into the national market. While only a handful of national magazines will buy my kind of photography, seven hundred to a thousand potential clients exist in Colorado—including art directors, graphic designers, ad agencies, and larger companies with in-house marketing departments. I often run into local, aspiring photographers who like to travel more than shoot, and they make the big mistake of shooting everywhere *but* Colorado. Today, our company's strength is still Colorado. However, we've broadened ourselves in order to sell the image of Colorado and the West to a national market.

When I began, I thought it was necessary to work at building a strong niche or area of specialization that would provide a foundation to build on. It can be helpful to try to define what you do in a phrase or a couple of sentences. For instance, I started with "large-format landscapes of the American West." Defining yourself is even more important when competing with today's big stock agencies.

It is smart business to look for an unfilled niche. When I started shooting, a Colorado landscape photographer was already shooting for the calendar and coffee-table-book market. It seemed like the perfect time to take a different direction—the growing field of commercial stock photography. Now we've expanded our coverage beyond landscape to include people in nature. We're using CD-ROM and Web technology to grow.

I looked to stock as a long-term commitment and envisioned what I'd have to show for twenty to thirty years of work and investment. I hope to have a cohesive body of work that is timeless and valuable. If you shoot just what the stock agencies want, such as model-released people, it will have more value in the near term but may have little value in ten years—little value to you either as stock or in defining you as an artist. I ask myself, will anyone want to look at this stuff in ten years?

The time is quickly coming when most stock submissions will be digital. Even so-called high-res files are often of only fair quality, but they seem to be acceptable. Large-format film is expensive to scan; when scanned, it becomes no different from anything else. Will 4″ × 5″ film be of any value to stock photography in the years to come?

Today, with a family and changes coming faster than ever, I think short- and medium-term. However, retaining *copyright ownership* of all my work is a long-term commitment. And I'm still always looking for new opportunities.

## THE STOCK-PHOTO INDUSTRY AND YOU

The stock-photo industry has gone through tremendous change since the mid-1990s. I'd like to provide a little background to help you decide how much money and effort you might want to put into stock. Like other industries, there has been a consolidation of many small, private agencies into relatively few publicly held companies. The climate is perceived as having plenty of photographers and relatively few agencies. Hence, agencies can be pretty selective and can write contracts asking for a greater percentage of sales and more exclusivity regarding your photos. It's believed that photographers are in no position to bargain.

The bigger agencies are trying to push everything onto the Web. It should be quite successful for these big companies, but I'm not sure if the individual will prosper on the Web. Directing photo buyers to your site and getting them to buy in sufficient numbers might well prove difficult.

I would seriously consider how rational it is to place too much of an investment in stock photography, considering the current and predicted business climate. It has become a game of big players, and it may be too late to get into the game. There's always opportunity, but reconsider some of what I said regarding niches and long-term commitment. I think five to seven years is a minimum start-up period before any money can be made. In all honesty, a financial stock mutual fund will probably perform much better and with very little risk and effort on your part.

## WHERE I AM AT THE START OF THE TWENTY-FIRST CENTURY

Kieffer Nature Stock consists of my wife Beth, an occasional assistant, and me. We sell my photography, which is best defined as large-format landscapes of the American West. We've expanded by representing other photographers in related areas such as lifestyles, recreation, and wildlife. A few years ago, we also began producing portfolios and stock-photo catalogs on CD-ROM and on the Web *(www.kieffernaturestock.com, e-mail John@kieffernaturestock.com)*. These are for stock photographers, stock agencies, and commercial photographers. We also have two daughters, eight and twelve years old, who've cleaned a lot of film holders and have spent more than enough time patiently waiting for me to finish up a shot.

## Model Release

In consideration of _____ Dollars ($_____), and other valuable considera-
tion, receipt of which is acknowledged, I, _____
_____ (print Model's name) do hereby give _____
_____ (the Photographer), his or her assigns, licensees, successors in interest, legal representatives, and heirs the irrevocable right to use my name (or any fictional
name), picture, portrait, or photograph in all forms and in all media and in all manners,
without any restriction as to changes or alterations (including but not limited to composite or distorted representations or derivative works made in any medium) for advertising, trade, promotion, exhibition, or any other lawful purposes, and I waive any right
to inspect or approve the photograph(s) or finished version(s) incorporating the photo-
graph(s), including written copy that may be created and appear in connection there-
with. I hereby release and agree to hold harmless the Photographer, his or her assigns,
licensees, successors in interest, legal representatives and heirs from any liability by
virtue of any blurring, distortion, alteration, optical illusion, or use in composite form
whether intentional or otherwise, that may occur or be produced in the taking of the photographs, or in any processing tending toward the completion of the finished product,
unless it can be shown that they and the publication thereof were maliciously caused,
produced, and published solely for the purpose of subjecting me to conspicuous
ridicule, scandal, reproach, scorn, and indignity. I agree that the Photographer owns the
copyright in these photographs and I hereby waive any claims I may have based on any
usage of the photographs or works derived therefrom, including but not limited to claims
for either invasion of privacy or libel. I am of full age* and competent to sign this release.
I agree that this release shall be binding on me, my legal representatives, heirs, and
assigns. I have read this release and am fully familiar with its contents.

Witness: _____          Signed: _____
                                                           Model

Address: _____          Address: _____


                                           Date: _____, 20____

---

**━━━ Consent (if applicable) ━━━**

I am the parent or guardian of the minor named above and have the legal authority to exe-
cute the above release. I approve the foregoing and waive any rights in the premises.


Witness: _____          Signed: _____
                                                        Parent or Guardian

Address: _____          Address: _____


                                           Date: _____, 20____


*Delete this sentence if the subject is a minor. The parent or guardian must then sign the consent.

# A

# Professional Associations

ADVERTISING PHOTOGRAPHERS OF AMERICA (APA NATIONAL)
P.O. Box 1647
Vencice, CA 90292
800-272-6264
*www.apanational.org*

The national office and its Web site can provide information on the regional chapters in Atlanta, Los Angeles, Milwaukee, New York, and San Francisco. Membership is open to photographic assistants and an assistants directory is published for larger cities.

ADVERTISING PHOTOGRAPHERS OF NEW YORK (APNY)
27 West 20th Street, Suite 601
New York, NY 10011
212-807-0399
*www.apany.com*

This organization was formed by a group of independent photographers in 1981, with offices in the heart of New York's photo district. It was formerly known as Advertising Photographers of America—New York (APANY). They have regular programs, but most importantly APNY works with assistants. There is a very complete on-line *Assistant List* and an *Assistant Photographer Program*.

AMERICAN SOCIETY OF MEDIA PHOTOGRAPHERS (ASMP)
150 North Second Street
Philadelphia, PA 19106
215-451-2767
*www.asmp.org*
E-mail: *info@asmp.org*

ASMP is an invaluable resource. It is the largest organization of professional photographers and is probably the best to get involved with. ASMP was formed in 1944 and has forty chapters. Therefore, outside the larger markets like New York, Los Angeles, and Chicago, it's likely to be one of the few sources of professional information. Contact the national office to locate regional chapters. Membership is open to assistants and students. The national office publishes the *Bulletin* newsletter. Local chapters usually publish an assistants list and a newsletter and have their own Web sites. Visit the ASMP national Web site and then go to the "Site Map" to find the local chapters.

PROFESSIONAL PHOTOGRAPHERS OF AMERICA, INC. (PPA)
229 Peachtree Street NE, Suite 2200
Atlanta, GA 30303-1608
404-522-8600 and 800-786-6277
*www.ppa.com*

Contact the national office for the membership list of your region. *Professional Photographer (www.ppmag.com)* is the official magazine of the PPA. The group is associated with the PPA International School of Photography.

PROFESSIONAL PHOTOGRAPHERS OF CANADA, INC.
Web address: *www.ppoc.ca*

Go to the organization's Web site to find links to other Canadian photographic organizations.

# B

# Creative Directories— Sourcebooks —Web Sites

AMERICAN SOCIETY OF MEDIA PHOTOGRAPHERS (ASMP)
150 North Second Street
Philadelphia, PA 19106
215-451-2767
*www.asmp.org*
E-mail: *info@asmp.org*
ASMP is producing its own stock photography catalog, due out January 2001.

AMERICAN SHOWCASE PHOTOGRAPHY
915 Broadway, 14th Floor
New York, NY 10010
800-894-7469
212-673-6600
*www.showcase.com*

THE ALTERNATIVE PICK
Storm Music Entertainment, Inc.
1133 Broadway, Suite 1408
New York, NY 10010
212-675-4176; Fax: 212-675-4936
*www.altpick.com*
Although specifically geared for the music industry, it includes photographers.

BLACK BOOK A.R. 100 (FOR ANNUAL REPORTS)
10 Astor Place, 10th Floor
New York, NY 10003
212-539-9800 and 800-841-1246; Fax: 212-539-9801
*www.blackbook.com*
The publication is for commercial photographers looking for corporate Annual Report work. Such work is often for location photographers.

THE BLACK BOOK
Black Book Marketing Group
10 Astor Place, 6th Floor
New York, NY 10003
Ph: 212-539-9800 and 800-841-1246
*www.blackbook.com*
The publication is perhaps the most prestigious source directory for photographers looking to work with advertising agencies.

CALIFORNIA IMAGE
Serbin Communications
511 Olive Street
Santa Barbara, CA 93101
805-963-0439; Fax: 805-965-0496
*www.serbin.com*
The sourcebook is distributed primarily in California.

THE CHICAGO CREATIVE DIRECTORY
333 North Michigan Avenue, Suite 810
Chicago, IL 60601
312-236-7337
*www.creativedir.com*
The market here is Chicago.

CREATIVE SOURCEBOOK
Sumner Communications, Inc
4085 Chain Bridge Road, Suite 201
Fairfax, VA 22030
800-800-9413; Fax: 703-385-5607
The sourcebook is nationally distributed to advertising agencies and corporations.

DIRECT STOCK
10 East 21st Street, 14th Floor
New York, NY 10010
212-979-6560
*Direct Stock* is a stock photography catalog in which photographers buy space to advertise their stock photos. Many stock photographers also shoot commercial assignments and use assistants.

ELYSE WEISSBERG CREATIVE CONSULTANT
212-227-7272
*www.elyserep.com*
Elyse is a creative consultant for photographers. Visit her Web site to find more up-to-date information on creative sourcebooks.

KLIK SHOWCASE PHOTOGRAPHY
American Showcase Photography
915 Broadway, 14th Floor
New York, NY 10010
800-894-7469 and 212-673-6600; Fax: 212-673-9795
*www.klikphoto.com*
The directory is for commercial photographers.

NEW YORK GOLD
10 East 21st Street
New York, NY 10010
Ph: 212-254-1000; Fax: 212-254-1004
The publication is distributed to the New York metro area and the northeast.

PDN'S PHOTO SOURCE
1515 Broadway, 11th Floor
New York, NY 10036
212-536-5196
*www.pdnonline.com*
*Photo Source* is a printed resource directory produced by PhotoDistrict News for commercial photographers, especially location photographers. It provides a national listing of photographic and creative services. Call to be placed on their assistants list. The Web site for *Photo District News* magazine, listed above, is designed for professional, commercial photographers and features photographers and much other useful information.

PHOTOSERVE
920 Broadway, Room 701
New York, NY 10010
212-375-1000
*www.photoserve.com*
The group provides a group Web site for commercial photographers.

SAN DIEGO CREATIVE DIRECTORY
Blue Book Publishers
7807 Girard Ave., Suite 200
LaJolla, CA 92307
619-454-9665; Fax: 619-454-8032
*www.sdcreative.com*
The directory is distributed in the San Diego area.

SINGLE IMAGE MAGAZINE OF ART AND ARTICLES
The Workbook
940 North Highland Avenue
Los Angeles, CA 90038
800-547-2688
The publication is printed three times per year.

WORKBOOK
940 North Highland Avenue
Los Angeles, CA 90038
800-547-2688
*www.workbook.com*
*Workbook* is nationally distributed to advertising agencies and corporations.

# C

# Photographic Equipment and Catalogs

ADOBE SOFTWARE
*www.adobe.com*
Makers of Photoshop software, the industry standard for photo reotuching and manipulation. Also: Adobe Illustrator, GoLive, InDesign, and LiveMotion.

ADORAMA CAMERA
42 West 18th Street
New York, NY 10011
800-223-2500 and 212-675-6789
*www.adoramacamera.com*
Large photo equipment retail store with catalog—everything for the professional.

B & H PHOTO AND VIDEO
420 Ninth Avenue
New York, NY 10001
800-947-9957 and 212-444-6657
*www.bhphotovideo.com*
Large photo equipment retail store with catalog—everything for the professional

BESELER PHOTO MARKETING CO.
1600 Lower Road
Linden, NJ 07636
Darkroom equipment, including enlargers.

BOGEN PHOTO CORPORATION
565 East Crescent Avenue
Ramsey, NJ 07446-0506
201-818-9500
*www.bogenphoto.com*
E-mail: *info@bogenphoto.com*
Distributes Bogen, Manfrotto & Gitzo tripods and stands, Gossen light meters, Lightform light control panels, Elinchrome lighting, and Metz on-camera flash units.

CALUMET PHOTOGRAPHIC, INC.
890 Supreme Drive
Bensenville, IL 60106
888-888-9083
*www.calumetphoto.com*
An excellent general-purpose catalog directed to the professional photographer. Features all camera formats, electronic flash systems, lighting hardware, darkroom supplies, and many related accessories.

CANON USA, INC.
One Canon Plaza
Lake Success, NY 11042
800-OKCANON and 516-328-5000
*www.usa.canon.com*
Canon 35mm SLR camera and lenses.

THE CHIMERA COMPANY
1812 Valtec Lane
Boulder, CO 80301
888-444-1812
*www.chimeralighting.com*
Excellent light-modifying devices, such as light banks and soft boxes.

DYNA-LITE
1050 Commerce Ave.
Union, NJ 07083
800-722-6638 and 908-687-8800
*www.dynalite.com*
Strobe lighting equipment and accessories. Known for lots of power with little weight.

FOTEK
PO Box 10028
Rochester, NY 14610
716-288-8526
*www.fotekphoto.com*
Image presentation and portfolio materials for the professional, including black cardboard mats for transparencies.

FUJI FILM
800-800-FUJI
*www.fujifilm.com*
Manufacturer of film and cameras.


GITZO TRIPODS
*www.gitzo.com*
The tripod to judge all other tripods by, distributed by Bogen Photo.


HASSELBLAD USA
10 Madison Road
Fairfield, NJ 07006
973-227-7320
*www.hasselbladusa.com*
Medium-format cameras. The most commonly encountered by assistants.


KODAK
343 State Street
Rochester, NY 14650-0811
800-242-2424 and 716-254-1300
*www.kodak.com*
Photographic films, papers, and chemicals.


LIGHT IMPRESSIONS CORPORATION
PO Box 940
Rochester, NY 14603
800-828-6216
*www.lightimpressionsdirect.com*
Excellent selection of portfolio-related materials, such as presentation boards and cases. Also has a photography book catalog containing a large and diverse selection.


LIGHTWARE, INC.
1329 West Byers Place
Denver, CO 80223
303-744-0202
*www.lightwareinc.com*
Cases for every kind of photographic equipment.

LOWEL-LIGHT MANUFACTURING, INC.
140 58th Street
Brooklyn, NY 11220
718-921-0600
E-mail: *info@lowel.com*
Tungsten photographic lighting equipment.


MAMIYA AMERICA CORPORATION
8 Westchester Plaza
Elmsford, NY 10523
800- 321-2205; 914-347-3300
*www.mamiya.com*
E-mail: *info@mamiya.com*
Mamiya medium-format cameras and Toyo view cameras.


MATTHEWS STUDIO EQUIPMENT
2405 Empire Ave.
Burbank, CA 91504
818-843-6715
Vast array of stands and studio hardware related to lighting.


MEGAVISION
888-324-2580
*www.mega-vision.com*
Digital camera backs.


METZ FLASH
See: Bogen Photo Corporation


MINOLTA CORPORATION
101 Williams Drive
Ramsey, NJ 07446
201-825-4000
*www.minoltausa.com*
Minolta 35mm SLR cameras and light meters.

NIKON, INC.
623 Stewart Avenue
Garden City, NY 11530
Photo Equipment: 800-645-6687
Digital Equipment: 800-645-6689
*www.nikonusa.com*
Nikon 35mm SLR cameras, digital cameras, lenses, and on-camera flash units.

NPC PHOTO DIVISION
1238 Chestnut Street
Newton Upper Falls, MA 02464
617-969-4522
*www.npcphoto.com*
Polaroid instant film backs for 35mm and medium-format cameras.

PENTAX CORPORATION
35 Inverness Drive East
Englewood, CO 80112
303-799-8000
*www.pentaxusa.com*
Pentax 35mm and medium-format SLR cameras.

PHASE ONE
888-PHASE-ONE
*www.phaseone.com*
Digital backs for medium- and large-format cameras.

PHOTOFLEX, INC
33 Ecinal Street
Santa Cruz, CA 95060
800-486-2674
*www.photoflex.com*
Lighting, light-modifying devices, and stands, including soft boxes and reflector panels.

POLAROID CORPORATION
575 Technology Square
Cambridge, MA 02139
800-225-1618 and 617-577-2000
*www.polaroid.com*
Polaroid instant film and film holders. A useful Web site.


QUANTUM INSTRUMENTS
1075 Stewart Ave.
Garden City, NY 11530
516-222-6000
*www.qtm.com*
Rechargeable battery packs, electronic flash units, and flash meters.


SEKONIC LIGHT METERS
8 Winchester Plaza
Elmsford, NY 10523
914-347-3300
*www.sekonic.com*
Sekonic light meters.


THE SET SHOP
36 West 20th Street
New York, NY 10010
212-255-3500
*www.setshop.com*
E-mail: *info@setshop.com*
Primarily products for the studio, including background materials and stands. But it also
has many hard-to-find supplies, like adhesives, props, and portfolio-related materials.


SINAR BRON IMAGING
17 Progress Street
Edison, NJ 08820
800-456-0203 and 908-754-5800
*www.sinarbron.com*
E-mail: *info@sinarbron.com*
Sinar view cameras, Sinar/Leaf digital backs, BronColor electronic flash equipment,
Foba studio stands.

SPEEDOTRON CORP.
310 South Racine Avenue
Chicago, IL 60607
312-421-4050
*www.speedotron.com*
Speedotron electronic flash equipment. Very popular with studio photographers.


TRENGOVE STUDIO, INC.
247 West 30 th Street
New York, NY 10001
800-366-2857
*www.trengovestudios.com*
Special-effects materials, such as artificial ice, custom replicas, and steam chips.


UNIQUE PHOTO
11 Vreeland Road
Florham Park, NJ 07932-0979
800-631-0300 and 973-377-5555
*www.uniquephoto.com*
Photography supplies.


THE F.J. WESTCOTT COMPANY
1447 Summit Street, PO Box 1596
Toledo, OH 43603
419-243-7311
Distributes a large range of light-modifying devices, including soft boxes.


WOLF CAMERA AND VIDEO
150 14th Street, NW
Atlanta, GA 30318
800-289-WOLF
*www.wolfcamera.com*
A broad selection of equipment for the professional photographer, including view cameras, electronic flash, and lighting accessories.

# D

# Periodicals

APERTURE
Aperture Foundation
20 East 23rd Street
New York, NY 10010
*www.aperture.com*
Features mostly finc-art photography.

ASMP BULLETIN
ASMP
150 North Second Street
Philadelphia, PA 19106
215-451-2767
*www.asmp.org*
The national publication for the American Society of Media Photographers.

B & W
Black & White Magazine
Picturama Publications
1789 Lyn Road
Amoyo Grande, CA 93420
805-474-6633
Covers fine-art photography and collecting, not technique.

DIGITAL CAMERA MAGAZINE
4050 Sunset Lane
Shingle Springs, CA 95682
*www.photopoint.com/dcm*
Technological and consumer information for digital photo equipment, especially smaller formats versus digital backs.

DIGITAL IMAGING
Cygnus Business Media
445 Broad Hollow Road
Melville, NY 11747
516-845-2700
*www.digitalimagingmag.com*
Focuses on all aspects of digital photography.

DIGITAL PHOTOGRAPHER
4800 Market Street
Ventura, CA 93003
805-644-3824
Technological and consumer information for digital imagery and products, especially concerning smaller formats.

NATURE PHOTOGRAPHER
PO Box 690518
Quincy, MA 02269
617-847-0091
A showcase for nature photography and technique.

OUTDOOR PHOTOGRAPHER
Werner Publishing Company
12121 Wilshire Blvd., 12th Floor
Los Angeles, CA 90025
*www.outdoorphotographer.com*
A magazine for landscape, travel, and wildlife photographic techniques, but no professional business information.

PC PHOTO
12121Wilshire Blvd., Suite 1200
Los Angeles, CA 90025
310-820-1500
*www.pcphotomag.com*

PHOTO DISTRICT NEWS
770 Broadway, 7th Floor
New York, NY 10003
646-654-5500
*www.pdnonline.com*
The *best periodical* for most professional photographers. Provides thorough coverage of many subjects related to professional photography, including business, marketing, and legal issues, plus trends in photographic styles and technology. Also, has classified ads for assistants. *PDN* can be found at better magazine stores and pro photo labs.

PHOTO ELECTRONIC IMAGING (PEI)
229 Peachtree Street NE, Suite 2200
International Tower
Atlanta, GA 30303
404-522-8600
*www.peimag.com*
A publication for commercial photographers that stresses the digital and business aspects of professional photography.

THE PHOTOGRAPHER'S MARKET
Writer's Digest Books
1507 Dana Ave.
Cincinnati, OH 45207
This book is published yearly and lists magazines, book publishers, stock agencies, and calendar publishers that buy photographs.

PHOTO LIFE
Canada's Photo Magazine
One Dundas Street West, Suite 2500
PO Box 84
Toronto, Ontario M5G123
800-461-7468
*www.photolife.com*

PHOTO TECHNIQUES USA
Preston Publication
6600 West Touby
Niles, IL 60714
A general-purpose photography magazine.

PETERSEN'S PHOTOGRAPHIC MAGAZINE
6420 Wilshire Blvd., 18th Floor
Los Angeles, CA 90048
A general-purpose magazine directed to the amateur photographer.

POPULAR PHOTOGRAPHY
1633 Broadway
New York, NY 10019
A widely circulated magazine for the amateur photographer.

PROFESSIONAL PHOTOGRAPHER
Professional Photographers of America Publications (PPA)
800-786-6277
*www.ppmag.com*
Presents business and technical subjects for professional photographers, especially those who specialize in wedding and portraiture. The official journal of the Professional Photographers of America, which also has a large educational facilty.

STUDIO PHOTOGRAPHY & DESIGN
Cygnus Business Media
445 Broad Hollow Road
Melville, NY 11747
516-845-2700
*www.spdonline.com*
Was directed primarily to wedding and portrait photographers, but has expanded to cover the digital aspects of photography.

TEST
Polaroid Corporation
575 Technology Square 2M
Cambridge, MA 02139-9878
800-225-1618
*www.polaroid.com*
*Test* is published by Polaroid Corporation in order to provide technical information on its film and equipment. Useful Web site.

VIEW CAMERA MAGAZINE
Steve Simmons Inc.
1400 S Street, Suite 200
Sacramento, CA 95814
916-441-2557

# Glossary

**Ambient light**—In photography, it refers to the light that is already present or available on the site. This might be sunlight or the uncontrolled light flooding a factory. The photographer brings artificial light.

**Angle of incidence law**—This states that the angle of incidence equals the angle of reflectance. Therefore, light striking a surface at a given angle is reflected from that surface at the same angle, similar to a banked billiard ball.

**Artificial light**—Usually refers to a light source such as tungsten or electronic flash that is supplied, positioned, and controlled by the photographer.

**ASMP**—American Society of Media Photographers. Generally, the best photography organization for professionals and assistants. *www.asmp.org*

**Available light**—The light that already exists in the scene to be photographed. A photograph made with available light implies that the photographer didn't supply professional lighting equipment. Also called ambient light.

**Background material**—An almost endless variety of materials that can be used as a background or backdrop for the subject.

**Back light**—A light source that's positioned behind the subject and points toward the camera. The subject is referred to as back lit.

**Bellows**—The flexible and lightproof part of the view camera connecting the front standard to the rear standard. Most often, a bellows is accordion shaped. A bellows for a wide-angle lens is also called a "bag" bellows. It's designed to allow the lens to be positioned very close to the film plane.

**Book**—Slang for a portfolio. You will show your "book" to a photographer.

**Booking**—A confirmed assisting job for a specific date. You can "book" an assisting job.

**Boom**—A horizontal crossbar placed on top of a stand, used to position lights and other objects over the set.

**Burn**—Usually in reference to "burning" a CD-ROM to store or archive files. The most common software is Toast. When making a black-and-white print, "burning" during the exposure process will darken that area of the print. It's the opposite of "dodging."

**C-41**—The chemical process used to develop color-negative film.

**Camera movements**—The movements that can be performed by a view camera to control perspective and the plane of sharp focus. The movements are rise, fall, swing, tilt, and shift.

**Changing room**—A lightproof room used to load and unload sheet-film holders.

**Changing bag**—A lightproof bag into which the hands can be inserted. It's most likely used to load or unload sheet-film holders while on location. The better ones are changing tents.

**Capture**—Used to describe making an exposure with a digital camera. The camera captures the image.

**Chrome**—A term referring to color-transparency film.

**Color-compensating filters**—Used to achieve precise color rendition by compensating for deficiencies in the color quality from a light source, the film, or reciprocity failure. Available in the primary colors blue, green, and red and in the secondary colors cyan, yellow, and magenta. They're usually a gelatin-type filter and are held in a filter frame.

**Color temperature**—A way of quantitatively describing the color of light. Midday sun, electronic flash, and HMI lights have a color temperature of about 5500 degrees Kelvin and is bluish (cool) in color. Light at dawn, dusk, and that produced from tungsten lighting is approximately 3300 degrees Kelvin and is yellow (warm) in color.

**Compendium**—A bellows-shaped lens shade used primarily on large-format lenses.

**Copyright**—Refers to the ownership of creative material, such as a photograph. When a photographer creates a photo, the photographer owns the copyright to it. When the photographer registers that photo with the U.S. Copyright Office, greater protection is afforded. When a photographer signs a contract with the dreaded words, "Work for Hire," the photographer is giving away copyright ownership. It is a terrible mistake.

**Creative directories**—Books published on a local or national level to advertise a photographer's services. Also referred to as sourcebooks and photography annuals. Most creative directories have associated Web sites.

**Cropping tools**—A pair of L-shaped pieces of black cardboard used to crop Polaroid prints and color transparencies.

**Dark cloth**—See focusing cloth.

**Dark slide**—The removable slide utilized in sheet-film holders and medium-format film magazines. It's designed to protect the film from unwanted light when the film holder or magazine is not attached to the camera.

**Day rate**—The base amount a photographer, stylist, or assistant charges for a day's services.

**Diffuse light**—The kind of light produced by a source having a large area, such as an overcast day or a soft box. Diffuse light doesn't produce sharp shadows and is thought of as having a soft quality. It's the opposite of specular light.

**Diffusion material**—A variety of translucent, white materials used to make a specular light source more diffuse.

**E-6**—The chemical process used to develop color-transparency films, other than Kodachrome.

**Electronic flash**—The brief but brilliant flash of daylight-balanced light produced by electronic flash systems. Also called a strobe.

**Fill card**—A lighting tool used to reflect light back onto the set. Although most often made from white cardboard, the cards' size and shape vary widely. Also referred to as reflector or card.

**Flag**—A light-modifying device, usually consisting of a piece of black cardboard. Positioned to eliminate lens flare or control a light source.

**Flash head**—The part of the electronic flash system that consists of the flash tube, modeling light, and cooling fan. It's connected to a power supply by a long cable.

**Flash meter**—A kind of light meter capable of measuring the brief duration of a flash of light.

**Flash tube**—The portion of a flash head that produces the flash of light.

**Focusing cloth**—A black piece of cloth used with view cameras to aid in viewing the ground glass. Also called a dark cloth.

**Freelance**—A photographer, stylist, or assistant who is an independent contractor and solicits work from a variety of sources.

**Full time**—In the context of this book, an assistant who's a full-time employee for one photographer or studio.

**Gaffers tape**—A specialized photographic tape, usually black in color and two inches wide. It's very strong yet doesn't leave a gummy residue when removed from photographic equipment.

**Ground glass**—The viewing screen found on a view camera. It is often protected by a fresnel lens.

**HMI lights**—Produce a continuous, daylight-balanced light using a metal halogen lamp. Popular in digital-photography studios.

**Hot lights**—Common term for tungsten or quartz lights, which produce considerable heat compared to electronic flash.

**Inverse square law**—A law of physics stating that the intensity of illumination is inversely proportional to the square of the distance between the light and subject. In other words, if the distance from the subject to the light is doubled, the illumination is decreased to one-fourth. Therefore, altering a light's distance is an effective means of adjusting the illumination.

**JPEG (pronounced: jay-peg)**—A common file format, used especially when you want to compress or reduce the file size, such as with Web use.

**Key light**—See main light.

**Kodak Photo CD**—An economical way to have film scanned and archived to CD-ROM, especially for 35mm slides. Visit a local photo lab.

**Layout**—A sketch or drawing representing what's to be produced on film or as a digital file.

**Live video**—The ability to view, on the computer monitor in real time, what the camera is seeing. A feature on some digital cameras and digital backs.

**Loupe**—Common abbreviation for a focusing loupe or magnifying loupe. Aids in focusing the view camera and viewing color transparencies.

**Main light**—The principal light source used in the photograph. Also called key light.

**Modeling light**—A low-wattage tungsten lamp built into a flash head. It's used to judge the approximate effect of the flash.

**Model release**—A form granting the photographer the right to use the photographs. It should be signed by the model shortly after the shooting session.

**Natural light**—Refers to the light produced by the sun.

**Notch code**—The notches found along one edge of sheet film. Allows the film type and emulsion side to be identified in the dark.

**Open-up**—To increase the size of the lens aperture, from f22 to f5.6 for example. The opposite is to stop-down the lens.

**Perspective**—The apparent size and depth of objects within an image. Perspective is the quality that creates the illusion of three dimensions in a two-dimensional photograph. Some aspects of perspective can be controlled through the use of the view-camera movements.

**Photoshop**—The industry standard photo-manipulation software, manufactured by Adobe. If a photo is digitally altered, it's often referred to as being "Photoshopped." Photoshop is also a file format with the suffix ".PSD."

**Plane of sharp focus**—That area of the scene which is most sharply focused. The placement of the plane of sharp focus can be controlled by proper use of the view-camera movements.

**Polaroid instant film**—A type of film that produces an instant print used to check focus, lighting, and composition. Polaroid instant film can be used with 35mm SLR, medium-format, and view cameras. Often referred to as a proof print.

**Pop**—Refers to the sound produced when a flash head produces a flash. An exposure may require multiple pops to produce sufficient light.

**Power supply**—A major component of electronic flash systems. A large capacitor or rechargeable battery that provides energy to produce the flash of light. Power supplies are rated in watt-seconds.

**Proofing**—Refers to using Polaroid instant film to check lighting, exposure, and composition.

**Pull**—To overexpose the film and then compensate by giving the film less-than-normal development.

**Push**—To underexpose the film and then compensate by giving the film greater or longer development than normal.

**Resolution**—Usually used in a digital context and defined in pixels per inch or dots per inch (ppi/dpi). A scan with a resolution of 72 ppi is standard for monitors, whereas a resolution of 300 ppi is standard for many four-color print jobs.

**Roll film**—Film that comes in a roll. Commonly used in 35mm SLR and medium-format cameras.

**Royalty-free photograph**—A purchased photo (clip art) that can be used for almost anything without paying additional fees. It's supplied as a digital file on CD-ROM or downloaded from the Web.

**Scan**—The digital file after a piece of film or flat art has been scanned.

**Scanner**—An electronic device used to convert film or flat art to a digital file so that it can be used by a computer. Today, virtually all film is ultimately scanned, whether it's to be used for print advertising, multimedia, or prints. Drum scanners produce the highest-quality scans, whereas flatbed scanners are low quality.

**Scheimpflug rule**—A law that states that to obtain overall sharp focus, the plane of the subject, the plane of the lensboard, and the plane of the film must either be parallel to each other or meet at a common point. Applies to view cameras and their movements.

**Sheet film**—Film that is cut into flat sheets, commonly measuring 4″ × 5″ and 8″ × 10″.

**Single lens reflex (SLR)**—A camera in which the image formed by the lens is reflected onto the viewing screen by a mirror. Most 35mm and medium-format cameras are of this design.

**Soft box**—A light-modifying device in which light passes through a large piece of diffusion material, thereby producing a diffuse light. Also referred to as a soff box or light bank.

**Specular light**—The kind of light that emanates from a specific point, such as a bare light bulb. It produces very distinct shadows. The opposite is diffuse light.

**Still life**—A type of photography involving the arrangement of objects into an aesthetically pleasing composition.

**Stock photography**—Photographs that already exist, as opposed to those produced on assignment for a specific use. The photo's usage rights are sold through a stock-photo agency.

**Stop-down**—To decrease the size of the lens aperture, from 5.6 to f22.0 for example. The opposite is to open-up the lens.

**Strip light**—A soft box that is long and narrow. Often used to light narrow objects.

**Strobe**—A term used to refer to electronic flash systems.

**Stylist**—An individual utilized during a shooting session to prepare the subject, usually a person and their clothing. However, due to the fickle nature of food, food stylists also exist.

**Sweep**—Refers to a background such as Formica or seamless paper that is swept up to form a concave surface.

**TIFF**—A common file format for saving Photoshop files; works on both Mac and PC computers.

**Toast**—The most common software to write data to or burn a CD-ROM.

**Tungsten lighting**—A continuous light produced from a thin tungsten filament. Often referred to as hot lights, due to the large amount of heat produced.

**URL**—Universal Resource Locator or a Web site's Web address.

**View camera**—A camera in which the lens forms an upside-down and backward image directly on a ground-glass viewing screen. The front and back of the camera can be adjusted to control focus and perspective.

**Watt-seconds(w-s)**—The unit used to rate the output from a power supply. The greater the number of watt-seconds, the greater the power.

# Index

# BOOKS FROM ALLWORTH PRESS

**Mastering the Basics of Photography** by Susan McCartney (softcover, 6¾ × 10, 192 pages, $19.95)

**The Photojournalist's Guide to Making Money** by Michael Sedge (softcover, 6 × 9, 224 pages, $18.95)

**Historic Photographic Processes: A Guide to Creating Handmade Photographic Images** by Richard Farber (softcover, 8½ × 11, 256 pages, $29.95)

**Travel Photography, Second Edition** by Susan McCartney (softcover, 6¾ × 10, 360 pages, $22.95)

**Mastering Black-and-White Photography: From Camera to Darkroom** by Bernhard J Suess (softcover, 6¾ × 10, 240 pages, $18.95)

**Business and Legal Forms for Photographers, Revised Edition** by Tad Crawford (softcover, 8½ × 11, 224 pages, includes CD-ROM, $24.95)

**The Law (in Plain English) for Photographers** by Leonard Duboff (softcover, 6 × 9, 208 pages, $18.95)

**ASMP Professional Business Practices in Photography, Fifth Edition** by the American Society of Media Photographers (softcover, 6¾ × 10, 416 pages, $24.95)

**Pricing Photography: The Complete Guide to Assignment and Stock Prices, Second Edition** by Michal Heron and David MacTavish (softcover, 11 × 8½, 152 pages, $24.95)

**How to Shoot Stock Photos That Sell, Third Edition** by Michal Heron (softcover, 8 × 10, 208 pages, $19.95)

**The Photographer's Guide to Marketing and Self-Promotion, Third Edition** by Maria Piscopo (softcover, 6¾ × 10, 176 pages, $18.95)

**The Photographer's Internet Handbook, Revised Edition** by Joe Farace (softcover, 6 × 9, 224 pages, $18.95)

**The Business of Studio Photography: How To Start and Run a Successful Photography Studio** by Edward R. Lilley (softcover 6¾ × 10, 304 pages, $19.95)